比较哲学与比较文化论丛

第11辑

吴根友 主编

湖北省人文社科重点研究基地 "比较哲学与文化战略研究中心"

武汉大学哲学学院

中国社会科学出版社

图书在版编目（CIP）数据

比较哲学与比较文化论丛. 第 11 辑／吴根友主编；武汉大学哲学学院，
武汉大学中西比较哲学研究中心编 . —北京：中国社会科学出版社，2017. 12
ISBN 978 - 7 - 5203 - 1207 - 3

Ⅰ.①比…　Ⅱ.①吴…②武…③武…　Ⅲ.①比较哲学—文集②比较文化—文集
Ⅳ.①B0 - 53②G04 - 53

中国版本图书馆 CIP 数据核字（2017）第 255480 号

出 版 人　赵剑英
责任编辑　凌金良　徐沐熙
责任校对　周　昊
责任印制　郝美娜

出　　版　中国社会科学出版社
社　　址　北京鼓楼西大街甲 158 号
邮　　编　100720
网　　址　http://www.csspw.cn
发 行 部　010 - 84083685
门 市 部　010 - 84029450
经　　销　新华书店及其他书店

印刷装订　北京鑫正大印刷有限公司
版　　次　2017 年 12 月第 1 版
印　　次　2017 年 12 月第 1 次印刷

开　　本　710×1000　1/16
印　　张　20.5
插　　页　2
字　　数　316 千字
定　　价　88.00 元

主　编：吴根友
副主编：郑泽绵　李健君
本辑执行主编：李健君

编辑部

主　任：李健君
副主任：王林伟　沈　庭　廖璨璨
编辑部成员：吴根友　郑泽绵　李健君　王林伟
　　　　　　沈　庭　廖璨璨

目　录

比较哲学视野中的"学以成人"（代序） ……………… 吴根友（1）

特　稿

西方核心价值的城邦源头及其批判 ……………………… 笑　思（3）

唯识学专题

唯识论的符号学诠释（总论）………………………… 桑大鹏（33）
玄奘求法的唯识学释疑
　　——基于当现二常观的探讨 ………………………… 袁经文（61）
再论近代唯识学复兴的原因及其本质 ……………… 沈　庭（77）

翻译、比较中的佛教与基督教

On the Nestorian Translation of Christian Scriptures:In Comparison
　　with the Buddhist Successful Model ……………… Vincent Shen（95）
Religious Traditions:Theory to Practice
　　Fostering a Form of Buddhist and Christian Spirituality that
　　Responds to Social Needs …………… Thomas Menamparampil（130）
心与道的差异
　　——《心经》对话《约翰福音》 ………………………… 谢劲松（153）

跨文化哲学理论探讨

The Project of Intercultural Philosophy and Intercultural
Communication ……………………………………… William Sweet(171)
From the Imitation of Nature to a Meeting between
Cultures ……………………………… Wojciech Golubiewski(189)
Lost in Translation? ……………………………… Peter Jonkers(206)
Universal Rationality across Cultures ……………… Zhang Lihai(224)

东学西渐的哲学史考察

欧洲三位哲学家论孔子的思想及其方法论的反思 ……… 吴根友(239)
"像中国人那样思考"
　　——论杜威对西方哲学的批评及其中西哲学
　　比较研究 ……………………………………… 许苏民(258)

访谈与对话

关于"理想人格"的对话 …………………… 吴根友　刘素民(287)

Contents

Preface:"Learning to be human"in the Perspective of
Comparative Philosophy ··· WU Genyou(1)

Special Contributions

An Examination of the Polis-based Origin of Western Values ······ Xiaosi(3)

Yogācāra Buddhism

An Interpretation of Yogācāra Buddhism in light of
Semiotics(A General Introduction) ····················· SANG Dapeng(33)
An Analysis of the Reason for Xuan Zang's Indian Seeking for
dharma on the basis of the Dispute about the
Actuality of *dharmakāya* ································· YUAN Jingwen(61)
A Re-discussion about the Reason for the Revival of Xuan Zang's Yogācāra
Buddhism and its Essence in the Early Modern Times ······ SHEN Ting(77)

Buddhism and Christianity in
Translation and Comparison

On the Nestorian Translation of Christian Scriptures:In Comparison
with the Buddhist Successful Model ····················· Vincent Shen(95)

Religious Traditions:Theory to Practice Fostering a Form of
 Buddhist and Christian Spirituality that Responds to
 Social Needs ································ Thomas Menamparampil(130)
On the Diffenrence between *ālāyavijñāna* and *logos*-The *Heart*
 Sūtra in Dialog with the Gospel *John* in the
 New Testament ································· XIE Jingsong(153)

Intercultural Theories

The Project of Intercultural Philosophy and
 Intercultural Communication ···················· William Sweet(171)
From the Imitation of Nature to a Meeting between
 Cultures ································· Wojciech Golubiewski(189)
Lost in Translation? ····························· Peter Jonkers(206)
Universal Rationality across Cultures ··················· ZHANG Lihai(224)

Investigations of the westward History
of Chinese Philosophy

A Methodological Reflection upon three European Philosophers'
 Reception of Confucius ····················· WU Genyou(239)
"As the Chinese think"-Dewey's Critique of Western Philosophy
 and his Comparative Research on the
 China-Western Philosophy ·················· XU Sumin(258)

Interviews and Dialogs

A Dialog on the"Ideal Personality" ··········· WU Genyou,LIU Sumin(287)

比较哲学视野中的"学以成人"
（代序）

吴根友

"学以成人"（Learning to be human）是 2018 年第二十四届世界哲学大会的主题。该次大会将在中国北京市北京大学召开。此次会议主题带有鲜明的中国哲学特点，但不能说只有中国哲学才关注如何成人的问题。古希腊哲学十分关注人对自己的认识，德斐尔神庙的格言就是"认识你自已"。近现代西方哲学的主题之一，就是在与基督宗教神学的斗争中，系统而深刻地阐述了现代世俗的人文主义思想，对于人的自由、权利等抽象的本性做了极其深刻而丰富的论述，为人的全面解放做出了巨大的贡献。因此，如何成为人，成为什么样的人，是中西哲学，也可以说是世界哲学共同关注的主要问题之一，如何从比较哲学的角度来开掘这一重要哲学问题，或许能给比较哲学提供一个极富理论价值与现实意义的哲学论域。

从不同的文化传统来看，"学以成人"这一问题有丰富的哲学思想可以讨论，首先，对于"学"如何理解，就非常值得讨论。从广义的角度看，"学"既指学习书本知识，也可以指在实践中、行动中尝试做某事。甚至宗教信仰活动中的仪式、人在宗教场所里宗教心理的培养，都可以看作是"学"；而在一种文化传统、习俗中不自不觉的耳濡目染过程，也是一种广义上的"学"。

不仅如此，在中华文化传统里，"学"还有"为学"与"为道"的区分。"为学"是知识的增长，"为道"是精神境界的提纯与提升，是知识与习俗偏见的被剔除或人的精神品质被升华的过程。而"为学"与"为道"的区别，实际上也是知识与智慧的区别，是专业技术知识与对人类根本意义的觉解、人文通识的区分。而无论是"为学"，还是"为道"，都属于广义的"学"。

至于"成人"问题，在不同的文化传统里，在同一个文化传统的古今时间段里，在同一个文化传统内部的不同学派、哲学家的思想体系里，也都有相当大的不同。当然也可以找到某些相似点。在古希腊的苏格拉底思想体系里，他所说的美德是偏重于对知识的把握，所以有"美德即知识"的命题。其反命题，人缺乏美德不是德性本身的问题，而是因为无知。但在中国儒家创始人孔子的哲学传统里，仁智相乐、仁礼相得益彰，才具有美德。"人而不仁如礼何，人而不仁如乐何？"人必须具备爱自己的同类，即爱人的本性，才有了美德的必备基础。无知者虽愚而不一定为恶德。孔子以后的儒家在讲人的德性问题时，常喜欢以"智、仁、勇"构成人的美德的三种大纲大目。如果从各大宗教传统来看，基督教的"成人"其实就是与神更为接近，或被神恩典而得救；在佛教传统里，则是一种解脱人间苦难，进入不生不死，没有烦恼的涅槃境界，即成佛；而在道教传统里，则是成为各种各样的仙人。

就世界范围内的现代文化而言，"成人"即是成为一个独立自主、具有自由意志、恰当地运用个人权利的自由人或现代社会的公民，按照中国化的马克思主义哲学家冯契的说法，即成为一个具有"平民化的自由人格"的普通人。这种"平民化的自由人格"的个人，能够恰当地理解个人与社会，个人与他者的关系，个人的内在性命与超越的天道的关系，如果用庄子的哲学来解释，即是一个拥有一技之长而又能上达天道的匠人，如解牛的庖丁，承蜩的佝偻者，削木的梓庆，蹈水的吕梁丈人等等。

简而言之，"学以成人"的哲学问题，在比较哲学的视野里可以有十分丰富的思想内容：一方面，我们可以从比较哲学的视野来丰富这一哲学问题的具体论述；另一方面，通过这一哲学问题的具体讨论，使得比较哲学由一种外在的比较转向一种以哲学问题本身为出发点的内在比较。这样，在深度全球化的时代里，通过比较哲学的途径逐渐形成一些具有全球共识的世界哲学问题意识。这也是我一贯主张的，通过比较哲学走向世界哲学。

特　　稿

西方核心价值的城邦源头及其批判

笑　思*

摘　要：希腊价值观过度受限于源自古希腊的城邦政治生活理念，这在根本上塑造了西方人的精神视野。本文分析了"城邦"如何规范了西方人对人性、道德、社会、文明与理想的理解，揭示出其城邦政治理念所留下的隐患。对于中华文化复兴、恢复文明自信来说，批评源于古希腊的西方政治文明，是迟早要面对的任务。

关键词：城邦　翻译误导　中领域主义　儒家　农业文明

东亚思想界，迄今还较少以东方经验为根据，对西方价值进行追根溯源式的批评。苏格拉底、柏拉图、亚里士多德等人及其许多追随者，成为这类放纵的受益人。古希腊本来有大的教训，然而却迄今鲜为人知。古希腊哲学三杰，今天仍然是许多东方人，因为不了解其失误，而予以过度尊敬的对象。

从东亚立场上看，由古希腊源起的西方价值的问题，至少有一点，就是过高依赖于城邦，以致使这种特定单位几乎成为其生活领域中的唯一规范。当城邦充满视野之后，古希腊人便很难再并行重视其他人类生活领域，以至于忽视了家庭小领域与天下大领域中丰富的人类资源、道德秩序与生活意义。

---

* 笑思：本名杨效斯，旅美华人学者。

有一条常识原理：不谋全局，不足谋一城。这可被看作就是在说古希腊：他们就是公然地不顾全局，仅谋一城。古希腊人对道德的界定、人性的说明、政治的理解、文明的确认、社会的观念、理想的看法，都过分地囿于城邦而带有明显的局限，这限缩了西方人此后的总体精神视野与情感关怀的范围。以上这些观点与判断就是本文的主题。

相较之下，古中国人的视野反而要宽广、全面些。《大学》并列身、家、国、天下，意味着小领域家庭，大领域天下，与其间的中领域国家同样重要。如果能对若干西方主要价值的城邦渊源与局限予以揭露批评，就能帮助我们补全关于古希腊的缺失信息，并且能为东方政治历史的名誉恢复与道德上的自信重拾提供根据。

古希腊道德与城邦生活的内在渊源 古希腊伦理道德文化，是受害于城邦中领域主义的主灾区。西方人后来因此很少再关注不同于城邦内部的道德——如东亚人熟知的家庭道德与天下大公之公德。追溯起来，荷马史诗中的德性和善观念，便已经明确地指向中领域性的城邦了。因为，"在荷马的理论中，美德概念从属于社会角色概念"①。麦金泰尔对西方伦理考察道："一个履行社会指派给他的职责的人，就具有德性。然而，一种职责或角色的德性与另一种职责和角色的德性是完全不同的。国王的德性是治理的才能，武士的德性是勇敢，妻子的德性是忠诚，如此等等。"②

显然，这里的德性观念，有些类似于当今的所谓"职业道德""社会角色责任"。而将妻子的德性并列于武士的德性，则可见家庭道德与城邦道德的混同，或者说小领域与中领域的混同，好像妻子只是一种社会角色（为什么不把它首先限于家庭角色？）或者说古希腊人无论如何都不愿意将家庭与城邦并列。

由此还能够引申出，家庭角色的需要名副其实，以及家庭单位有可能并列于城邦、社会，尚未被古希腊人意识到——这一点后面还要再

---

① ［苏格兰］阿·麦金泰尔：《追寻美德》，宋继杰译，译林出版社2003年版，第236页。

② ［苏格兰］阿·麦金泰尔：《伦理学简史》，龚群译，商务印书馆2004年版，第31页。

论。在西方传统中，家庭是社会的附属；家庭角色被认为低于、下属于社会角色；家内道德被看作社会道德的亚种，并不作单独看待。——这也是使西方人迄今很难深刻地懂得"以家为道德源头的儒家思想"的原因。

当阿伽门农打算偷偷占取阿基里斯的女奴布莱斯时，内斯特对他说："虽然你是善的，但不要夺走他的姑娘。"这里不是说，"因为阿伽门农是善的，他不应强占那姑娘；也不是说，假如阿伽门农占取这姑娘，他就不是善的。而是说，无论他是否占取那姑娘，他都是善的"①。

能够看出，这里的善观念，并不紧密地关涉于人如何对待别人、是否尊重别人的财物（这里先不考虑将女人当作财物这一点本身的缺德）或者如何善待别人。阿伽门农所属的文化中的对于"善"的理解，显然不同于"善待别人"中的善，不同于汉语中所谓"善良""善人"中的善，而是与特定的社会角色、与完成角色的能力及其相关的评价有关。

先于苏格拉底、柏拉图、亚里士多德等古希腊哲学三杰，而比较集中地论及道德者，是古希腊所谓的智者们。他们把所有的道德，与城邦或者社会生活等，紧密地联系了起来："一个人的德性（ἀρειή）就在于他完满地履行了作为一个人的职责。在城邦中作为一个人的职责履行得好，就是一个有成就的公民。…离开了成功，就没有德性的标准，离开了每个特定城邦占主导性的实践，就没有正义的标准。"②

智者们假定，城邦是所有一切的背景。一个人的职责是否履行，有无德性，唯一的评判标准就是所为该人背景的城邦。智者服务、教授、取财于斯的，仅是城邦公民。而公民关注的，也仅是城邦事务，或者城邦术（目前翻译为政治）。智者的职业与收入，与他们的善观念一起，都出自城邦。

"智者不得不教的是在每一不同国家被认为是正义的东西。你不能

---

① ［苏格兰］阿·麦金泰尔：《伦理学简史》，龚群译，商务印书馆 2004 年版，第 31—32 页。

② 同上书，第 40—41 页。

提出和回答这个问题：正义是什么？而只能问，在雅典什么是正义的？在科林斯什么是正义的？"① 换句话说，道德与价值，因城邦的不同而彼此区别。城邦成了构成正义的标准单位或定义者。"没有超越城邦的道德"——这正是希腊文化的局限性所在。

道德，于是随城邦的不同而转移。这就是西方后来著名的社会性道德相对主义，它开了晚近各种围绕不同社会而有的道德相对主义的先河。总之，在古希腊道德的理解与实践中，城邦的决定性作用太大、太过分了。古希腊道德过于决定于、附属于和限制于城邦单位了，这使其未能顾及生活中其他同样有道德需求的单位。

古希腊哲学三杰由城邦定义人性 以苏格拉底为首的古希腊哲学三杰，与其先驱一样，具有强烈的、彻头彻尾的"城邦情节"。他们不仅同意、继承了关于道德仅对于城邦来说才有意义的传统，而且代表古希腊思想界，概括出了一个更著名的中领域主义信念，即"人是生活在城邦里的动物"，或者说"人是城邦动物"（Zoon Politikon）。

"人是城邦动物"，后来在西方思想史上，尤其是在政治思想史、道德思想史、哲学思想史上，变得无人不知。它成为无人敢挑战、不曾被批评的最基本原则。它经常还被看作同义于另外一组说法：人是政治动物，人是社会动物，人是群体生活的动物，人的本性即社会性，等等。

结果，古希腊的这一特殊的人性定义，后来变成为整个西方文明所接受、传承的定律、常识。西方人从未把它与其他不同的观点进行认真对比，乃至从未对之进行深刻的研究、批评、改进。"人是城邦动物"，作为西方共识，意味着真正的人，不仅事实上生活在城邦里，而且应该在那里生活，不能不在那里生活。

例如，亚里士多德的美德观念，基本上就是只有联系于城邦才有意义、才能被理解的观念："美德在城邦的社会语境中有其位置，就成了雅典人共同的前提。所有的希腊人都认为，做一个好人至少与做一个好

---

① ［苏格兰］阿·麦金泰尔：《伦理学简史》，龚群译，商务印书馆2004年版，第42页。

公民是紧密相连的。那使人成为好人和好公民的美德是什么？与此相应的恶行又是什么？"①

需要注意，这种中领域主义道德观，与东亚儒家的小领域主义道德观，恰成对照。按照孔子—儒家的看法，好人，首先意味着从幼年起，就做好一个儿子、女儿。德行，不如古希腊那样仅为少数的、作为城邦公民的成年人个人所有，在东亚儒家文化圈中，它是中领域团体需要的素质。德行，是从小在家就联系于亲人、家规、家礼，而于幼年家庭生活中形成的。

中国人以往懂得，只有从小在家善待家人，即亲亲，从而形成孝悌仁爱等基本德行，长大才能成为一个好人。幼时不孝父母，不敬兄长，便已经缺德而无异于禽兽了。一个人是有德而成长，还是缺德而为禽兽，这在这个人达到公民、国民的年龄资格之前，就可以也应该确定了。总之，按照中国的看法，那些进入成年社会之后才考虑道德的人，已经太晚而被严重耽误了。

古希腊人—西方人，除了由城邦定义道德、人性，而且还局限于城邦意识之内去看待人类的秩序治理。他们以城邦为唯一的范式，来理解和定义政治。这个特殊而意义深远的西方特色，本身没有普遍意义，消极影响却特别巨大，成为西方人中领域主义秩序治理观的源头。

"城邦术"被误译为"政治" 西方许多的基本词汇，从形式上便离不开城邦词根，这一点后文还要谈。西方语言中"政治"（Politics）一词是以"Polis"（城邦）作为词根的，它是西方文化中最重要的语词之一。"Politics"，在适当考虑其词根的巨大限定作用的前提下，本应译为"城邦术"而非"政治"。

西方人凡说到 politics 时，其语言心理总是毫不含糊地意识到城邦这种源头、词根。而东亚—中国人以往在说到"政治"时，语言心理则几乎完全不包含他们不熟悉的"城邦"。因此可见，东西方的政治观念其实区别很大。目前这种很大的区别，被予以了各种掩饰，并造成了

---

① ［苏格兰］阿·麦金泰尔：《追寻美德》，宋继杰译，译林出版社 2003 年版，第 171 页。

严重的误解后果。

这里，我们首先必须加以明确的是，中国人思想、语言中的政治一词，与城邦这种古希腊人所强调的单位，几乎没有多少关系。中国传统的政治观念，至少是对政治的主流理解，很早就由儒家文化予以明确的定义了，尽管道家、法家等，亦皆有其特殊的政治理解，或者说政治界定。

根据孔子—东亚人的见识，一、"政者，正也"，也即政治可以被一般地解为"正当的治理"。二、需要正当治理的单位，并不专门、唯一，而是有广泛的多元性。凡是人类的生活单位，无论如何，都需要某种"正治"。三、特别重要的一点是，治家是首先需要、非常必要的，这被中国人称为"齐家"。四、齐家先于治国。治家，既独立于治国，又能从本身出发，外推而启示治国。五、治国以后，还要进步到平治天下，也即家国天下需要一体治理。

用汉语词"政治"对应翻译"Politics"，这等于是将东方主流理解中的"正当的治理"对应于"城邦治理术"。后者完全没有前者那种正当与否的考虑，而前者则完全没有后者那种对古希腊式城邦的特殊偏爱。古希腊人关心其城邦术，是想要在城邦世界的武力竞争中成为取胜者。这种关怀，是强权政治的关怀，而与孔儒所偏重的"正"治相去甚远。

此外，用"政治"对译"Politics"，掩盖了东亚多元治理与西方城邦单治之间的重大区别，掩盖了东方对是否正治的关切。它同时掩盖了，在东亚政治思想中，几乎完全没有城邦与城邦术、没有中领域主义的地位强调这一基本事实。此翻译会让东方人严重地误会，以为东西方人对政治的理解没有重大差别，而可以看作大体一致。

可见，"Politics 即政治"，或者以城邦术等同于政治，构成了一个因翻译导致的、东西方思想沟通上巨大的陷阱。"Polis"这个词根，本来必须在其汉语对应词中显现出来，不可或缺，以突出西方所理解的政治的城邦根源。将"Politics"直译为"政治"，便让"城邦"这个词在"翻译中迷失"了，这是导致数亿人彼此误解的重大误译。

从今以后，思想界需要保留中国那种以"正治"解政治的特殊传统，保留此传统所高扬的德治正当性，以及正治适用范围的多元性，及其完全没有"关于城邦的特殊针对性"等中领域主义的东方特点。只有这样，我们才能容易地感觉到西方政治思想与东方对应物的不同，才能开始理解西方文明的城邦如何导致了西方的政治中领域主义。

后来的西方政治思想中的几乎全部核心观念，如自由、权利、民主、公正，都受到其文明源头处的古希腊城邦术的局限——这是西方思想史界的共识。它们既不产生于也很难立即应用于家庭与天下。因此，亚里士多德的那部名著，不应该译为"政治学"，而必须译为"城邦术"。为了突出东亚更为宽广的见识，翻译应该反映城邦术的局限。今后，"Politics"要译为"城邦术"为好。

值得指出的是，柏拉图—亚里士多德的城邦术哲学，就是在西方史家眼里，其实也并不成功。著名的西方思想史家萨拜因说："柏拉图与亚里士多德的政治哲学在当时完全没有理论上和实践上的影响。事实上，如果以亚里士多德死后的两个世纪来判断这个哲学所起的作用，那么它只能被看成一个巨大的失败。"

另外，在一部普及性的而非意在创新的《西方文明史》中，专门列有一节，题为"希腊政治的困境"。其中说："斐力（亚历山大）征服城邦，暴露出希腊政治的根本弱点。虽有内部危机和连绵战争，希腊人却没有形成除城邦外的任何别种政治形式。城邦很快变得不合时宜，但是希腊人却看不到在一个向着大国或帝国发展的世界中，小小城邦是无法与之抗衡的。"①

上面提到的"希腊政治"，就是古希腊城邦术。上面提到的"政治哲学"，就是"Political philosophy"②，即实际上应该称之为"城邦术哲学"的体系。证诸历史记录中的城邦术哲学体系的巨大失败，应该首先被看作是用城邦这种单位来定义人性，来束缚整个政治思想及其应用范围这种西方传统做法的失败。

---

① 参见［美］马文·配里主编《西方文明史》上卷，胡万里等译，商务印书馆1993年版，第89页。

② 萨拜因：《政治学说史》，第123页。

以"城市化"作为"文明"定义　城邦观念，应该说其核心含义有二。一是前边已经说过的、以公民团体作为人类核心组织样态的道德秩序单位来定义政治；至于第二种含义，是指从价值上区分人的居住地，即城里城中和野外乡村。以下要就这第二种含义，即西方人用来当作文明区别标准的城里与乡村之别，来展开讨论批评。

就古希腊城邦观念的第二种含义而言，也即就城邦所内含的城里—野外乡村的区别而言，西方人认为，城里与乡村野外间的区别，等同于文明与不文明的差别。"Civilization"这个词，既指城市化，又指文明，这二者实际上被等同起来了。这个事实，迄今还没有引起东亚思想界的充分注意与讨论。

因此，城邦观念不仅塑造了西方人的道德观、人性论、政治观，而且塑造了西方人的文明观。人们生活文明与不文明的区别标准，根据古希腊价值观，要看他们是否已经被城市化，或者说已经被城市化到了什么程度。Uncivilized，未城市化，即意味着未文明化，或者说仍然是野蛮、无教养的。

古代西方人游牧渔猎的生活方式，往往不稳定、不安全，缺乏组织纪律，缺乏社会组织性。与此有关，一旦筑城而定居，能有效保护自己，能就中建立社会，形成法制、纪律，生活便改善了。古希腊人珍爱这种善化机制，于是将城市生活高高置于其他生活形式之上。这是可以理解的。城市化对于游牧渔猎者，意义非凡。

崇尚古希腊城邦者，此后便开始认为，野外、农村一般就是丛林、战场，是野蛮人（或者希腊人在其较为野蛮的时候）为非作歹、无法无天的地方，是低等阶级的人生活的地方。那里缺少人性、秩序、文化、安全，因而不文明。于是，城市化即社会的组织化、人的行为的纪律化、文明化，城市化于是变成文明的定义了。

然而上述的这种西方对观念价值的处理，在全部人类的历史经验中，仍然过于特殊，并没有普遍性。以城市化作为文明的标准，意味着"农业、农村、农民"原则上只能与"不文明"的生活相关。或者说，如"农业文明"这种说法，在西方对于文明的严格界定上，相当于自相矛盾，因为就其内在逻辑而言，"文明"这个词乃是对农业的否定。

然而历史事实是，与发达的家庭文化相结合的农业文明，是西方世界以外的伟大存在。西方人没有将资源与建设重点置于乡村、家庭，西方的农业—家庭文化贫乏，那是西方的问题，并不是全人类的问题。农村，只要有家源道德，完全可以有高度的文明。家庭生活及其家规，一般总是先于社会生活与法律，而使幼年人接受道德教化的。

西方以城市化为文明的标准，也是因其农—家文化双双不发达而被迫作出的选择。于是，古希腊人选择发展城邦，歧视农村家庭，只是偶然事件。古中华文明所走的道路，完全不受古希腊的影响。可见，凡用"城市化"来定义文明的人，很可能是西方中心主义的受害者，是对东亚农业—家庭型文明知道太少的无知者。

应该由家庭道德水平的高低来判别文明与野蛮 农业中的农民，同样可以是具有高度组织性的。农民的组织机制、良好习惯，不必同于城邦的团体，不必出自社会，不必靠组织单位的中领域化，不必靠国家法制。中华文明中农民的主要生活组织形式、纪律形式、自律形式，是家庭及其礼教，靠的是儒家总结、推广、教育出来的家礼家规、孝悌德行。

东方这种非中领域化的文明，是东亚广大的农村人民依循儒家的家庭化教养而产生的结果，它曾经造就了世界上最丰富的善德体系、造就了最大的善人群体。农村家庭化文明，可以如此高度地提升"野外"的文化程度，以至东亚人都熟悉这样的至理名言：礼失求诸野。对西方人来说，其城邦价值观使他们完全无法理解这种观念。

而东方人则把野外农家看作是文明地区，至少可以是道德的保存地。所以，非城市化便不文明的这种观点，完全是偏见与误会。西方农家生活量少质次，农业次于游牧渔猎与工商业；农民因为农奴化而地位从来没有高过；家庭文化与道德没有特别重要过；缺少成熟的乡绅文化传统；缺少孝悌家德体系；农村总是有待城市化。但这只是西方的特殊问题。

西方的精英—绅士们，或许都聚居在城里，或者主要住在城里。然而在中华文明中，却始终存在着"乡绅"这种紧密联系于乡土的特殊精英。中国人直到晚近的西化时代，都没有真正地贬低过农村。所以，

"城里""城市化"，在东亚从来没有像在希腊化的西方那么重要。

根据道家的价值观，野外自然本身就有极高的内在价值。道家对东亚文化的影响极为深刻，且年代长久。"道法自然""顺其自然"、重视风水等深刻智慧，是深入东亚人心的东方文化精髓。由于基督教将自然基本上看作是由上帝创造出来、送给人类的礼物，人类因此便对之具备拥有权。西方缺乏道家的价值观。

士与农，这两个最高阶级，在古代东亚社会中是紧密相关、紧密相连的。这是古代东亚社会中脱离了奴隶—奴隶主这种阶级差异过大的阶级制之后，显现出的阶级差异弱化的特点。由于"耕读传家"的朴素生活理念对人民之德性潜移默化的塑造，以往中华文明中的士与农这两个阶层的活动及其联合，大多都在农村，而不一定发生在城里。

特别重要的是，当天下一统、天下大治实现之后，农村中的安全能够得到保障。当农村能够依靠家训、族规、乡约以及乡绅领导的宗族组织进行自治，农村就可以是有精英阶层作为榜样、有秩序治理、伦理道德的地方，因而就可以有高度的文化。换言之，大领域与小领域应各自具有秩序治理，而且可以联合起来，从而减少中领域秩序治理的负担。

此外，祖坟对于高度发达的家庭文化，对于儒家价值观来说，是特别重要的。儒家哲学认为祖坟的存在具有极高的道德价值和历史意义，而不远离野外—祖坟—家乡山水的道德生活，便只能是农村生活。这些是西方文明论者所不熟悉、不了解、没有过的，但是那也只是西方特有的无知。

由于不同的文明观，东亚儒家至少中性地、经常正面地看待农民。东方的"人民"主要是指农民。而西方则只能据其政治哲学的逻辑相应地抬高"市民"的地位，说到"人民"时其实主要指城里的市民。东方于是重视和肯定农家社会、宗法社会；西方人便只能强调"市民社会"、城里人了。

"市民社会"成为社会观念的最早源头　　"社会"一词在西方影响下的当今，成了描述与评价人类时不可或缺的基本词汇。舍此一词，人们对于人类、人世、人道、人生，将完全无从谈论，张口结舌。然而究其根源，社会与城邦有渊源深厚的历史联系。没有关于城邦的意识，人们对于西方式的"社会"一词的理解，就不会明了其所具有真正的脉络。

在古希腊，最为基本与核心的团体，是公民—武士团体。这个团体，如果不是从城邦术、城邦法律等方面去看，而是从文化、经济生活、日常生活方面去看的话，便是所谓的"公民社会"。在这个意义上，当今人们对于来自西方的"社会"的理解，是不能脱离其古希腊根源的，更是不能脱离古希腊"公民社会"的。

"公民社会"，在汉语翻译中，也经常被译为"市民社会"。中国人没有中领域主义倾向，对城邦的意识非常薄弱的一大证据，一个重要表现，就是汉语使用者往往不知道应如何理解和使用"市民社会"一词。市民社会，基本上没有东亚文明中的历史对应物、语言对应物，它是一个舶来品。中国人以往的对于社会的理解，基本上都深植于强烈的家族性因素，因此一般都从"宗法社会"而来。

从根本上看，Civil Society 在汉语中应该首先被译作"公民社会"，以此来显示其不可磨灭的城邦术（或者说"政治"）含义。但是，"市民社会"这种翻译并不是错误的，因为它特别明显地突出了 Civil Society 与城邦的关系。同一个外文词的两种不同的翻译，及其在中国人心中造成的困惑，突显了城邦在面对汉语、中国道德思想、秩序治理文化的传统时所表现出的外来性。

"市民社会"中的"市"，就是指城邦所是的那种"市"。这不是中国人一般理解中的，天下范围内的某个城镇之市，也即有"Market Place"（市场）的地方，而是指整个国家的城邦之市。换言之，"市"即国家。正是在这个意义上，市民就是公民；市民社会就是公民社会；城市就是城邦国。

所以，通过市民社会，城邦成了"社会"这个词的、西方式扭曲理解的源头。由于与城邦的这种不解之缘，社会只能被看作是一种中领域单位、一种特殊的人类群体。这种群体，讲究成员的资格；对成员之外的人有排斥性、排除性。今后，在意识到了西方"社会"一词的中领域性质、城邦根源之后，东方人需要警惕自己对这个基本观念的理解与使用，尤其是要注意分清中西文明间"社会"一词或者来自城邦或者来自家族及其扩展的不同渊源。

柏拉图的理想与邦国　城邦特殊的中等尺寸，不仅限定了希腊人的德性、人性、政治、文明观，而且规范了西方人的理想意识与理想追求。柏拉图，作为苏格拉底的学生，在其最有影响的著作《理想国》中，不仅将城邦国刻画成了理想国，而且间接塑造出了西方人可以就某个对象而追求理想的整个传统。

柏拉图将理想这个重要的观念，以一种特殊的方式与城邦国联系在了一起，构成了一种决定性的、塑造了整个西方文明的范式（para-digm）。这种范式暗示着：理想应该首先联系于国家，甚至仅被容许联系于国家，至少必须联系于中领域。于是，理想国的权威，在西方思想史上逐渐变得牢不可破。理想国，以及等价的理想社会，成为西方人的全部追求。

理想国家，类同于理想社会，或者理想的中领域单位。这些关系，恰巧吻合于基督教传统中的"上帝之城"、天国观念、基督教团体生活能够达到教会单位中的完美等观念。于是，中领域主义理想观，城邦单位的优先性，先后得到了古典传统与宗教传统的双重支持。

当国家或者如教会这样的中领域团体，成为能够达成理想的唯一组织样态时，理想国、天国也就被绝对化、独一化，乃至永久化了。但是西方人没有意识到——尽管柏拉图绝望地看到了——理想国至少在城邦国这种形式上，是很难乃至不可能达到的。柏拉图把城邦国视为理想，其实意味着这种理想国反而缺乏现实性。

理想国不可能理想及其道理　国家不可能单独地成为理想的存在，因为还有国外、世界上是否已经普遍地达到了理想化的问题。国家毕竟只是一个局部。当天下各民族都和谐相处、讲究德行时，才谈得到国族间的安全，从而才谈得到一国的理想。然而当天下统一时，原来的各国则连彼此间是否有必要清楚地划清界别，亦会成为问题。

中国历史上，君民曾经为了天下大治而不断地弱化国家，乃至通过天下统一而去除国家。这说明连国家的存在是否有必要，都有商量的余地。又例如，欧盟正在挣扎着去否定、模糊原来的欧洲国族间的界限。这是为什么？这反过来又对城邦术、城邦间区分以及对理想国观念表达了什么？

此外，人类需要秩序治理、伦理道德，原则上不限于国家、社会、团体等中领域。任何可持续的人类单位，任何这种单位所需要的秩序治理、伦理道德，都必然内在地联系于全部的人类秩序治理，这就需要某种秩序能够相对全面地覆盖全部生活。下不治家，上不治天下，国怎能居间而单独得治？

换言之，"理想家庭""理想世界"与理想国是必然相关的。否决了家庭、天下的不断完善和理想化，则这两者相对于国家所具有的脉络作用，或于国之两端所起的限定作用，就减少至零了。相应地，西方人便不再会去争取家庭生活的改善和理想，不再去争取世界和平的改善、世界秩序的统一。

如此断绝了"齐家""平天下"，应该说是理想国观念让西方文明付出的最大代价，也是其不可能实现的主要原因。因此，对于东亚思想界来说，甚至连"单看治国还是西方人更强"的这个说法，都是有问题的。它回避了太多方面，回避了家庭理想化、天下统一化与国家治理之间的关系，而难以服人。

理想国观念，在西方文明史的实际之中，确实导致了大小生活领域不重要、不必要、不理想等后果。异常狭隘的思想，导致了严重残缺的文明。下而牺牲家庭小治与小公公德，上又不求天下大治与大公公德，仅偏治和求德于家与天下之间，只顾中段而大小皆失，则西方人能够达到的只能是局部性得治。局部性，本身就意味着不理想和对理想的否定。

单治本国，不顾邻国，就像古希腊时代的雅典那样，一旦发生战争、强邻入侵，便难免国破家亡。城邦国，离不开这种单国—孤军—局部—地方的窠臼，原则上置更高层次、更大范围的脉络环境之治于不顾，致使其不可能在超国家范围上建立起道德秩序。城邦国已经被历史反复证明其短命，还谈什么理想？

人类的生活，必然地涉及身、家、国、天下。大学四维三领域框架的深刻、宏大、理想，是无与伦比的。人类需要国家好、社会稳定，这就要求人应该首先建设其家庭以达到理想，并且最终统一其天下来达到理想。古希腊人囿于其城邦生活经验，只能产生出中领域主义理想观。这需要东亚的家庭文化、天下文化来予以教育、纠正和扩充。

翻译中的加法与减法，文明差别如何被欺骗性翻译弥平 "城邦"，即 Polis，这个词后来构成了西方语言中一组关键词的词根，其对外人了解西方价值观的特殊重要性，往往在翻译中被掩盖乃至牺牲，而未能被东方人所充分地了解、理解和领悟。例如，警察、礼貌、政体、政策、政客等西语词，都以城邦为词根。

然而很明显，这个词根的含义，在上面所列举的词语的汉译过程中，从字面上被舍去、抹杀了。这是导致中国人误解古希腊思想、西方文化的一大根源。由于后来变得日渐重要的"社会""团体"（Community）"公民"（市民）"市长"等词，实际上亦联系于"城邦"，故"城邦"成为适当理解西方生活—语言—政治—社会—文化最重要的一个源头词、关键词。①

但是，目前东西方翻译界的惯例，是容许在东西方语言的两个翻译方向上，分别施行一个有欺骗性的"加法"或"减法"。当那一组西文词语被翻译为汉语时，必做一种减法，也即在对译所用的汉语表达词中，将上举诸西方词中统统具有的、起关键作用的词根词"城邦"，一一减去。没有多少中国人意识到了这种减法所产生的误导效应。

结果，中国人不再能够意识到"城邦"这个词根的存在与作用。中国人在看到上举西方词语的汉译时，尽管自以为懂得了西方诸词的意思，自以为对上举诸词翻译后的理解与西方人一致；然而他们不知道，欧美人在每一次用到这些词时，都在强化这个词根——城邦——及其不可避免性的意识。

问题是，中国人在用到这些汉语对应词时，完全没有西方人的那种涉及城邦的历史意识与语言心理。西方由城邦词根携带进来的语言心

---

① 以英文为例，警察即 Police，礼貌即 Polite，政体即 Polity，政策即 Policy，政客即 Politician，政治即 Politics。这些词语，都含有"Polis"这个词根，故而都来自城邦、指向城邦、服务城邦。就城邦中的"城市"部分，它反映在西方"市民即公民""市长即基层行政首长"等观念。然而所有这些的汉语对应词，则完全没有反映出这些概念的城邦源头性及其市民指向性，而掩盖了极其重大的实际文化差别。

理、中领域价值观，与中国思想风马牛不相及。中国人晚近的那种"只知有天下，不知有国家"的知识结构，首先表现为不知道城邦文化，甚至已经薄弱于所有的国家文化、中领域文化。

中国语言中，由于以往长期没有城邦这个词，故而城邦之于中国文化、历史、思想、语言没有产生西方式的塑造。至少从秦汉之后，中国人开始逐渐步入与天下大治相适应的历史趋势，一城一地，变为过渡性的存在，变为本身缺少稳定性、可靠性而不再是值得认真对待的东西。然而这类与东亚特殊文化历史有关的事实，却在翻译过程中被完全掩盖掉了。

反过来，当中国人所说的"礼貌""政策""警察""政治"等词汇被一一译为西文时，西方人都实际上——经常是无意识的——在暗中做了一种加法，即为每一个词汇加上中国人意识中所没有，但是西方人却当作理所当然的"城邦"词根。经过这种加法以后，西方人对这组汉语词语，便自以为能理解（误解）了。

这时，西方人会以为，中国人在用这一组词时，一定与西方人一样，意识中总是联系着"城邦"这个词根的——尽管这与中国人的实际情况相去甚远，乃至背道而驰。所以，翻译过程中的加减法，人为地"弥平"了一种东西方间本来巨大而不能忽视的有城邦—无城邦的区别。这种因翻译中的弥平引发的误导所产生的消极影响是非常巨大的。

所以，尽管城邦在塑造西方核心价值上作用极大，然而另一方面，城邦却没有对中华文明具有同样的影响力。下面来看一看城邦本身的可疑、脆弱之处，借此可以表明，何以城邦就算是在西方，亦不是一种本身就能够始终延续的存在，因而很难成为一系列西方核心价值的定义基础。

城邦有尺寸要求　城邦的一大问题，是本身尺寸较小。城邦并不像当今"社会"一词在西方人心目中那样，被允许随心所欲地到处套用，尺寸上具有几乎无穷无尽的灵活性、弹性（尽管社会一词本身源起于城邦）。恰好相反，城邦是最小的国家，是有特定尺寸要求的东西，在大小上没有多少弹性。

亚里士多德曾说，如果一个人站在城邦中心的广场呼救，而立于城门者却已经听不见这种呼救了，则这个城邦便尺寸过大了。亚里士多德的这个观念，至今谈论者不多，其意义、影响却很大。更一般地说，一个能够自治的团体，必须满足一定的尺寸要求，例如小到能让每一个成员都多少了解其余的任何一个成员。

联系于西方的中领域主义价值观，我们会发现上述要求是非常重要的。它在西方经常是一种认真、严肃、必不可少、到处尊重的、针对团体的尺寸要求。例如，美国高等教育体系中的一大批文理学院，就倾向于保持一两千人的尺寸，而拒绝随意扩张或缩小。这能保证其中的每一个人，都有可能在一定时间范围内，认识其他所有人。

这对于东亚人能够深刻地了解古希腊城邦、了解中领域单位、了解什么叫做团体（Community）、了解中领域主义文化精髓，是十分重要的。没有满足特殊的尺寸限定要求，则中领域团体成员们，将无法充分地彼此了解，无法理由充分地按照个人专长，来进行角色安排、分工合作。西方人的团体建设、单位设定、民主选举、人际关系，直到今天仍然特别重视这种尺寸要求。这是东亚人所不熟悉的。中领域有特定尺寸，是中领域主义的重要特征与内涵。

小尺寸城邦扭曲之后的放大应用（1） 城邦的尺寸很小，并且按照原则是不得随意将其放大的，然而西方人却经常于此不顾，滥用城邦范式，以扩大其应用。基督教神学的创立者之一、圣奥古斯丁对上帝治下的所有神圣界的称谓，便类似于古希腊人那样，称为"上帝之城"。这显然令城邦观念在古希腊时代之后，能够于基督教主导的很长的一段历史时期中继续被使用。

然而对比于前述城邦本身要求的小尺寸，我们于西方宗教史上，却不难看出存在着一个关于天国范围究竟有多大、上帝领地的尺寸有多大的巨大讽刺与明显矛盾。这个讽刺、矛盾，既表明宗教界对中领域团体、中领域主义精神的坚守，又表明这种坚守，在他们实际使用"城邦"一词的时候，可以不合情理到什么程度。

一方面，基督徒宣传说，上帝无处不在，无所不能，创造并领有整个宇宙。因此天国原则上应该是无穷大的，乃至无远弗届。另一方面，上帝所管辖的范围，又被奥古斯丁看作和称作（尺寸很小的）"上帝之城"。大宇宙等同于小城邦，上帝创造的一切，都在一个城里——这究竟是恭维上帝及其宇宙，还是贬低袖？是在扩大还是在缩小神圣界的版图？

但是奥古斯丁不是唯一这样扭曲城邦、忘记其尺寸要求而滥用城邦观念的人。西方晚近仍然存在扭曲使用城邦范例的事件。

小尺寸城邦扭曲之后的放大应用（2）　如果说"上帝之城"使城邦在中世纪里被虚幻地继续使用，那么美国人的政治中领域主义，便让"城邦"一词于近现代继续被扭曲地使用。美国人将自己版图巨大的国家，称为"山巅之城"（City on the hill）。这是美国人对自己国家的一种美誉，而非贬低。显然，这与当年的基督徒一样，是在"将大范围看作小城邦"。

如美国所有的、几百万平方公里这么大尺寸的一只脚——这种面积在以往曾经让中国人产生过天下统一、天下大治的观念——是不可能套上城邦这种小鞋的。然而西方人对城邦制的执着，却如此顽固，以至为无论多么巨大的国家，总要硬是套上小鞋。这反映了城邦观念对西方思维的支配、渗透，使人已经不在乎逻辑、不顾情理了。

用城邦形容上帝所领有的整个宇宙，把巨大的国家称为城邦，这反映出几个特点：第一，城邦观念已经被固化，已经形成了价值观中的中领域主义，并且对之西方人几乎非用不可，连尺寸要求、逻辑一致性也可以置之不理；第二，关于城邦的使用，至少就其原始的尺寸要求来看，到晚近已经变得越来越"名不副实"，并且西方人已经习惯于这种名不副实的使用了；第三，基督徒、美国人，经常将自己的国度，既称为城邦，又看作是整个世界，这是典型的中领域自我中心、将中领域视为世界的思想模式的反映。

古希腊的城邦，基督教的上帝之城，美国的"山巅之城"，仅从这三大例证来看，城邦的扭曲应用便超过其合理应用。这是古代、中古、现代西方思想中，城邦已经拥有霸权而足以迫使人不能不用的例证。三个案例反映出，城邦这个观念对西方的主流思想的禁锢，已经达到了不分青红皂白的程度。西方人什么时候才能进行一次思想解放，把自己从城邦中解放出来，去考虑非城邦的政治思想？

城邦在时间上的短命　如果说城邦空间上很小，人口不多，在西方历史上常被夸大而扭曲地使用，那么从时间上看，城邦亦相当短命。古希腊人歌颂城邦的最大讽刺之一，古希腊哲学家依赖城邦定义道德人性的最不可靠处，就是城邦本身无法持久——它在西方文明的整个历史上，从来难以稳定长存。

古希腊城邦体系内部，任何一个城邦总是面临被邻居征服、入侵的威胁，从无安全保障，例如雅典便被斯巴达征服过。同时，由于城邦之间并不团结，结盟脆弱，古希腊城邦的整个体系，在外部大帝国的征服面前，抵抗力有限。

亚历山大（即前边引文中说的斐力）征服古希腊城邦世界时，费时不长，困难不多，一气呵成，乃至一劳永逸。古希腊城邦此后没有复辟过，而是开始向古罗马帝国这种巨大的新政治单位过渡。古罗马帝国，无论如何是城邦观念"装不下"的，此相当于否定了城邦在其历史阶段中的存在。当然，古罗马帝国这种大单位，于历史上同样未能长存下来。这一点多少挽救了城邦的尊严，使其威信不至于完全扫地。

城邦并没有胜过其他竞争政治形式的历史记录　西方的政治开始于城邦，然而城邦在西方实际的政治历史上，又并非主流形式。例如，古罗马帝国，就是伟大而又宝贵得多的西方实践。它本有可能令西方产生天下大治的文化，今后亦能成为西方人接受东亚天下文化的基础。然而古罗马帝国却不是应用城邦政治就可以予以说明的。

从古罗马帝国开始，到中世纪城堡，再到近现代民族国家，直至晚近出现的欧盟等，这些政治形式或单位，都不同于城邦：中世纪欧洲封建领主的城堡单位，一般尺寸上小于城邦；近代西方的主要秩序治理单位——"民族国家"——又大于城邦；欧盟这种由民族国家组成的单位，更是极大地超越了城邦的尺寸。

这些超城邦的政治形式，在西方历史上占有更重要的地位，起到了更大的作用。而城邦单位与这些政治形式竞争，在历史上并没有表现出优势。拿"民族国家"来说，它比城邦大得多，在西方晚近历史上也重要得多。它在保障安全、赢得国力竞赛、发展社会化经济上，至少从西方近代史上看，要比城邦要有效得多。

那么，民族国家是否在西方政治思想中，享有至少与城邦同等的地位？实际情形并非如此。时至今日，民族国家在西方政治思想中，作用仍无法与城邦—城邦术相提并论。西方政治文化有一种内在的讽刺：在理论上重要的城邦，在实践中并不重要。在实践中重要的民族国家，在政治理论上又没有如城邦那样的影响力。

西方人因此而不幸，其政治思想在民族国家出现之前便已经被城邦政治塑造定型，并且变得十分顽固。西方政治思想界一直被几个恰好熟悉和热爱城邦政治的人所把持，并因此形成了排外传统。例如，除了古希腊哲学三杰是彻头彻尾的城邦主义者以外，马基雅维里为晚近的西方奠基的政治学实则应该是被称为城邦术学的体系。

马氏的思想、经验，主要出自于 16 世纪意大利尺寸较大的城邦文化。新教创始人之一的加尔文，以及后来对近代西方契约论影响很大的法语系思想家卢梭，这两个人均恰好偏爱日内瓦这个城邦。上述思想家的偏爱，并没有得到多少历史主流的支持。

近现代西方于世界上的强大，是靠民族国家获得的。然而这却没有改变西方思想家、政治家始终聚焦于城邦与城邦术意义上的政治的传统。这令人怀疑，西方的政治思想家们，究竟是如何尊重自己实际的历史实践经验的，或者说他们能否实事求是地依据实际经验的检验结果，来评价和确定其政治理论。

其他中领域单位形式同样短命，使已经退出现实的城邦继续被使用

城邦这种政治形式之所以能够持续拥有威信而勉强维持下来，可能恰恰是因为其他具有竞争力的政治形式同样没有稳定的存在、成功的记录。例如，古罗马帝国便从未被复制；中世纪封建领主建立的庄园城堡短命；民族国家——至少从引起过 20 世纪两次世界大战，逼迫欧洲人寻求欧盟来看——也是不能稳定长存的。

西方人在 20 世纪两次世界大战之后，也即在对民族国家这种政治形式表示失望之后，理论上仍然有机会重回城邦体系，重拾小城邦这种政治形式并再次尝试古希腊文化。然而欧洲人却并没有回到小城邦体系中去，反倒朝向相反的方向，选择了更大尺寸的单位，去力求统一欧洲。

这相当于表明，城邦对于西方人的实用政治，早就没有实用价值、没有前途了。它之所以尚未被完全抛弃，只不过是因为其取代者自身迄今也都还脆弱堪忧。西方人尝试过的秩序形式，无论是城邦、民族国家，还是欧盟，都还在试验，都还未成熟，对之都没有真正的把握、确定性，它们都只是西方人最终迈向天下大治途中的里程碑。

这就不禁令人感慨，西方人今天对于采取什么尺寸的人类政治单位才能长治久安，看来并无历史根据、文化自信。他们在找到一种适当尺寸、能够保障安全与稳定、能够帮助定义人性的政治单位这件事上，仍在探索的路上，尚无可靠的结论。如此，则西方政治文化，总体来看，还有什么可以拿来吹嘘的呢？

教会对城邦传统的间接支持　事实上，犹太—基督教等西方宗教传统，对城邦受到持续的尊重，做出了核心的贡献。由于教会属于中领域团体，它与尺寸类似的城邦有亲缘性。在城邦政治垮台之后，教会接手过来，一方面否定俗世间城市的价值，另一方面宣称上帝之城的重要，如此就继续维持了城邦的某种威信。

教会在古希腊城邦秩序溃败之后，在政治上无法达到统一、只能在各国并存的混乱的西方世界里，对西方人进行了千年的社会化训练，是西方历史中实行中领域化的主要操纵者。受过教会社会化训练的人，很容易接受尺寸与组织形式上与教会非常类似的城邦。所以，政治性中领域主义开其头，宗教性中领域主义续其体，实行了前短后长的轮流坐庄。

教会在城邦世界湮灭之后，挺身而出，用教徒团体取代了公民团体。这种多元化，增加了中领域的选项、价值与生命力。城邦政治上的脆弱、失败，教会精神上的扭曲、狭隘，本来都较丑陋，然而双方竟然在彼此协助中，通过互相弥补、互相遮羞，使两者面目双双改善了。

中领域成为西方社会生活的重心，于是在从城邦形式到教会形式的历史接力中，获得了保障，维持了它本来可能丧失的声誉。这可以看作古希腊传统与犹太—基督教传统之间最为重要的一种协作。后来，到了近代，由城邦与教会合作培育的中领域文化，还得到中领域经济——所谓国民经济与国民经济学——的进一步巩固。

城邦本身脆弱却极大地影响着西方的秩序治理文化，这一点，应该大大有助于东亚人重拾信心，以积极的态度，尊重自身天下大秩序治理的历史实践与理论传统。城邦之外，不是还有家庭与天下吗？只有在更小加更大的单位中，例如在东亚人所重视的家庭与天下中，发展出成功的小大秩序治理、伦理道德文化，才能为国家—社会中领域的秩序治理，建立适当的脉络或上下层级。

当然，在小领域与大领域德治有可能复兴的情况下，城邦这种小单位的独立存在价值、绵延便可能更成问题。中国人早就全面、系统地认识到家国天下，在这种宏大框架中清楚地区别了三种版图的尺寸，同时又能兼顾三者，统一系统地发展出三种领域中的道德人性观。这才应该是西方政治思想界认真参考的范式。

热爱城邦其实是一种阶级偏见，是少数人观点 城邦作为公民团体而被热爱、固执，其实与城邦本身一样，具有偶然性。这种偶然性，首先体现为阶级偏见、贵族偏见。谁最热爱城邦？——组成城邦的人最热爱城邦。但是组成城邦的人，是古希腊人中的少数。能够介入城邦团体的公民，往往仅占古希腊城邦全体人口中的一二成，是所谓的贵族，是少数人。大量的妇孺老幼与非公民们，生活于公民团体之外，也即无从介入城邦生活。这些与城邦存在距离的人，有人性吗？然而因为不能参加城邦活动，他们的人性从哪里来？怎么定义？可见，"人是城邦动物"，其实描述的是贵族们的自我定性，服务于其自我认定的高贵，或者说是一小撮古希腊高阶级者能够自吹的根据。

西方历史上的少数高阶级者，对自己享有的特权，有一种自我中心式的感受与宣示。它表现公民们的一种对只能活动于家户中的奴隶们和妇孺老幼们的优越感、不屑感。以城邦—团体来界定人性，于是不过是仅适用于极少数、极小比例人的阶级社会中的阶级偏见，无法覆盖古希腊甚至世界中的多数人。

另一方面，政治参与范围的不断扩大，公民团体容纳范围、容纳成员的不断扩大，是贯穿于西方文明史中的一种趋势。本来，公民身份是一种精英的、贵族的、少数人的、特殊阶级的身份，但是这种传统，只能在西方价值观的后来发展中，引起人们对等级制、阶级制的厌恶和对政治平等的强烈追求。

晚近西方追求平等的历史，也就是政治团体降低吸纳资格、扩大吸纳范围的历史。先是吸纳本族、非公民的欧裔成年男性，然后吸纳外族的欧裔成年男性，最后才轮到妇女、奴隶。这个过程，既是城邦团体扩大的过程，也是城邦在尺寸上、含义上异化自身的过程，也即前述的城邦如何被超尺寸应用的过程。

所以，"城邦"这个词，在西方语言史上，不断被扩大地、扭曲地、违背城邦本身时空限定性地使用和形容，应该看作既是合理和有进步意义的，又是讽刺和自我否定的。

城邦不足以定义人类基本价值，因为后者比城邦要稳定永久得多

城邦，无论在空间上还是时间上，都不是一种长期稳定、能靠得住的人类组织单位。道德、人性、政治、文明、社会、理想，如果基于城邦而定义，就会因此而无法稳定。事实上，古西方人的道德，确实随着城邦的消亡而发生过重要的变化。

例如，斯多葛学派的伦理道德，出现于古希腊城邦时代之后，而不再以城邦为背景。这种取代之所以可能，就在于城邦业已消亡，而新的庞大世界需要新的道德观。欧洲北方的野蛮民族后来入侵中南欧时，古希腊式小城邦或古罗马式大帝国，连同其道德、人性观，都没有显示出顽强的抵抗能力、坚韧的组织生命力，而是统统被毁灭，令西方进入千年的黑暗时期。

需要强调指出，在非西方地区，城市与其周边地区的关系，不同于古希腊。城邦的存在，在一些古老文明中，既不长久也不普遍。埃及人和中国绝大多数人，或许还有大量印度人，住在农村、认同农村居所的更多。中华帝国以往的财源和文化主体，皆在农民、乡绅、农业和农村。

这么多古老文明、成功文明中的人，难道都因为不住城里，不重视城邦，就缺少道德、人性、文明、政治、社会、理想了吗？甚至就连西方人自己，现在也已经不再依靠城邦生活了，那么他们是否便不再能够确定道德、人性了？可见，问题应该说还是出在古希腊，出在古希腊人囿于城邦范围内的见识还不够宽广、深刻上。

农家可以有优越的道德、丰富的文化 根据儒家与道家的价值观，农村的生活是正常的生活。儒家认为，家庭道德秩序，可以作为所有道德哲学的源头与根基。道家在农村、乡野与城市之间，只会更崇尚自然的农村。其他单位的道德秩序，完全可以从家庭的道德秩序中予以外推。

例如，晚清政治家、军事家曾国藩，在招用人才包括军人时，特别看重朴实、普通的农家子弟，看重其能够吃苦耐劳、勇于担当、可以不顾个人利益乃至个人安危、不怕牺牲的优秀品质。相反，对于常年游荡于市井城垣的人，曾氏反而会多加警惕，以免令奸诈狡猾、自私懒惰之人加入而败坏军风士气。

可见，在这个意义上，东亚儒道可以说发展出一种"家庭小领域—农家道德化—农村生活优异—农民有优秀品质"的世界观。没有这类宝贵资源，中华文明在近代那些主要依靠农民取得的巨大、神速的进步，包括历次革命的成功，中国军队在 20 世纪中期表现出来的强大战斗力，是完全不可能的。

东亚—中国的农民，其勤奋、勇敢、吃苦耐劳、质朴可靠、自律上进、积极乐观、和平谦让、与人为善等优秀品质，可以说是世界上其他人类群体所少有的。东亚家庭文化的丰富成熟，家庭道德的基本作用，使得以农家为本的文明内容可以丰富成熟、成就非凡，可以使之造就高尚的道德体系，这些对于世界都具有重大意义。

于是，修改西方式的家庭观，向其引入儒家家哲学，发展高度的家庭内部伦理道德；同时重视道家对自然—乡野的价值评价——这两方面必然会影响人们去考虑修改其农村观、城市观、社会观、文明观与世界观。这些修改，对于人类整体而言，是提高和改善，是迟早需要普遍完成的。

总之，古希腊关于家庭的盲点，其家庭伦理道德修养的低下，使其错过了更好、更普遍适用的文明标准。古希腊城邦之外的一片荒芜、野蛮可怕，令古希腊人只好选择"城市化"作为文明标准。但是，贫乏、失误、地方特色的偶然，并非理由。西方人需要大力发展其农村文化与农家文明，发展其孝悌等家庭道德，如此才能为真正可靠的新文明观奠定基础。

一种具有普适性的人性论，应该能够最广泛地说明、应用于大多数人，而不可能因其住在城内或是乡村而变化。近代西方人更熟悉民族国家，那么人性是否也要由民族国家来定义？西方人现在更热心于大尺寸的"欧盟"，那么道德定义要不要接着修改？如果比城邦更适用于当今现实的民族国家、欧盟，都没有影响西方人的人性定义，为什么更短命的城邦，具有能够定义人性的资格？

上述追问表明，古希腊少数贵族公民，太看重自己了。他们以自身熟悉并特别热爱的居住形式，原封不动地拿来当作定义人性的根据，实在是太偶然、太专门、太自恋、太自我中心了。中华文明始终存在，历史上没有断绝过。古希腊城邦，今天在哪里？人性是否更应该参照成功存在的文明来定义，才更有说服力？

所以，西方人以城邦为人性的源头，实际上是因为西方文化本身已经具有了强烈的中领域主义惯性。这种惯性逼迫西方人，只能推崇城邦，以保持自身传统文化的逻辑一致。短命的城邦，居然开启了长期的文明中领域化。长期的中领域化文化，于是反过来帮助追认早已脆弱灭亡的城邦。这倒颇为"公平"。

东亚人直到现在，对于城邦这个词，仍然在作消化、容纳仍然不熟悉、不了解它的作用与规范功能，也很少用它。中国人从语言心理到生活体验上对城邦都体会不够，在相关的哲学性、语言使用的认识上当然也只能忽略。但这并不妨碍中华文明在历史中造就伟大与成功，不妨碍中国人从家国天下的角度定义人性。

没有走城邦政治的弯路，是中华文明晚近崛起的运气　本来，按照西方政治思想史的核心，按照近代一大批精神上严重西化的中国学者的初衷，中国人应该从古希腊城邦开始，学习中领域文化。但是中国人事实上并没有在城邦上浪费时间，而是直接瞄准了民族国家开始补课。就这一点看，中华文明因直接进入了更有用的民族国家文化而少走了弯路，是何其幸运！

或许因为还来不及深入地了解西方的政治理论，或者因为很早就专注于西方和全世界的政治实际，近代中国并没有系统地引进西方的城邦文化。这也表明中国人何以迄今仍然会对古希腊的城邦文化感到陌生。事实上，对具有天下大治思想的中国人来说，民族国家的缺点很明显：德国作为一个民族国家的历史，严格地说不足百年，虽发动了两次世界大战，但仍然无法分享其它靠海西方强权所攫取的殖民地。德国历史只是显示了民族国家有多不稳定。

今天，欧洲德语区已经开始成为欧盟的主干力量。这或许也间接反映了他们在民族国家期间的失败经验，以及对这种形式在情感上的不再留恋。在卷入了几次国际战争之后，欧洲民族国家体系其实已经很难正常存在了；西方人终于开始意识到大尺寸政治单位的优势，而开始寻求统一，并建立了比民族国家大得多的欧盟。

中国人在春秋战国年代就经历了这种试图抛弃国家，而寻求更大范围内一统天下的政治文化演化过程。但是，由于过早也过于坚决地固守了城邦这种单位，西方人没有从思想逻辑上给自己接近、发展天下一统的思想留下多少余地。这一点，在当今世界的全球化趋势面前，只能让中国更具有领导人类的资格与能力。

农村文明被低估，会造成过度城市化　东亚人的生活，部分地因为强调家乡、祖坟、农业劳动、耕读文明、自立自养的重要，以及因为道家总结农民的价值观而崇尚自然的文化传统，因而具有天下一统的独特秩序优势，从来不歧视、反而特别崇尚农村、农业、农民。东亚—中国农民的素质，简直可以说是世界第一。以中华文明为代表的农村文明，应该是人类最为宝贵的文化遗产之一。

包括日、韩、越等地区在内，东亚人看待社会，首先看重以家为轴心的宗法社会，看重家乡、祖坟，看重农村的自然环境。西方人则更重视由团体契约形成的陌生人社会，看重人为建设的城市。其宗法社会的薄弱，相应于家庭的薄弱，西方这两方面均没有高度发达过。但这是西方的一种贫乏，而贫乏是不能作根据的。

城内，在东亚人心目中，绝不自动地文明于乡村。至少，以高下来看待城内与乡村生活，是不具有明确的道德性质的评价的。以城市化为文明，作为一种阶级偏见，远不如"具有孝悌的道德与否"这种东亚人定义文明的标准。人的文明与否，在东亚的文化立场上看，在于人是否懂得和实行父慈子孝一类的家庭基本道德，而不可能特别取决于生活在城里城外。

东亚—中国当今的过度西化，一个重要的表现，是在于过度地迎合西方的城市化文明价值观，过度地自我贬低了农业文明价值观、农村生活的大量宝贵经验，过度地常规化了城镇生活方式，过度地宣传了农村生活的过失与过时，过度地追求农村的城市化。当今中国的农村城市化，或许早已经过头了。而其中的教训，是中国人并没有真正透彻地研究过、懂得过古希腊城邦在历史上的功过，没有在系统的对照中，考察东亚人在几千年里发展出来的农村生活，其价值究竟何在。

人类如果想要有普遍发达的、不止于城市化的文明，便必须依靠农村文明丰富的东亚文化资源。这一点，对于当今东亚文明的评价、全人类文化的走向，具有紧迫性。东亚人晚近对于自己文明实践与历史的不公平对待，包括过度否定以往的农村生活方式，否定农业文明，是荒谬、短见而根据不足的。

如何为人类彰显农村文明，如何就农村建设做出样板，如何让农村生活中人与自然间的道家式妥协得到与城市生活同样的认可，如何防止因为过度城市化乃至高度城市化而出现偏颇，将是今后东亚文明伟大复兴的重要内容。那种仅仅以城市化居住，能够提供高效率的公共服务体系为理由，否定农村生活的看法，其说服力仍然有限。它将被历史证明为因小失大。

西方人从未接触过"人是家庭动物"的人性思想　古希腊人在把人性看作是出自城邦之后，从来没再认真反思过，"人类是生活在家里的动物"是否更为合理。人类是否具有家庭性、天下性？家庭与人性之间，有没有些特殊的联系？——这方面，东亚儒家具有丰富的理论，重要的发言权。

人类，是否离开家庭就不能存在？古希腊人—西方人是不是从根本上就缺少关于家庭的哲学水平上的思考活动、深刻思想？家哲学—家文化上的贫乏，令西方出现什么问题？如东亚儒家那样，把人说成是家庭动物，比把人说成是城邦动物，是否更贴切些？家庭只能附属于城邦，还是城邦—社会也可以看作是家庭的外推与延长？家庭有没有相对于中领域社会的独立并列性？

　　——上述问题不仅古希腊人很少问，而且在整个西方历史上，直迄今天，始终很少有人问。现在，是西方人开始重视儒家，重视从家看人的东亚历史文化，重视人的家庭性这种东亚价值观的时候了。

唯识学专题

唯识论的符号学诠释(总论)

桑大鹏[*]

摘 要： 释迦说法四十九年，其所建立的全球性的宗教、哲学、教育体系，是按两条并行不悖的理路展开的，即因果律的揭示及其唯识论的说明，二者一方面揭示了因果律作为宇宙间的总规律，另一方面解释了因果律发生的唯识论因由。其中唯识论是其全部体系的理论基础，它为释迦设立的无量法门作出了理论说明并以其本身构成了一个独立的体系，这一体系可用符号学理论作出部分阐释：再现体（符号）、对象、解释项分别对应性地诠释了佛法的世界相续、众生相续、业果相续，而其中"心识涌动""意识渗透""因果控制"分别关联起世界相续与再现体、众生相续与对象、业果相续与解释项。但符号学只能阐释其形之于言的部分，涉及功夫论、超验论的部分却有待吾人实证。

关键词： 唯识论 因果律 符号学

一 释迦四十九年说法的教义演进历程与唯识经论的安置

释迦说法四十九年，创一代时教。此四十九年被天台智者大师在

---

* 桑大鹏，教授，三峡大学文学与传媒学院。

《法华玄义》中细分为五个时段①：华严时；阿含时；方等时；般若时；涅槃法华时。其中华严时为释迦在菩提树下初成道时向法身大士说法，历十四天，后集结为《华严经》，此经直接描述佛境，并历叙进趋佛境的阶梯，将佛的最高境界与佛法大意和盘托出，表明往后四十九年的历阶而升并非释迦知识本身有变化，而是依其弟子心智的成长而渐次演述、逐步展开的，是胸有成竹的安排。

阿含时，佛十二年间说法于印度十六国，后人集结为四《阿含》（长阿含、中阿含、增一阿含、杂阿含），佛为四众弟子开显四谛八正道十二因缘三十七道品，指陈因果律显现的经验事相，同时隐说唯识，代表最初级、最浅显的佛法，被称为小乘佛法。

方等时，方等——方正平等，佛八年间观察四众弟子的根性并观机逗教、因病予药，是时佛察知利根弟子中有人已能接受大乘，乃向他们斥小赞大，将其引入大乘，乃有《维摩经》《胜鬘经》《楞伽经》《般舟经》《净土经》等；从空有二理角度广说因果之理，并有他方佛土显化的因果由来。唯识经典在此时段出现，《楞伽经》提出著名的"八识说"（眼识、耳识、鼻识、舌识、身识、意识、末那、阿赖耶识——后文有解说），此是佛为利根弟子初种唯识之根。

般若时，此时段历二十二年。佛广说般若空相，以六百卷《大般若经》为代表，并有《金刚经》《心经》为眷属和提纯，广显唯识性相理体的空性空相，以明空性不碍因果，因果不碍空性。

涅槃法华时，此时段历近八年，佛说《法华经》《解深密经》《大般涅槃经》等。其中《法华经》解释佛到人间向人类开示悟入佛之知见的终极迷案，而小乘极果阿罗汉不过是趋向佛境的"化城"，是暂时休歇之处，激励弟子回小向大，走菩萨的普度众生之路而趋向佛境。《解深密经》为佛将要取涅槃时所说，佛涅槃后集结经典时被小乘弟子们归入方等部，实则不了佛意。此经是唯识论派的著名经典，佛在经中彻底打开究竟密意，提出"三自性""阿陀那识"等著名概念，并为自己

---

① 五时判教出自智者大师《法华玄义》卷9、卷10，华严宗也有小、始、终、顿、圆之五层判教，与智者判教暗合，学界以智者判教影响较大，故多用。

四十九年说法划分时段，即初转说阿含、二转说般若、三转说唯识。此与智者大师五时段相合，唯识代表最高最后的阶段。《大般涅槃经》为佛趋向涅槃时一日一夜为弟子所说，佛追问弟子们还有何疑虑并一一扫除，提出著名的"眼见佛性说"，指出菩萨证悟空理后可肉眼洞见实相，依此眼见之实相而任运自在，必趋佛果；并向四众弟子和盘托出因果律发生的始源地，表明"万法皆空，因果不空"的终极因由，显示佛境作为人的因圆果满的完美性，佛就是"人的完成"，或"完成的人"。涅槃法华时与华严时遥相呼应，表明佛走完了四十九年的度生里程又回到极境。

纵观四十九年的佛法理路，我们发现其中贯穿两条并行不悖而互为表里的主线：因果律的揭示及其唯识论的说明。此两条主线一方面揭示了因果律作为宇宙间的总规律，在精神与物理层面无不应验，佛以此警示四众尊重因果，遵守戒律，诸恶莫作，众善奉行；另一方面解释了因果律发生的唯识论因由，识知因果律的由来，佛以此教戒行者循因果之路趋向佛境，取路回家。

智者五时段说既然与释迦的三时段说若合符契，而两条主线又贯穿始终，对此我们就应该思考其中的密意。我们发现，唯识学思想其实是佛说法四十九年彻始彻终的思想。华严时全面展示佛在证悟唯识极理后双具道种智与一切种智而遍知遍在的法身境界；阿含时因弟子不具备接受唯识的心智水平，故佛隐说唯识，四谛八正道初显唯识表象，十二因缘以阿赖耶识为源头和起点，展开一路流衍的过程，三十七道品深隐唯识精神；方等时正式提出唯识论，并在《楞伽经》中细说八识。般若时解释阿赖耶识性相皆空，倡导弟子放弃我法二执，归于唯识空理。涅槃法华时将唯识的终极源头彻底展露，解释阿赖耶识不生不灭、感生万物之不可思议的非能动品质，以及阿赖耶识理体如来藏纯净无染、万德圆备的性状，呼应华严时的法身遍在。故一代时教唯说唯识。

然而，我们仍然要将那些相对集中细说唯识的经典搜寻出来，其中《解深密经》《楞伽经》《密严经》《佛说不增不减经》《大乘本生心地观经》《央掘摩罗经》奠定了唯识学的思想基础，《楞严经》《佛藏经》《维摩经》《胜鬘经》《华严经》《佛说入胎经》等旁赞前经，是唯识思想的进一步展开。这些经典系统构建了唯识论体系，是我们了解释迦唯识论思想的必读书目。

公元四五世纪，即释迦涅槃千余年后，一大批著名学者因不满般若空宗无法合理解释现象界的迷妄，开始系统阐释唯识思想。其中无著、世亲兄弟最为有名，他们共推弥勒菩萨为唯识学派（又称瑜伽学派）创始人，而在释迦经典中，弥勒长于唯识已有明载。史籍记载，无著在禅定中上升兜率内院（最后身菩萨住处）听弥勒菩萨说了一部《瑜伽师地论》（一百卷），此为阐释唯识论的首部也是最重要论著。其后，无著造《摄大乘论》，具体阐述了阿赖耶识的存在和作用；世亲造《唯识三十颂》《唯识二十论》《大乘百法明门论》。《三十颂》将洋洋大观的《瑜伽师地论》义理浓缩为简练的三十偈颂，简述了瑜伽行派（唯识论派）的本体论、认识论、功夫论要义，从正面成立唯识论思想；《唯识二十论》则针对外人的非难，提出了"唯识无境观"，从反面成立唯识论思想；《大乘百法明门论》从五位百法的角度论证了唯识论成立的必然性。此外，更有马鸣大士造《大乘起信论》，从一心（如来藏心）二门（真如门、还灭门）的角度阐述了唯识论极理。释迦阿含时的"十二因缘论"也可作唯识观。

公元七世纪，中国玄奘西行求学天竺回国，依据《瑜伽师地论》《唯识三十颂》及世亲诸多弟子的阐释，结合自己的领悟造《成唯识论》，其弟子窥基作《成唯识论述记》，师徒俩在国内成立"法相唯识宗"（中国佛教八大宗派之一），代表了中国佛教最高哲学水平，至此，中国唯识论思想走向圆满。20世纪三四十年代，新儒家代表熊十力用儒道两派思想重解唯识，创"新唯识论"，颇不合原意，早已为梁漱溟所破，此不赘。

二　唯识论概说①

佛法唯识论是本体论、认识论、功夫（修证实践）论一应俱全的

---

① 因唯识论经论太多，故本文不一一引证，具体引证会在分论中出现。

完整体系，是佛法解释宇宙与生命的由来以及何以如其所是的完整学说。在四十九年的说法历程中，只有当四众弟子的心智与知识水平成长到足以接受唯识论时，佛才向他们开显此一真理。因此教内对唯识论有着这样一致的认识：唯识论代表佛的最高智慧，即代表佛的道种智、一切种智与差别智，是法身遍知遍在的智力因由。笔者今以浅陋学识妄叙此一真理体系，难免言不及义、挂一漏万。笔者今先行忏悔！

正如任何一种宗教与哲学体系一样，唯识论表达的是对人的终极关怀，这种终极关怀表现为对如下问题的解释：1. 生命从何处来？其本质是什么？2. 以轮回为表现形式的现实迷妄如何发生？3. 吾人所见证的物质世界何以如其所是？4. 生命的终极状态是怎样的？如何达到这种终极状态？以佛的洞见，生命与世界本为一体，而此二者一体所表现出来的轮回与现象界的迷妄，尽从无明发生，是由吾人迷失了金刚心不生不灭、非粘非滞的光明性而来，《楞严经》对这些问题有纲领性的表述：

> 佛言：若无所明，则无明觉，有所非觉，无所非明，无明又非觉湛明性。性觉必明，妄为明觉，觉非所明，因明立所。所既妄立，生汝妄能，无同异中，炽然成异，异彼所异，因异立同，同异发明，因此复立无同无异。如是扰乱，相待生劳，劳久发尘，自相浑浊，由是引起尘劳烦恼。起为世界，静成虚空，虚空为同，世界为异，彼无同异，真有为法。觉明空昧，相待成摇，故有风轮执持世界；因空生摇，坚明立碍，彼金宝者，明觉立坚，故有金轮保持国土；坚觉宝成，摇明风出，风金相摩，故有火光为变化性；宝明生润，火光上蒸，故有水轮含十方界；火腾水降，交发立坚，湿为巨海，干为洲潬，以是义故，彼大海中，火光常起，彼洲潬中，江河常注；水势劣火，结为高山，是故，山石击则成炎，融则成水，土势劣水，抽为草木，是故，林薮遇烧成土，因绞成水。交妄发生，递相为种，以是因缘，世界相续。复次，富楼那，明妄非他，觉明为咎，所妄既立，明理不逾，以是因缘，听不出声，见不超色，色香味触，六妄成就，由是分开见觉闻知，同业相缠，合离成

化，见明色发，明见想成，异见成憎，同想成爱，流爱为种，纳想为胎，交遘发生，吸引同业，故有因缘，生羯啰蓝，遏蒲昙等，胎卵湿化，随其所应，卵唯想生，胎因情有，湿以合感，化以离应，情想合离，更相变易，所有受业，逐其飞沉，以是因缘，众生相续。富楼那，想爱同结，爱不能离，则诸世间父母子孙，相生不断，是等则以欲贪为本，贪爱同滋，贪不能止，则诸世间卵化湿胎，随力强弱，递相吞食，是等则以杀贪为本，以人食羊，羊死为人，人死为羊，如是乃至十生之类，死死生生，互来相啖，恶业俱生，穷未来际，是等则以盗贪为本，汝负我命，我还汝债，以是因缘，经百千劫，常在生死，汝爱我心，我怜汝色，以是因缘，经百千劫，常在缠缚，唯杀盗淫，三为根本，以是因缘，业果相续。富楼那，如是三种颠倒相续，皆是觉明，明了知性，因了发相，从妄见生，山河大地，诸有为相，次第迁流，因此虚妄，终而复始。（《楞严经》卷4）

此中，佛以累世历练、冷然洞观的智慧叙述了三种相续（物质界、众生界以及因果律控引下的业因果报）及其所以发生的因由，为轮回着的人之终极关怀提供了一种思考和答案。三种相续是如何发生的呢？这正是唯识论所要致力破解的问题。

唯识论认为，吾人皆有八识，此八识可分四大部分表述：一、前五识：眼识、耳识、鼻识、舌识、身（触）识；二、第六识：意识；三、第七识：意根，又称末那识，即吾人之自我意识；四、第八识：阿赖耶识。其中阿赖耶识是前七识的始发地和回归地，所谓唯识，即"唯此阿赖耶识，万物唯识所成所变"。今结合唯识论之其他方面分叙之。

（一）六道轮回：此为佛法对生命轮回的基本认识，通大小乘。六道即天道、人道、阿修罗道、畜生道、饿鬼道、地狱道，是六种生命层次与形式。其中人道因寿命短促（七八十年，故生起年光有限的紧迫感），具备理性（认知功能）和五官感知（全面感知世界），反倒最优胜。驱动吾人轮回六道的是因果律，因果律利用善恶业报指引生命数数六道往返，尝尽一切苦乐境界。若不能证悟阿赖耶识，则轮回永无穷尽。佛法的全部目的就是要超越生死，永断轮回。

（二）六根：眼耳鼻舌身意，前五种是吾人应对外界的五种肉身构件，而"意"则是属于心灵的识知官能，此"意"既与前五根相渗透，又自身独立，外界表象信息通过前五根渠道为吾人所捕获，并被"意"所了别。五根又分胜义根与浮尘根，浮尘根就是吾人可见的肉身构件，如眼如葡萄、耳如蒲扇、鼻如悬胆、舌如卷叶、身如肉桶手如勾爪（身手一体），胜义根就是与此五种外在肉身相应的神经系统，为浮尘根所依，集中在脑部。意根是无色根，即第七识，又称末那识，并无物质性器官。由于六根是外在信息所入之处，故又称"六入"。

（三）六尘：色声香味触法，与六根相应，是六根触知与把握的对象。此六尘又分内相分与外相分，外相分是由无数众生阿赖耶识大种姓自性生发叠合而成的物质世界，内相分即阿赖耶识依此物质世界而在吾人五根门头幻现的一模一样的影像。其中法尘之"法"具有"轨则""界别"之意，在佛法里，一切可以言名之的事相（精神、物理）皆可名"法"，因一切精神物理事相均依一定的轨则和界别而成立，法尘是意识和意根所攀缘的境界，此中法尘具有精神性。

（四）六识：眼耳鼻舌身意识，是六根接触六尘发生的六种识知了别功能，即关于形色、声响、气味、味道、滑涩、善恶的识知判断。当状如葡萄之眼球摄取外在形色时，此形色只是外在事物投射视网膜上的影像，尚未受到识知判断，与此同时，胜义根起用才对此作"何形何色"的分别识知，此即眼识的完成。余四根均如此。

今单说意识：意识由意根（第七识）与前五识结合而成，以意根为归，又以前五根为功能施设场地，协助前五胜义根完成对各自内相分的识知，其最活跃的特征是认知性、了别性，是"审而不恒"，其了别性来源于阿赖耶识。它一面对内五尘作出善恶美丑的了别判断，一面又将此信息提供给意根，由意根作出去留取舍的决断，同时能在前五根与意根不间断的情况下独自成立，故号"独头意识"，本质是生灭法。意识在睡眠位、闷绝位、正死位、无想定、灭尽定五种状况下是可灭的。因意识随死亡而灭，随新生命的孕育而生，故吾人每一世的意识都是全新的，上一世的意识不可能转生到此世，此世的意识也不可能转生到下一世，故吾人世世要从头学习关于世界的知识，尽管这些知识中有无数知识以往曾反复学过，但对意识而言始终是全新的。

六根六尘合称"十二处"，六根六尘六识合称"十八界"，"界"是方位界别之意，十八界描述了吾人可知可感的一切身心物质境界。

（五）第七识意根：又称末那识，即吾人自我意识，其特点是"恒、审、思量"。末那识恒以阿赖耶识为主体的"我"并因此紧紧与阿赖耶识绑定——吾人恒有自我意识，同时以前六识为"我"的功能，此为"恒"；意根时时刻刻在攀缘一切法，但因为攀缘很广——既攀缘误认作主体识的阿赖耶识为"我"，又攀缘六识的普知功能，所以祂的了别性很差。故当吾人意识觉知心不在的时候（譬如眠熟、入无想定中），吾人还是有很少分的觉知性，此即意根的觉知，因为意根不曾一刹那中断、不曾一刹那停止其攀缘、执着和很粗很差地了别，此为"审"，故说意根"恒"而又"审"；每当法尘有重大变化之时，第七识意根会做主、会决断，譬如睡眠被惊动时，它会决定我是否要醒过来，如果意根认为需要醒过来，就会把我唤醒，那么吾人意识等觉知心就会生起，识阴六识就会全部现行，开始分别应该如何响应，我们将此刹那做主的功能称为"思量"。

意根的恒审思量性，使其生出了其他一些特性及相应的名称：由其坚执阿赖耶识为"我"，引得阿赖耶识感应此执带来的善恶无记之识而永续流衍、世世不绝，故名"业识"；依此永动之识起于见相见分，如波恒转，故名"转识"；时时现起决定并引逗阿赖耶识起现身心世界，故名"现识"；驱六识分别善恶染净、好恶美丑，故名"智识"；恒持六识念念不失，并使无量世之善恶业报无分毫差违，生命因之永续流转，故名"相续识"。

意根本身了别性极差，只能恒时认同意识的认知判断并将此判断执持起来，吾人因之有了"记忆"。又，一般凡夫在无量世轮回流转中不能断此意根，但阿罗汉可断，阿罗汉断尽七识，驻于纯粹的阿赖耶识理体如来藏中，阿赖耶识无可感应，故阿罗汉不再轮回，即超越生死，"不受后有"，他们在入灭时会唱言"诸漏已尽，梵行已立，所作已办，不受后有"，这是阿罗汉最自豪的时刻。

（六）第八识阿赖耶识：此识有很多别名，如心、本体、本体识、入胎识、如来藏、异熟识、无垢识、金刚心、实相、佛性、空性、真如等。总之，此识在不同语境中有不同名称。其特点是"恒而不审"，与意识体性刚好相反。阿赖耶识是万物的渊源，吾人生命的本体，六道轮回的主体。其体性需分别解说：

1. 三藏：即能藏、所藏、执藏。能含藏前七识造作的一切善恶无记种子，故能藏；一切善恶无记种子尽落阿赖耶识中，是为所藏；这些种子不仅被收存，还被执持，在无量世的六道轮回中，于机缘成熟之时又经由前七识流注于吾人命运，显现果报，是为执藏。就所藏而言，是"现行生种子"，就执藏而言，是"种子生现行"，由此三藏，因果律永远起作用。

2. 四种大种性自性：阿赖耶识具有地、水、火、风四种大种性自性。地水火风是佛陀时代古印度人对物质世界基本元素的普遍看法。佛说法有一原则，即利用人类已有的认知能力、知识与概念阐述更高的真理而不坏世俗概念，故佛承袭了当时印度人的哲学范畴。地即坚凝性；水，润湿性；火，烧燃性；风，流动性。阿赖耶识以此四大种性因应七识之妄动，生出主体适以自存的世界，无数众生的阿赖耶识同此造作，叠影而成的结果是构建了外相分——物质世界，阿赖耶识又将此外相分投射给五胜义根，成为五胜义根所见的内相分。换言之，吾人从未见过真正的"物质世界"，所见到的只不过是此物质世界的内相分，但吾人何以又觉得此世界如此真实坚固、是真正的"物质"呢？原来，意识的本性是刹那生灭，每 0.18 秒生灭 2000 余次，即每秒生灭 10000 余次，当意识触知五胜义根提供的内相分时，其刹那生灭性异化了内相分的心识本性——电影放映机每秒钟放映 24 格同一胶片，银幕上就呈现出一个固定的画面——意识的刹那生灭性固化了内相分，使我们感知到的内相分具有坚固性和物质性，好像是外在世界。其实我们从来不曾接触过由阿赖耶识大种性自性生出的外在世界，所谓的"物质世界"不过是阿赖耶识提供的内相分，被我们的意识固化的结果。究极而论，吾人所见"世界"不过是一个幻象。

3. 四分：即相分、见分、自证分、证自证分。见分即指诸识的能缘作用，为认识事物的主体，亦即能照知所缘对境（即相分，为认识的对象）之主体作用。"见"即见照、心性明了之义，谓能照烛一切诸法及解了诸法义理，如镜中之明，能照万象。换个方式说，见分即心识的缘虑作用，亦即主观的认识主体。相分即自心体上变现出的为见分所缘的境相，在唯识学上摄尽一切所谓的客观现象。心识是能缘虑之法，心识生起时，识体变现出相、见二分，见分是能缘虑的作用，相分是所缘虑的境相。由于宇宙万法皆为阿赖耶识之所变现，故所谓相分，即是第八识的色法种子——所谓相分色所变现的境相。自证分，又作自体分，"自"是自体，"证"为证知，即自觉的证知作用。四分中的见分有缘虑、了别相分的作用，但不能自知其所见有无谬误，故必须另有一证知见分的作用，即是自证分。自证分即识之自体，故又名自体分。自证分还有一种再度知的作用，与自证分互相为证，以证二者有无谬误。证自证分，这是识体作用的一部分，即是对自证分再加以证知的作用。自证分有证知见分的作用，但谁来证知自证分有无谬误呢？于是识体更起能缘作用，以证知自证分的所证是否正确，此再度证知的作用，即是证自证分。但谁来证知证自证分有无谬误呢？就是原来的自证分，因为自证分和证自证分二者有互缘互证的作用，所以就不必另立一个证自证分了。八识各有四分，各自四分又有相当差异，其共同特征即如上所述。

4. 五蕴：即色蕴、受蕴、想蕴、行蕴、识蕴，又名五荫。蕴者集聚，荫者遮蔽，因集聚而有遮蔽，故性相相通，此二名之用依据不同语境而有所选择。五蕴即指吾人肉身生命及其适以自存的世界，色蕴即吾人六根六尘六识（十八界）蕴积而成，指十八界遮蔽吾人光明空性的粗重相状；受想行识蕴全属精神部分，指遮蔽吾人空性光明的四种心理状态。五蕴如交芦，互相借力架设，抽一芦则余者皆灭，五蕴之生全因阿赖耶识而来。

5. 情世间与器世间：即生命与物质世界，用"世界"一词主要强调其形而下品质。"五蕴"主要解释肉身生命的根身构成与精神性，兼及由"色蕴"而来的六尘。在情世间与器世间中，情世间单指一切生命；器世间单指物质世界，也包括肉身六根所对之六尘。这二种世间都是阿赖耶识的形而下显现。

6. 永恒性：阿赖耶识不生不灭、不垢不净、非动非静、无始无终，不与万物为侣而恒随万物流转。从物的主体性立场观之，阿赖耶识"非我、不异我、不相在"，行者若能开悟而破重关，则可于万物之上以肉眼洞见此识。

7. 非能动性：阿赖耶识之生成万物并非主动创生，祂并不具备能动的主体意志，而是感应而生、因应而生，即因应于七识的种子与动性感生身心世界，因此具有被动性。这与上帝、神我、梵天等第一因在主体意志驱动下不得不创世有根本差异。阿赖耶识性相体用俱空，故能不失分毫地执持因果律而无碍于空性的永存，因其空性故无碍于万物的发挥，故"万法皆空，因果不空"。或问：既是空相，何能以肉眼洞见？既能被"见"，则此空相还是一个"相"。须知，此"见"是开悟者之"见能"结合体验所得。

8. 性体如来藏：阿赖耶识性体名如来藏，此即阿赖耶识最纯净无染的部分，万德圆备、不假修成、本然如是。人之能成佛，就是修除了阿赖耶识的染污部分而得以纯净无染，故万德圆备、万法庄严、遍知遍在、福德智慧无穷。

9. 异熟识与无垢识：此二者是阿赖耶识在不同阶段被净化之后的别名。阿罗汉与八地菩萨之识名异熟识，因累世（异世）修除无明与我法二执的功行至此成熟，故名异熟识；佛地则称无垢识，因没有任何垢染、纯真一如，故名无垢识。

10. 转识成智：即转八识成四智。佛地仍具八识，但因佛累世修除无明达到纯真无染，故此佛地八识已不同于凡夫八识。其八识在道种智的渗透中获得了性能的转换，即转我执的了别为无我的直觉，显现为"纯智"，此即所谓"转识成智"：转前五识为成所作智，转第六意识为妙观察智，转第七识意根为平等性智，转第八识阿赖耶识为大圆镜智。佛地四智圆明、冷然洞观、遍知遍在、与物为春。

（七）三性三相：八识因其间性质与功能的差异而有三性之说，即依他起性、遍计所执性、圆成实性。前七识的每一识都是依"他"而起，没有独立而永恒不变的自性与主体性，如眼根色尘相触才生眼识，此眼识依根尘之触才发生，具有典型的依他而起之性；意识依末那识与前五识而起；意根依阿赖耶识与前六识才能成立。凡具依他起性者都是可断灭的生灭法——身心世界——一切精神的与物理的——全为生灭法所囊括。第七识末那识又具有遍计所执性，因其恒审思量，普遍计度阿赖耶识为"我"、前六识为"我"的功能并执持不失，是为"遍计所执"。第八识本自圆成，不受染污与轮回，虽含藏一切种子而不为种子所变，具有"圆成实性"，是唯一真正的"实相"。与此三性相应地显现"三相"即三种相状。

（八）入胎、轮回与因果：末那识因恒执阿赖耶识为"我"而与之绑定；阿赖耶识不作任何分别顺应此"我执"，而我执最突出的表现是存在感以及直接印证此存在之为存在的性快感、性冲动。当主体（人、人类、一切有灵性生命之物）一期生命结束之后，阿赖耶识因其不灭性带着末那识出离肉身而漂移，此时的灵体状态称为"神识体"，因其是介于前后两世之间的阴性能量，由记忆而显现为前世的影像，故又名"中阴身"，即民间俗语所说的"灵魂"。第七识并不适应这种漂移状态，祂急需找到一个肉身以确证自己还"存在"，基于存在感需要的性冲动驱使祂去寻找有缘的父母。当此父母发生性关系时，中阴身乐观其事，一旦受精卵出现，中阴身即扑向此受精卵，如果中阴身喜欢性交中的女性，受精卵将来会形成男性肉身，反之则为女性——这可解释弗洛伊德潜意识之女性的恋父情节与男性的恋母情结。在中阴身看来，祂重又获得了一个坚实沉重的肉身而实现了存在感，其实是入胎而使受精卵具备了"识"，具备识的受精卵开始利用母体子宫的精血吸摄四大（地水火风）滋养自身，此即胎儿的发育。四个月时，胎儿形姿初具，阿赖耶识利用肉身五根使前六识现起，于是八识齐备。九至十个月，胎儿成熟而出生，经历童年、少年、青年、中年、壮年、老年，直至死去，于是这一期生命结束，完成了一个轮回过程。

主体前世的善恶业与定力决定了其下一世的六道（天、人、阿修罗、畜生、饿鬼、地狱）轮回与生命走向。当具备识的受精卵出现后，收存于阿赖耶识中的善恶业种流注于受精卵、胎儿、成人而影响此人命运，是即"种子生现行"。如果主体前世善业大于恶业，感得阿赖耶识流注善的种子，在形貌、事功、幸福感等方面都流注出符合社会正面评价的因素，使主体模样端正、事业成功、心理幸福；如果恶业大于善业则反之，此即显现为善恶业报的因果律现行。当然，因果律至少要通观三世方能获得事相上的验证，用主体一世的命运来确证因果会多有龃龉。佛曰："假使百千劫，所作业不亡，因缘会遇时，果报还自受。"（《大集经》）只要阿赖耶识含藏着善恶业种，则必然会显现善恶果报，无论跨越多少世。

（九）开悟与念佛往生：开悟是教内教外一切行者的毕生使命，也是最神秘最不可思议的事件。佛住世时，释迦四众弟子中很多人在佛陀三言两语的开示下当下证悟（开悟）；佛涅槃后，众生开悟愈益艰难，但并非没有。我国隋唐时代仍有大量行者开悟，六祖慧能、唐僧玄奘、南泉普愿、赵州从谂、圆悟克勤等不仅开悟，并有言论行世，《五灯会元》《景德传灯录》等在在有言。当代，有台湾在家居士萧平实先生彻悟实相并有一百多部著作问世。悟，有小乘极果阿罗汉、辟支佛二乘之悟与大乘菩萨之悟。阿罗汉断尽前七识，入驻阿赖耶识中，独存如来藏而不再出生后世色身，但此并非触证了阿赖耶识而是信顺佛语知有阿赖耶识不灭，乃驻于阿赖耶识而永超轮回，因而只是个人的解脱，故佛并不完全认同，佛将阿罗汉所证之涅槃称作"化城"，认为此涅槃只是暂时休歇之处；菩萨触证阿赖耶识，破重关洞见实相、破牢关生起差别智，了知阿赖耶识的不生不灭性而不断第七识，用第七识的引生性引发自己无惧于轮回并无数次重返六道来普度众生，使众生也趋向佛境，与此同时自己也积功累德而成佛。纵然有很多人早已成佛，也会重入轮回，倒驾慈航，重新开始度生大业，如观世音菩萨为正法明如来再来，文殊菩萨为龙种上如来再来，他们都是以菩萨的身份倒驾慈航的典范。

若没有善知识的开示，一般人很难通过自己努力而开悟。于是佛为吾人开设"念佛往生"一途，即在满足净业三福（孝养父母，奉事师长，慈心不杀，修十善业；受持三皈，具足众戒，不犯威仪；发菩提心，深信因果，读诵大乘，劝进行者）之后以信愿行称佛名号，口诵心惟，以期这一期生命结束之后以神识体往生佛国。在我们银河系周围都有佛国，其中特别是西方极乐世界的阿弥陀佛，发四十八大愿，感召十方众生，迄今已有无数众生往生此佛土，不再轮回。

（十）四种涅槃与中道：不生不灭、非生非死谓之涅槃，中道即驻于涅槃之境。涅槃共有四种：无余依涅槃；有余依涅槃；本来自性清净涅槃；无住处涅槃。二乘（阿罗汉、辟支佛）圣人所入的是无余涅槃，即信顺佛语断尽七识，入驻不生不灭的阿赖耶识中，永断轮回，没有任何再生的可能，故名无余依涅槃；断一切烦恼而绝未来生死之因，然尚余今生之果报身体，谓之有余依涅槃；菩萨触证阿赖耶识，现观一切境界都依光明心如来藏而施设，此心离见闻觉知，不执六尘，本具妙性，非修而得，光明晃耀，永离尘染，故菩萨不畏生死，不惧轮回，数数往来六道而不动道场，永不入无余涅槃，此之谓本来自性清净涅槃；佛已登佛地，已证真如，不住生死，不入涅槃，大慈大悲，利乐有情，虽已不再流转生死，但亦不脱离世间，穷未来际度脱众生而无有穷尽，是谓之佛地无住处涅槃。

三　唯识论的符号学介入

前文从十个方面叙述唯识论学说，尚不能尽唯识论之少分，其间或有谬误，笔者敬待方家。读者若欲了知唯识论全体，当深入经论，细寻其理。从大处说，唯识论代表佛陀无数世理证与实证的最高智慧，其名相之繁多、教义之宏富、推理之严密，非世间其他学说可比。

唯识论可用西方形形色色的哲学与文学理论进行诠释，但任何一种纯理论的诠释都只是触及了唯识论可以言说的部分，其不可诠释的部分则有待精神实证（非物理实证），得之于悟性、验之于超越，即顿悟实相超越轮回。换言之，其实证处超言绝思，"于不可言说处我们应当保持沉默"（维特根斯坦）。因此，康德的做法是聪明的——他对"物自体"本身不置片言，只是以之为最高命令，而为信仰与伦理留出地盘。

当我们用符号学诠释唯识论时，我们首先感受到的居然是符号学本身的有限。尽管符号学分支繁多，但其中最能用于诠释唯识论的是认知符号学与意义符号学。自索绪尔以来直至如今，意义符号学已渐趋成熟，但认知符号学迄今尚无完整的体系与成熟的方法，所以我们只能从皮尔斯逻辑符号学（本质也是认知符号学）中拿来范畴、理路与方法对唯识论加以诠释。索绪尔与皮尔斯思想是我们介入唯识论的工具。

人是追寻意义的动物。吾人追寻意义、承担意义并在意义中安身立命。生命延续的过程就是意义繁衍延宕的过程，生命因体验意义流衍而"具有意义"，而意义又必须因形形色色的符号（语言、图符、图像、行为、礼仪、仪式、旋律、建筑等）而获得。事实上，符号本身就内含着意义，是知性嵌入符号的结果，因而，符号关联着认知。"符号学作为一种对普遍意义活动规律的思索，目的就是为了理清人类表达与认识意义的方式，符号被认为是携带意义的感知。意义必须用符号才能表达，符号的用途是表达意义。符号不仅是表达意义的工具或载体，符号是意义的条件，意义不可能脱离符号而存在。"① 故符号本身是认知性的，人经由符号创造并体验意义，是故，人又是符号的动物。

唯识论是由一系列庞大宏富的范畴、概念铺就的终极关怀的理路。汉译佛经根据玄奘规定有五不翻的原则：（一）多含不翻：如"薄伽梵"，指世尊，是佛陀的名号之一，又含有自在、炽盛、端严、吉祥、尊重等义。又如"摩诃"，含有大、殊胜、长久及深奥等义。（二）秘密不翻：如楞严咒、大悲咒、十小咒，以及各种经咒，一经翻出，就会失去它的神秘性。为什么咒语不翻？为的是怕持咒的人，知道太多文字意义，反而有了文字上的障碍，即"所知障""文字障"。（三）尊重不翻：如"般若"，不可直译为智慧，"三昧"不可直译为"正定"，"涅槃"不可直译为圆寂或解脱等。（四）顺古不翻：如"阿耨多罗三藐三菩提"不可直译为"无上正等正觉"，"阿罗汉"不可直译为"无生"，"菩萨"不可直译为"觉悟"等。（五）此方无不翻："此方"指中国。如印度的庵摩罗果，形似苹果，其意为"无垢清净"，食之可除风热，但中国没有。佛经中常以"庵摩罗果"来比喻地球的形状。

因有此五不翻，故中国人对这一系列符号关涉着的别样意义就无从

---

① 赵毅衡：《关于认知符号学的思考：人文还是科学？》，《符号与传媒》2015 年秋季号，第 107 页。

体验，而只能在由《周易》奠基的文化语境里体验已经翻译过来的符号意义。唐代李通玄站在《易》理的前见立场诠释《华严经》，使《华严经》玄义向《易》理生成，树立了一个异域经典中国化的典范。故经典意义之发生是具体的文化语境培育的结果。

即便尊重五不翻，但吾人仍可根据上下文语境体验其不翻符号的意义，这既为符号学所允许，更是符号学之意义体验的必由之路。在此符号学语境中，我们可根据佛以唯识论推演的三种相续所显现的终极关怀介入符号学，使其意义向符号学生成。

（一）世界相续：再现体的生成与意义的发生

> 佛言：若无所明，则无明觉，有所非觉，无所非明，无明又非觉湛明性。性觉必明，妄为明觉，觉非所明，因明立所。所既妄立，生汝妄能，无同异中，炽然成异，异彼所异，因异立同，同异发明，因此复立无同无异。如是扰乱，相待生劳，劳久发尘，自相浑浊，由是引起尘劳烦恼。起为世界，静成虚空，虚空为同，世界为异，彼无同异，真有为法。觉明空昧，相待成摇，故有风轮执持世界；因空生摇，坚明立碍，彼金宝者，明觉立坚，故有金轮保持国土：坚觉宝成，摇明风出，风金相摩，故有火光为变化性：宝明生润，火光上蒸，故有水轮含十方界：火腾水降，交发立坚，湿为巨海，干为洲滩，以是义故，彼大海中，火光常起，彼洲滩中，江河常注：水势劣火，结为高山，是故，山石击则成炎，融则成水，土势劣水，抽为草木，是故，林薮遇烧成土，因绞成水。交妄发生，递相为种，以是因缘，世界相续。（《楞严经》卷4）

佛在这一段文字中详细阐释了物质世界发生与流变的过程，解释了空轮、风轮、水轮、金轮（坚实的物质）形成的因由，其中世为迁流，界为方位，此即时空的由来。我们可将此视作一个系统命题的总纲领（后二种相续与此同观）。在佛的阐释中，与此命题相关的一系列范畴、概念（四种大种姓自性、五蕴、六尘等）以及相关理路都是我们给予符号介入的圈域。事实上，这一系列命题的表述本身就是符号，是符号学关注的范围。根据皮尔斯符号的三分构造说，一个完整的符号体系可从再现体、对象、解释项三个方面来考察，我们既可对唯识论的某一概念作如是思考，也可对其命题表述系统作如是观待。本文在对唯识论作符号学思考时，使试图针对三种相续及相关范畴分层作再现体、对象、解释项的考察。读者以此进行互文性的统合，当会获得全面的了解。

佛陀解释世界相续时，创造了一系列再现体：其一，"世界相续"本身就是一个再现体，它以全称肯定命题的形式表述了一个动态相；其二，为使"世界相续"这一命题与表述成立，佛再创空轮、风轮、水轮、金轮、四种大种姓自性、五蕴、六尘等范畴并将其引入表述，走向某种意义。

何为"再现体"？再现体与符号同名，"它一方面由一个对象所决定，另一方面又在人们心灵中决定一个观念……思想，如果不是唯一的，也是最主要的再现体类型……"① 皮尔斯此论道出了什么呢？笔者认为应有如下意涵：1. 吾人在创造一个符号时，必须考虑对象的性质，因为对象的性质决定了符号的性质，唯识论正是从现象世界入手创设了一系列的符号并以此为基础展开程式化推演，即所谓因明逻辑的展开。2. 符号一旦生成，就会在吾人心中引生相应的意识体验与观念，因此唯识论的推理过程就是伴随着主体的意识体验的一系列观念的建构过程。3. 由观念建构的思想体系本身又构成了符号体系，故唯识论不仅义理无穷，还可自我繁衍，符号经由意义的推演之路可自我生成。4. 思想本身是运动的，故符号体系在运动中会不断衍生新的符号体系，如此繁衍，以至无穷，达到思想的无限丰富与流衍，唯识论以此而生生不息，可接纳任何哲学的诠释而不为所动。

唯识论有一个预设，即"三界唯识，万法唯心"，又说，万物无不是"唯心所现，唯识所变"。这就是直面现象世界并直指其心识本性，以此而产生的观念符号具有与现象世界的同质性，即均是主体意识体验

———————————

① ［美］皮尔斯：《皮尔斯：论符号》，赵星植译，四川大学出版社2014年版，第31—33页。

的产物，而在由此繁兴的思想体系与符号体系之中时时处处涌动着心识之流。因思想的运动性，符号系统时时展开着。

世界何以相续？因心识涌动。故佛陀在表述世界相续，解释空轮、风轮、水轮、金轮的形成与运动时，本质都是在表明"心识涌动"的符号显现。换言之，物质世界的形成、运动与展开本质上都是符号的表现。既如此，唯识论用以指陈物质对象的范畴如五蕴、六尘也都是心识涌动的符号了。

再现体即符号，是为了将某种确定的意义围住的手段。皮尔斯的符号建立在现象学的基础上，故符号本身就是意识体验的产物，其因被灌注了某种心智与认知而与主体意识息息相关。根据皮尔斯对符号之品质、事实、法则的规定与考量，当佛陀创造一系列符号进行唯识论表述时，其符号所固有的品质、事实、法则因素在佛陀的归纳、演绎、试推中已注定会走向必然的终极结论。

皮尔斯对符号品质、事实、法则尤其是品质的思考极有价值。他写道：

> 一个真正的一般物不可能具有任何存在，除非它存在于这样一种前景中，即它在某个时候有机会被具体化到一个事实之中，而这个事实自身不是一种法则或者任何与法则相似的东西……它（品质）不是某种在其存在方面依赖于心灵——不管这种心灵是以感觉形式出现，还是以思想形式出现——的事物；它也不在其存在方面依赖于这样一种事实，即某种物质性的东西会拥有它。认为品质依赖于感觉，这是概念论者所犯的一个严重错误；认为它依赖于它在其中得以实现的那种主体，这是一切唯名论者所犯的一个严重错误。品质仅仅是一种抽象的潜在性……我们可以把现象的这一面向称为它的"一元观相"，而品质就是把自身呈现于一元观相的那种东西。[①]

---

① ［美］皮尔斯：《皮尔斯：论符号》，赵星植译，四川大学出版社 2014 年版，第15—20 页。

我们可将此种论述用之于阿赖耶识及其四种大种姓自性之中，用之于阿赖耶识生发万物的创造性活动之中。就阿赖耶识本身而言，祂正是一种"不可能具有任何存在"的存在，而只会在具象（前景）中显现，其存在与显现既不依赖于任何感觉的心灵，也不依赖于任何形式的思想，更不会被某种"物质性的东西"所拥有。换言之，任何唯灵论、唯实论、唯名论的言说都是一种与唯识论的疏离，相对于唯识论，这些言说只会渐行渐远而不可能切近祂。万物之中的阿赖耶性永远是一种潜在性，祂只能显现，却不能被创造。而且吾人欲瞥见这种显现只能通过实证的直观，通过物的"一元观相"直接切中，这可能是吾人切近阿赖耶识的唯一道路。

然而，物质世界的"事实"毕竟实实在在地向吾人显现着。在皮尔斯的符号学语境中，"事实"是这样一种东西：

> 这些（品质、法则）被排除在外的事物留给事实范畴的，首先是那种被逻辑学者们称之为"偶然的"东西，即偶然的实在之物……假如我们撇开别的事实，去考虑某个个别事物的任何状态，我们就有了这样一种现象，即它是实在的，但其自身却又不是必然的。我并不打算把在此处称为"事实"的东西视为全部现象，它仅仅是现象的一种成分——它甚至属于一个特定的地点以及时间。[1]

这就是说，"事实"是一种偶在！它的存在和出现需依赖于时空。这种界定与西方哲学语境尤其是普诺提诺、胡塞尔等话语中的"质料"十分接近，它是普诺提诺精神抵达的最后场地、是启示胡塞尔意向性之被构建的神秘力量，在一定程度是"被造"的，是现象——符号最遥远的边界。由于心识涌动，事实不能不出现，不能不向吾人显现。

---

[1] ［美］皮尔斯：《皮尔斯：论符号》，赵星植译，四川大学出版社 2014 年版，第 23—24 页。

在阿赖耶识四种大种姓自性中隐含着地水火风的物化趋势，只是在被意根（第七识）搅动之前，此种趋势隐而不发、永远蛰伏。换言之，阿赖耶识内部（请读者原谅笔者不得不用"内部"表明此种情势）永远潜含着被符号化的可能性，一旦心识涌动，四种大种姓自性终于得以显形，于是事实现前而符号形成。事实与再现体、与对象各有交叉部分，但不可能完全重叠。就其显现而言，它是意根搅动阿赖耶识的"被生"之物，故此与心识关联，无论其与心识多么遥远；就其功能而言，它又是启动主体哲思、进行形而上思考的引发之物，此与对象具有同一功用。

事实的形成与出现不可能是无缘无故的，而一定有某种理路运载事实之出现，此理路即皮尔斯的"法则"。按皮尔斯的理解，"连续性几乎完美地再现了第三性，每个过程均从那头开始发生"①。此中的"第三性"即是法则，是一种支配事物之出现的必然律。此法则在唯识论体系中，就宏观语境而言即为"因果律"，就物之形成与出现的微观语境而言可名之曰"因缘"。体现法则的"连续性"何以名之？一定是事实不间断地次第涌现，乃有了主体有关连续性的意识体验。皮尔斯并没有论及连续性的因由，只是推断出有一法则在支配着此种连续性，但唯识论比皮尔斯走得更远，唯识论断言：无论是事实之发生，还是其运演之理路，无不受因果律支配。佛法研究了因与果交织而成的多种形式与关系，佛陀四十九年说法，就是在事相与理论上表明因果律，最后深入唯识，才揭破了因果律的根由。这是符号学刚刚触及皮毛而唯识论已然培育成熟的领域。

总之，主体"心识涌动"带来两个结果：1. 世界相续；2. 符号（再现体）发生。心识涌动的本质是无明妄动，阿赖耶识感应此无明妄动生成永续流转的世界，而立足于现象学的符号正是意识流动的产物。主体借此心识涌动体验生命的意义，符号借此心识涌动言说意义的流动，此二者深刻地关联着。

---

① ［美］皮尔斯：《皮尔斯：论符号》，赵星植译，四川大学出版社 2014 年版，第 14 页。

(二) 众生相续：对象的"被造"

> 佛言：复次，富楼那，明妄非他，觉明为咎，所妄既立，明理不逾，以是因缘，听不出声，见不超色，色香味触，六妄成就，由是分开见觉闻知，同业相缠，合离成化，见明色发，明见想成，异见成憎，同想成爱，流爱为种，纳想为胎，交遘发生，吸引同业，故有因缘，生羯啰蓝，遏蒱昙等，胎卵湿化，随其所应，卵唯想生，胎因情有，湿以合感，化以离应，情想合离，更相变易，所有受业，逐其飞沉，以是因缘，众生相续。(《楞严经》卷4)

此一部分侧重论及皮尔斯符号体系中的"对象"。前述所引文字中，佛论及生命的形成与流变：由隐含无明的前七识扰动具有无限可能性的阿赖耶识，阿赖耶识以其明性因应此种扰动；代表本觉的"明"被固化、僵化，显现为某种知觉性，这种知觉性能反观自身，所谓"觉明为咎"，即僵化的明性已失去本初的无限可能性，只能在对立中有限地发挥原有觉性的作用——听不出声、见不超色，故形成前六根的妄知妄觉，是谓之"能（见）"——六根；为使此"能"最终演现，阿赖耶识用自己的大种姓自性为此"能"提供演现的场所，是即"所（见）"——六尘；六根六尘相触，发生六识，生命开始跃动。个体生命在交往的过程中，爱憎业种交缠，善恶业果升沉轮转，形成胎（生）卵（生）湿（生）化（生）四种生命形式和六道轮回的层次升降，交互发生，绵延无穷，是谓之"众生相续"。

在因果律的表述中，佛将个体生命的肉身看作正报，将其生活的环境视作依报，即个体依之展开活动与命运的场所。我们可以看出，无论是正报还是依报，都是展现因果律的果报显现，其本质都是皮尔斯符号系统中的"对象"。

那么，皮尔斯如何界定对象呢？细读《皮尔斯：论符号》一书，笔者发现，由于皮尔斯总是在一种三元关系中理解再现体（符号）、对象、解释项这些概念，所以当他解释对象时，便不可能摆脱符号与解释项来解释对象，这就使其对对象的解释一再地落在了对符号与解释项的解释上，对对象的说明反而显得次要了。皮尔斯说：

> 任何东西为了成为符号，都必须"再现"其他的事物，这种事物就叫做它的"对象"……符号可以被理解为它的对象的某种"流溢"……每个符号都独立于自身而代替一个对象，但它只能是那个对象的符号，只因这个对象本身就具有符号或思想的本质。因为符号不能够影响对象而是被对象所影响，因此，对象必然能够传达思想，也即它必然具有思想或者符号的本质。每一个思想都是一个符号。①

可以看出，符号与对象互相出生，符号可以出生对象，对象也可以出生符号——符号可以被理解为它的对象的某种流溢。符号是对象的符号，对象是符号的对象。由于皮尔斯的符号体系是建立在现象学的基础上，这使其对象不能不具有某种心识本性。换言之，我们必须从意识体验的角度来理解对象。

在唯识论语境中，对象如同主体一样，都是"被生"之物——被阿赖耶识所生，这使得主体与对象都具有心识特征。对象依于主体而生，因此对象必具有识性，所谓"心生种种法生，法生种种心生"即是此意。同时，对象之发生全因主体而改变，由于主体的无明妄觉，对象随时发生并因主体之千殊万类而显现形形色色，换言之，主体随时创造着对象并陷入与对象的对立之中，主体甚至将自身都当作对象。具有认知能力的主体只能从对象中发现存在与生活的意义——对象为主体提供意义，对象在一定意义上其实是主体的意义载体。主体正是在与对象的交互关系中演现着命运轨迹与种子生现行、现行生种子的永恒因果律——这正是皮尔斯对象之意义"流溢"的价值所在。

皮尔斯是在一种三元关系中解释对象的，这种思维兼及后两者，即

---

① ［美］皮尔斯：《皮尔斯：论符号》，赵星植译，四川大学出版社 2014 年版，第 41—43 页。

使我们任取两者作深观，那遗漏的一元也会因时需而随时参与进来，以充实两两静观的意义。当我们在考虑对象时，必须同时将解释项与符号考虑进去。

总之，在众生层面，阿赖耶识由于受主体的无明扰动而被固化、僵化，使主体通过肉身感知渠道将意识辐射到万物，由此构建起充满精神性的世界，演绎自身的流转；在符号学体系中，主体只能通过被意识渗透的对象才能表达自身，一个表达式少了对象的被借喻将是不可思议的，主体的价值与意义只有借助于对象才能被表达。这是两种体系的深刻关联所在。

（三）业果相续：因果律关联的三种解释项

> 佛言：富楼那，想爱同结，爱不能离，则诸世间父母子孙，相生不断，是等则以欲贪为本，贪爱同滋，贪不能止，则诸世间卵化湿胎，随力强弱，递相吞食，是等则以杀贪为本，以人食羊，羊死为人，人死为羊，如是乃至十生之类，死死生生，互来相啖，恶业俱生，穷未来际，是等则以盗贪为本，汝负我命，我还汝债，以是因缘，经百千劫，常在生死，汝爱我心，我怜汝色，以是因缘，经百千劫，常在缠缚，唯杀盗淫，三为根本，以是因缘，业果相续。（《楞严经》卷4）

此一部分侧重论及符号的解释项。前文已述及，阿赖耶识由于具有三藏本性，前七识造作的一切业因皆会被阿赖耶识收存，尤其是第七识意根坚执阿赖耶识为"我"的主体、前六识为"我"的功能，感得非动非静的阿赖耶识因应此种执着而万象繁兴，而诸种执着中能量最大者莫过于贪执，此贪执具体表现为杀、盗、淫，故佛发言即直指本质——想爱同结，爱不能离……是等则以欲贪为本；贪爱同滋，贪不能止……递相吞食，是等则以杀贪为本……死死生生，互来相啖，恶业俱生，穷未来际，是等则以盗贪为本……唯杀盗淫，三为根本，以是因缘，业果相续——表明杀盗淫在吾人命运流程中的演现事相。

佛不仅论及因果律的事相，而且论及其本质，即揭示因果律发生的唯识论根源。细思佛的因果论表述，我们至少可作如下领悟：1. 因果律是运载万物流变的总规律，万物不出因果之外，因果是万物演现的理路；2. 因果不仅决定物的流变，还是催生和诱发物之发生的唯一与根本力量，以此名为"因缘与果报"，有因有缘即有果，因缘具备，果就发生，若有因无缘或有缘无因，则果的出现是不可想象的；3. 因与果的关联形式有多种，一因一果、一因多果、多因一果、多因多果都是其表现；4. 因果律不仅决定了物之发生，而且决定了物之意义，而此物之意义是由它与余物的共时性与历时性关系决定的，因此，因果律其实是物之本身以及物物之间的根本意；5. 阿赖耶识虽然非动非静，但因果律必然是运动的，这决定了万物的生灭流变。

唯识论对因果律的阐释使我们联想到符号学的解释项。在三元关系模式中，皮尔斯对解释项有多层面、多角度的界定：

> 符号在解释者的心灵中创造了某种东西，而这种东西是由符号创造出来的，并且符号的对象也通过某种间接的或相关的方式创造了这种东西。符号的这一产物叫做"解释项"……符号的解释项就是符号所传达的所有事物，也即必须通过间接经验才能获得的、与其对象相熟悉的那些东西……符号把某种事物代替为它所产生或所改造的那个观念，或者说，它是把某物从心灵之外传达到心灵之中的一个载体。符号所代替的那种东西被称为它的对象；它所传达的东西，是它的意义；它所引起的观念，是它的解释项。再现的对象只不过是一个再现，而后面这个再现的解释项则是第一个再现。这种"前一个再现后一个"的无止境再现系列，可能会在其极限之处存在着一个"绝对对象"……这里存在着一种无限的回归。最后，解释项只不过是另一种再现，真相的火炬传递到后一种再现之中，而这种再现同样也具有解释项。①

---

① ［美］皮尔斯：《皮尔斯：论符号》，赵星植译，四川大学出版社 2014 年版，第 43—49 页。

皮尔斯规定了解释项的多种类型，他根据符号的适合意指效力将解释项分为情绪解释项、能量解释项、逻辑解释项，这三种解释项均可与前文所述之因果律的基本效能关联起来。

我们已知，因果律是由意根的无明我执之扰动、由阿赖耶识因其无限可能性成就此扰动而来。作为万物演现的理路，意根的每一次妄动都决定了万物的命运——但这种妄动却是主体自为的结果，不能求之于外因，故佛说"因果自承"。因果律的律动决定了物的根本命运，它是催生和诱发物之发生的唯一与根本力量，我们可将此关联到皮尔斯的"逻辑解释项"。皮尔斯写道：

> 逻辑解释项产生一种心灵效力，但它不是一个符号，而属于一种"普遍应用"，因此，心灵效力是一种"习惯改变"。习惯改变意味着一个人会修正自己行为的习惯性倾向。这种修正行为可能源自其意愿的或行动的先前经验或前期努力，又或者是上述两种原因共同造成的结果。①

意根的作用正在于决断，决断行为发生的方式与思想的方向，修正前期的意愿与经验，即"习惯改变"，从而形成一种心灵效力，并且这种心灵效力还可"普遍应用"。换言之，意根决断导致习惯改变，习惯改变引生行为链条，如此而导致顺次发生的意义之流，此为逻辑解释项的意趣所在，也是因果律根本价值的验证。

皮尔斯认为，"符号自身会产生一种感觉……以致我们将其解读为我们了解符号适合意指效力的证据……我将这种感觉称为'情绪解释项'……在某些情况下，它就是某些符号能够产生的唯一意指效力"②。皮尔斯的"感觉"显然具有认知的意义，即符号具有反观以达

---

① ［美］皮尔斯：《皮尔斯：论符号》，赵星植译，四川大学出版社 2014 年版，第 46 页。

② 同上书，第 45 页。

到自我认知的能力。这种能力在单一的范畴逻辑中，其价值并不了然，但在命题与表述中，其作用相当明显——这难道不是符号意义的自显自明吗？

在一个语流（即命题的展开与表述的完成，按皮尔斯之意，一个表述系统也构成一种符号）中，符号一方面达到意义的自显自明，另一方面又有一种能力来认读这种自显自明的意义。请注意，这正是因果律发生关键作用的时机！因为因果律不仅决定了物之发生，而且决定了物之意义，主体的每一次决断都不过是因果律的复制与延伸，借此以显示并体验生命的意义而已。此种意义的显示与被体验既与个人、种族的历史相关联，又与其所自来的社会文化相关联，即具有共时性与历时性特征。如此，符号的情绪解释项又与因果律关联起来了。

借助于情绪解释项这一媒介，符号的意指效果将会卷入更多的意指行为，亦即情绪解释项的延伸会带来符号意义的繁衍与延宕，显示符号具有意义的创生功能，是一个蕴含生机的能量系统，此即皮尔斯的"能量解释项"。能量解释项之意义的无穷创生性使我们联想到因果律控引物之发生与意义生成的能动性。我们知道，只要主体永不触证不生不灭的阿赖耶识而以意根之执扰动之，主体就将陷入无尽的轮回之中，受因果律支配，因果律不仅决定主体正报与依报之发生，而且决定主体生命的意义。换言之，对于主体而言，因果律就是一个能动的能量系统。在主体这个动态文本中，我们正可用能量解释项来诠释主体的命运与生命的意义，而主体永远处于"被"诠释的状态。

总之，"因果控制"不仅决定了主体的命运，而且引导着三种解释项的价值与方向，形成解释项言说的理路，使唯识论与符号学具有了高度的趋同性。

因此，佛所阐述的三种相续以及相关的范畴与理念都可用于符号学的考量与诠释，即用符号、对象、解释项作出分析。笔者在对此三种相续的符号学诠释中虽有各别侧重，但读者却可作出全面的观照，以期对唯识论进行符号学的系统把握。

（四）符号学无法触及唯识论超验部分

应该特别注意的是，唯识论中有一种思想，即当主体开悟即触证阿赖耶识之后，主体即超越了轮回，由被动生死转为主动掌控生死。这种超越可能以两种形式体现出来：阿罗汉永驻如来藏，断尽前七识而入无余涅槃，没有任何生缘故不再参与轮回；而菩萨却因了知生死本幻，因此无惧于轮回而数数重返六道继续度化众生的大业，引导众生与自己一同趋于佛境。此种思想涉及实证的功夫论，非吾人意识心可知，绝言思、绝情虑，所谓"言语道断，心行处灭，境智双泯，法我皆空"之意即是，唯识论并用四种涅槃与中道思想概述之。

而符号学建立在现象学的基础上，举凡意识与意义的视域我们均可用之于符号学的考量，故唯识论有关生命意义等可知可感的轮回与因果的阐述，我们都可以符号学介入，但有关超言绝思的菩萨阿罗汉心行本非意识心可以测度，当然也不是符号学可以举问的。虽然古人有"言已尽而意无穷"之说，似乎符号终止了但意义还在因联想而发生，但此命题只有在吾人面临意识可把握的文本时才显得有效，而"意"在阿赖耶识看来正是妄念，阿赖耶识绝不与此相应，其性、相、体、用皆空是意识不可能抵达的超验之物。换言之，当阿赖耶识被意识把握而成为一个意识对象时，阿赖耶识也已经妄念化而失其本真，已经成为一个意识事件、经验事件了，吾人所领悟到的阿赖耶识之意义其实只是主体自身的经验意义而已。

据《大梵天王问佛决疑经》所载：

尔时如来，坐此宝座，受此莲华，无说无言，但拈莲华。入大会中，八万四千人天，时大众皆止默然。于时，长老摩诃迦叶，见佛拈华示众佛事，即今廓然，破颜微笑。佛即告言："是也，我有正法眼藏、涅槃妙心、实相无相、微妙法门，不立文字、教外别传、总持任持，凡夫成佛第一义谛。今方付属摩诃迦叶"。言已默然。（《大梵天王问佛决疑经·拈花品第二》）

这段"释迦拈花，迦叶微笑"的典故几乎无人不知，迦叶在符号（花）的引领之下领悟独立不羁的如来藏（阿赖耶识）而破颜微笑时，符号其实终止了，故如来藏是意义也就是符号的终极边界，佛陀使用符号的手段恰恰是为了斩断符号，斩断意识之流。

玄奘求法的唯识学释疑

——基于当现二常观的探讨

袁经文*

摘　要： 玄奘在潜研佛籍时遇到了唯识义理的困难，这主要来自对汉译佛经文本与梵文原本存有差距的疑惑和忧虑；其直接后果是："双林一味之旨，分成当、现二常；大乘不二之宗，析为南、北两道"。为此，玄奘才决定"投身入万死之地"，历尽艰险，西行印度取经。但至今，学界对"当、现二常"所指含义，以及对玄奘求法归来后是否解决了这一问题，均未有详尽而令人信服的研究涉及。本文即针对这一主旨展开考证。

关键词： 当常　现常　玄奘　窥基　灵泰　唯识学

一　玄奘之惑与西行动因

自两汉之际佛法西来，至玄奘（602 年—664 年）之时，已过六百余载。唯识学的传承，在中土已出现三大系统：地论学派、摄论学派和唯识宗。

唯识宗为玄奘、窥基师徒所创；在玄奘西行求法前，汉地已流传

＊ 袁经文，教授，广西大学马克思主义学院哲学系。

地、摄两派学脉。据考，玄奘曾跟随汉地诸师研学《摄大乘论》并在多地讲授之；在印度那烂陀寺求学期间，应戒贤论师之邀还在当时这一佛学重镇——印度佛教的最高学府讲授《摄大乘论》和《唯识抉择论》。

玄奘对唯识思想的精通，已是远超时人。但玄奘师承所学基本属于真谛一系的摄论学派，并兼习地论学派的南北二宗。

在潜研佛籍的过程中，玄奘遇到了义理上的困难。这主要来自对汉译佛经文本与梵文原本存有差距的疑惑和忧虑。玄奘取经归来后，将菩提流支、勒拿摩提、佛陀扇多和真谛等天竺僧人所译的唯识学典籍（史称"旧译"），几乎重新翻译了一遍（史称"新译"），显然是对这些外来僧人的译本不甚满意。

玄奘在西行印度途中，到达高昌王城（今新疆吐鲁番），受到高昌王麹文泰的礼遇，二人结为兄弟。在对高昌王的"启谢"中，玄奘对由"旧译"典籍引发的疑惑有一番表述：

> 遗教东流，六百余祀①，腾、会振辉于吴洛，谶、什钟美于秦凉，不堕玄风，咸匡胜业。但远人来译，音训不同，去圣时遥，义类差舛②，遂使双林一味之旨，分成当、现二常；大乘不二之宗，析为南、北两道。纷纷诤论，凡数百年；率土怀疑，莫有匠决。③

此中有二句"腾、会振辉于吴洛，谶、什钟美于秦凉"，每句头两字，是合指四位外来译师，即摄摩腾、康僧会、昙无谶、鸠摩罗什。玄奘认为，这些外国僧人翻译的佛经文本，其读音、释义必然与梵文原本有异；更由于"去圣时遥"，释义和传续不免差错频出，其直接后果是严重的，已导致了大乘义理的割裂支离，"双林一味之旨，分成当、现二常；大乘不二之宗，析为南、北两道。"

---

① 祀：世，代；商代对年的一种称呼。这里是指后者。
② 差舛，chà chuǎn：差错。
③ 《大唐大慈恩寺三藏法师传》卷1，《大正藏》第50册，第225页下。

虽然未予具指，但这显然是对盛行于当时的摄论学派和地论师南北二宗的批评。"双林"，是指佛陀行将涅槃时所倚的娑罗双树；"双林一味之旨"是佛陀进入涅槃前的最后宣示，此喻指佛教终极究竟之义。

此中局面状况是"纷纷诤论，凡数百年；率土怀疑，莫有匠决"。为此，玄奘才决定西行求法，"投身入万死之地"：

> 信夫汉梦西感，正教东传，道阻且长，未能委悉。故有专门竞执，多滞二常之宗；党同嫉异，致乖一味之旨。遂令后学相顾，靡识所归。是以面鹫山以增哀，慕常啼而假寐；潜祈灵佑，显恃国威。决志出一生之域，投身入万死之地。①

玄奘这里再次提到"二常"（上引文的"当、现二常"）和"一味之旨"（上引文的"双林一味之旨"），足见他受这一问题困惑之深，以及此与历尽艰险、西行印度取经之间的因果关系。又，据"专门竞执，多滞二常之宗；党同嫉异，致乖一味之旨"中的"多滞""致乖"等断语，可以获知玄奘的弦外之音：西行取经后，他找到了解决这些疑惑的佛义真旨。

玄奘的疑问，集中于"当、现二常"。但至今，学界对"当、现二常"所指含义，以及对玄奘求法归来后是否解决了这一问题，均未有详尽而令人信服的研究。这是大乘佛教重要而关键的命题，也关涉到玄奘研究中不能回避的舍身求法的逻辑主轴。本文即针对此主旨展开考证。

二　玄奘弟子窥基释当现二常

当常和现常二说，最早由勒拿摩提和菩提留支两系导出，《续高僧传·道宠传》便指出，"当现两说自斯始"：

---

① 《大唐大慈恩寺三藏法师传》卷7，《大正藏》第50册，第261页上。

初，勒那三藏教示三人，房、定二士授其心法，慧光一人偏教
法律。菩提三藏惟教于宠。宠在道北，教牢、宜四人。光在道南教
凭、范十人。故使洛下有南北二途，当现两说自斯始也。①

这里的"洛下有南北二途"，就是上文玄奘所言"大乘不二之宗，
析为南、北两道"之义。"勒那三藏"即是勒拿摩提，"菩提三藏"即
是菩提留支，二人均属地论学派，该学派由研习和传播《十地经论》
而形成于南北朝。

《十地经论》是印度瑜伽行派的重要传承者世亲为了阐释《华严
经·十地品》而著；此论于永平四年（公元 511 年），由菩提留支在中
土主持译出汉文。据菩提留支的《金刚经》讲稿《金刚仙论》记载，
他是世亲的四传弟子，有世亲的传承法脉。此外，参加翻译的还有勒那
摩提、佛陀扇多等外来僧人。

关于《十地经论》的翻译，流传有多种说法，大概可以说明菩提
留支和勒那摩提的见解分歧，以及地论学派分为南北二道的端倪。

从菩提留支出，以道宠为开祖，称为北道；从勒那摩提出，以慧光
为开祖，称为南道。

由于从相州②至洛阳有南北两条通道，菩提留支及其徒裔多居北
道，所以这一派系又被称为相州北道或相州北派；勒那摩提及其门下多
居南道，所以这一派系又被称为相州南道或相州南派。

但据日人布施浩岳考证，南北二道，当指洛阳城内御道之南和御道
之北，因勒那摩提和菩提留支分居于御道之南北而得名。③

地论南、北二道的分歧，无法从其二道的早期传承人那里直接知
晓，因为相关的资料典籍已经荡然无存。但在地论师后来的相关文献
中，偶有探寻当、现二常含义的文字。

---

① 《续高僧传·道宠传》，《大正藏》第 50 册，第 482 页下。
② 相州，当时的邺都，今为河南安阳县，另说为彰德，或说为河北临漳。
③ 吕澂：《中国佛教源流略讲》，中华书局 2002 年版，第 142 页。

　　由于玄奘本人没有在文献中论释当、现二常的具体所指，但善于将玄奘之讲授记作笔录的弟子窥基对此却有一番陈述，所以，本文便以窥基之述作为探索玄奘本意的重点。为了突出玄奘一系的主题性解读，这里选择以玄奘弟子窥基的解释为行文线索的基调；其他文献的观点，在结语时略及。窥基在《成唯识论别抄》中以答问方式提到：

　　　　问：何者当常、现常？
　　　　解云：魏时有二"三藏"，同于内，各在别处翻译。
　　　　南院安置勒那三藏。云：众生身中，已具三十二相、一切功德，皆悉是常；但由障故，不得显现；后时断障剩①，此则佛身，更不别从净种而生。故名"现常"。由在南院，故曰南②道法师，非是吴蜀，故云南道。
　　　　菩提留支在北院翻译。立云：一切众生，后时成佛，得有常之身，必从净种而生，生已常住；非谓众生已得常身。故曰"当常"。以在北院，名曰北道法师也。③

　　"南道法师"，便是勒拿摩提；"北道法师"，便是菩提留支。
　　从这里可知，勒拿摩提所持的"现常"观认为，众生身中本来已有如来三十二相和一切功德，这一切是恒常存在的。凡夫断去障碍后，便可显现本有佛身；佛身是本有具备的，而不是从其他净种生出的。
　　菩提留支所持的"当常"观认为，凡夫众生尚未得佛地的常身，佛身是由清净种子生出，生后才得佛地常身。
　　显然，"当常"观与"现常"观是相互对立。
　　由于"现常"观提到三十二相的本有，便隐含凡夫现时已有佛地报身之意，因为三十二相、八十种好属于佛地报身所现应化身的庄严瑞相。谓凡夫在因地拥有应身之三十二相，并不确当；此或许是与法身混

---

　　① 剩：据《大正藏》注，原为"部"，并视"部"为"剩"字之讹；今从此。
　　② 南：《大正藏》原文为"有"，但据上语境"南院"及与下语境"南道"，"有"当为"南"字之讹；今依此改。
　　③ 窥基：《成唯识论别抄》卷10，《卍新纂续藏经》第48册，第848页上。

讹所致。显然，勒拿摩提的观点是错误的。

由于"当常"观提到佛身是当来之身而不是本有身以及佛身是由净种生出等义，此观便隐含有佛地报身是由外来清净种子而生的寓意。如此，就在陷入本无今有的因缘生法之错失的同时，也否认了佛性本有。显然，菩提留支的观点也同属错误。

但是，二人却同有可取之意蕴。勒拿摩提强调了本有，菩提留支强调了外缘熏起净种，这均是佛法正确的路向。即谓，若勒拿摩提所提是法身，而非报身应身，其认识便是正确，如此便彰显佛性法身的本有。若菩提留支在认可清净种子本有的基础上，从需待外缘熏发的角度去谈及清净种子的成熟现行，便也是可取之认识。窥基接续上文道：

> 十地论颂云：定灭故者，定灭二字，双标二种。定即本性涅槃，灭即方便涅槃。以本定之，称为定也。断障显故，称为灭者，如其次第成；同相本性，不同相为方便得也。①

窥基引述世亲《十地经论》之偈颂，以"定"（决定、确定）表述了佛性本有，即"本性涅槃"；以"灭"表述了本有佛性待断障后便可得显，即"方便涅槃"。"灭"之谓，强调了依过程次第而得成佛；在这一过程中，诸佛虽在因地时均有同相的本性涅槃，但诸佛却是各各依不同因缘方便而得至佛地果位的。

考世亲《十地经论》之偈颂，其原文表述与窥基所引，不尽相同：

> 偈言：
>   定灭佛所行，言说不能及。
>   地行亦如是，难说复难闻。
>   此偈云何彼智以②显"方便坏涅槃"？复示"性净涅槃"？偈言"定灭"故，"定"者，成同相，涅槃自性寂灭故；"灭"者，

---

① 窥基：《成唯识论别抄》卷10，《卍新纂续藏经》第48册，第848页上。
② "以"，《大正藏》作"已"；现据【宋】【元】【明】等其他版本的大藏经改作"以"。

成不同相，"方便坏涅槃"。①

窥基将"性净涅槃"表述为"本性涅槃"，将"方便坏涅槃"表述为"方便涅槃"；"方便坏"之谓，世亲用以指依因缘方便而使诸障坏失终证佛地涅槃灭谛。此文义与窥基的理解是一致的。

但是，世亲这里提到"彼智以显'方便坏涅槃'"，"彼智"即是菩提，即四智心品。显然，世亲这里已有将涅槃和菩提进行分述的隐意，即"性净涅槃"是涅槃，"方便坏涅槃"实质是菩提即四智心品，据此智，才能方便断除诸障。

此中《十地经论》涅槃和菩提之意，被地论师们不当地释解为现当二常。在玄奘师徒看来，地论师们并未深得《十地经论》要旨。

这里先行点过，此中深刻之义，笔者将在后面考察玄奘取法归来后宣明的正法意旨时，再作阐绎。

诚然，此上所论，是辗转获知的所谓勒拿摩提和菩提留支的观点。勒拿摩提和菩提留支二人是否真的会持这种认识，我们不得而知；这种分歧也或许是各自门人赓续门风旨蕴时误会所致。毕竟，此中佛义深晦，且地论南北二道的分立，是由双方门人肇始的，而相关资料又已经佚失阙如了。

三　玄奘的唯识学正义

玄奘求法回来后，对当现二常是如何释读并阐明立场的呢？

我们似乎没有直接找到玄奘本人对此的显明陈述，但据窥基的弟子灵泰所著之《成唯识论疏抄》提供的信息，我们可以明确，玄奘在《成唯识论》中，已经迂曲表明并解决了当现二常的谬误。

灵泰在《成唯识论疏抄》卷18中，在"疏：若初唯生，后不灭者，便违佛说乃至违比量故者"一句之后，提出"此文即是破当常、

---

① 《十地经论》卷2，《大正藏》第26册，第133页上。

现常也"。

为了掌握此中灵泰疏释的含意和背景，宜先对《成唯识论》的相关内容进行考析。

《成唯识论》卷10提到四种转依义，分别是"能转道""所转依""所转舍"和"所转得"。最后一种"所转得"，含"大涅槃"和"大菩提"两义：

> 所转得，此复有二。
> 一、所显得。谓大涅槃，此虽本来自性清净，而由客障覆，令不显。真圣道生，断彼障故，令其相显，名得涅槃。此依真如离障施设，故体即是清净法界。①
> 二、所生得。谓大菩提。此虽本来有能生种，而所知障碍故不生。由圣道力断彼障故，令从种起，名得菩提。起已相续，穷未来际。此即四智相应心品。②

此中之"大涅槃"和"大菩提"，在《成唯识论》的后续文句又称为"此前二转依果"，此即是"究竟位"。《成唯识论》的下述引文，便谈到"究竟位"及其八"相"：

> 后究竟位，其相云何？颂曰：
> 　　此即无漏界，不思议·善·常，
> 　　安乐·解脱身，大牟尼名·法。③
> 论曰：前修习位所得转依，应知即是究竟位相。此谓此前二转依果，即是究竟无漏界摄。④

---

① 《成唯识论》卷10，《大正藏》第31册，第55页中。
② 同上书，第56页上。
③ 按：这里用圆点和逗号标示出究竟位的八相：无漏界、不可思议、善、常、安乐、解脱身、大牟尼名和法。
④ 《成唯识论》卷10，《大正藏》第31册，第57页上。

笔者以圆点和逗号标示出偈颂"究竟位"共有的八相：无漏界、不可思议、善、常、安乐、解脱身、大牟尼名和法。此中的"常"，便是当现二常之误读所涉及的内容。以下出于主题论证的需要，只对八相中"无漏界"和"常"二相进行考释。

其一，关于"无漏界"相的考释。

在谈到涅槃（清净法界）和菩提（四智心品）具有无漏相的原因时，《成唯识论》是通过提问和释疑展开的：

> 清净法界，可唯无漏摄；四智心品，如何唯无漏？
>
> 道谛摄故，唯无漏摄。谓佛功德及身、土等，皆是无漏种性①所生，有漏法种已永舍故。虽有示现作生死身、业、烦恼等，似苦、集谛，而实无漏，道谛所摄。②

据此段引文，能与上一段引文回互推衍证知，"二转依果"指的正是"大涅槃"和"大菩提"。

因为此段引文接续其上提到的是八相之一的无漏相，所以此中的清净法界即是指涅槃，四智心品即是指菩提。若此与上一段引文的"所得转依……究竟位相……此前二转依果"，进行合释，便可表明，"大涅槃"和"大菩提"正是指具有八相的"究竟位"（"二转依果"）。

其二，关于"常"相的考释。

当现二常，实质上是对"大涅槃"和"大菩提"这"二转依果"的八相之一的"常"的误读。玄奘针对八相之一的"常"，有如下阐示：

> 此又是"常"，无尽期故。清净法界，无生无灭，性无变易，故说为"常"。四智心品，所依"常"故，无断尽故，亦说为

---

① "性"，【宋】【元】【宫】【圣】等其他版本的大藏经作"姓"。
② 《成唯识论》卷10，《大正藏》第31册，第57页上。

"常"；非"自性常"，从因生故，生者归灭，一向记①故，不见色心非无常故；然四智品，由本愿力所化有情无尽期故，穷未来际，无断无尽。②

清净法界（涅槃）无疑是"常"。四智心品（菩提）因依于涅槃之"常"而得，也具有永无断尽、永无终结的"常"义。但由于这是有起始的因缘生法，缘生法必归于灭，这是一直以来明知的理则，因为从未见过色法和心法不是无常的。但是，四智心品却是例外，祂是有始无终的；四智心品是依靠愿度化众生永无穷尽之期的本愿力量而成，而众生既然是永无穷尽的，那么，救度众生的四智心品因于无尽愿力而起，也不会中断、不会灭尽。

这便是佛法真义。显然，在"当现二常"中，对菩提四智心品的恒常义以及涅槃与菩提的复杂关系，均作了错误而简单化的处置。

那么，何以知之，玄奘的此段引文，针对的正是当现二常？

唐朝的灵泰是宗依窥基的门徒，他著有《成唯识论疏抄》，此中就有针对《成唯识论》上段引文的疏释，灵泰在这里提出了"此文即是破当常、现常也"：

> 疏：若初唯生，后③不灭者，便违佛说乃至违比量故者。
> 此文即是破"当常"、"现常"也。
> 然智者法师，执有"常当"者，说一切众生，若未得成佛，即色心是无常。若三大劫修因，当来得成佛已。众生若未得成佛，即色心是无常。若三大劫修因，当来得成佛已，佛色心即常住、不生灭，由如④真如是凝然常也。

---

① 记，【宋】【元】【明】等其他版本的大藏经作"说"。
② 《成唯识论》卷10，《大正藏》第31册，第57页下。
③ 后，《大正藏》原作"得"；据《大正藏》"得疏作后"之注，"得"当为"后"字之讹；从之，改为"后"。
④ 由如，即犹如；下二处同。

"现常"者，智法师说，一切众生身中，常有佛子①，无生无灭。此佛子故，鼻眼耳一切皆是，由如母胎中有娠儿，由母数数吃食津闰，今此娠儿，渐渐长大，后即出胎。众生身中佛子亦尔，由三大劫多闻令熏习，此身中佛子，渐渐长大，后时即得成佛。

今破云："生者皆灭，一向记故。"又作量云：佛色心等定有生灭。因云"从因生故"，由如凡夫；或应返显凡夫色心应不生灭；"从因生故"，由如来也。②

引文第一行，便是就菩提（四智心品）有始无终即"初唯生，后不灭"进行释疑的起语。引文最后一段，以"今破云"，照应了第二段"此文即是破当常、现常也"。而且，此中之破斥文"生者皆灭，一向记故""从因生故"，正是引用玄奘原文即八相之一的"常"的原语以进行疏释的。

毫无疑义，据灵泰此文可知，玄奘上一段阐述"常"的引文，正是针对当现二常而展开的，此中义旨，便隐含了玄奘对当现二常观的全面破斥和修正。这正是玄奘取法东归后得到的唯识学正义。

能够与玄奘的上述思想进行比对旁通的，还有灵泰援引《庄严论》提起的三种"常"义。不妨再看灵泰之疏：

疏：庄严论说三种常，如常施食，乃至断别，不尽相续。常义者，谓法身名凝然常，彼身不断常，化身相续常。虽说报化二身是常，还有生灭，如言此人有施食，此人举时等，即有施食，掖中③即不施食。又如言此人家势富贵，常受快乐，然此人亦有不受快乐时。今言报化是常者，非如法身常住不灭，报化身等，还有生

———————————

① 子，据《大正藏》注，"子疑性"；此认为是"佛性"之讹。但本文不从此，因为"佛子"与语境中的"母胎"、"娠儿"及"长大"、"出胎"等合释，"佛子"指的正是成佛的幼胎、幼子；尽管此喻此说不当。

② 《成唯识论疏抄》卷18，《卍新纂续藏经》第50册，第494页上、中。

③ 掖中，有二义：把东西塞入衣袋中；掖，通腋。承上文，当是指举手施食之双臂贴腋窝而暂时中断施食。

灭也。

问：何故如来报化二身，得常有耶？

答：由如来昔在因中，有法空智，断［*］不所知障，证法空理穷尽故。故成佛已，即自受用不断，常尽未来际故。声闻人，唯断烦恼障，同假择灭无为，法空智故。又，不证法空理，即证理不穷尽故。声闻人不得自受用身，即灰身灭智。又如由昔日中有悲愿，誓度一切有情，利乐他故。后成佛时，即得他用。及变化身，亦无尽也。若声闻人，无悲愿故，不拟利他故。声闻人，不得受用及变化身也。理实断所知障，证法空理，正得自受用身，傍亦得他受用身、变化身。若悲愿正，得他受用及变化身，傍亦得自受用身。由如所知障，正障菩提，兼障涅盘；说烦恼障，正障涅盘，兼亦能障菩提。此断所知障，及悲愿等，亦尔也。①

此中文义详尽深刻，富于启发性。显然，玄奘在《成唯识论》中对菩提“常”义的解释，并不是孤证独发，其思想实是与《庄严论》一致的。

四　结语：奘基师徒以外的认识

我们不能由上认为，奘基师徒围绕当现二常展开的理解和抨击，是唯一的。也许，正是由于有关地论师文献资料的缺失，以及佛法深义的晦涩难懂，才导致对当现二常的释读不是整齐划一，而是呈现出多维意义。

我们先看灵泰在上文所引“当常”和“现常”的含义。

这里提到，智者法师和智法师，各执当常和现常，显然二人已是受地论南北二派影响的后人。

现常，指众生身中常有佛性之子，此子之性，“无生无灭”，但又

----

① 《成唯识论疏抄》卷18，《卍新纂续藏经》第50册，第494页上。

如胎儿之可长养，由修习而能渐长，最后此子便能成佛。

当常，指在众生尚未成佛时，色身和心法均是无常；成佛后，佛色身和心法便常住，不生不灭，犹如真如之常。

在窥基上引勒拿摩提所持的"现常"观中，认为众生身中已有如来应身三十二瑞相，断障后此相可现；而此中智法师所持则是，众生身中具有的佛性之子，既是不生不灭的，也是依因缘而能变异长养的。显然，对佛子"无生无灭"的强调，与长养成佛已是非自洽了。由此，前者勒拿摩提所说是常法；后者智法师所说既是常法，也是缘起生灭之法——如果不是智法师思维逻辑的荒谬或一知半解，就是因辗转相传而远离了智法师的原意。

菩提留支所持的"当常"观认为，凡夫众生不得常身，至佛地才得常身。智者法师的当常观认为，众生色身和心法无常；成佛后佛色身和心法常住不生不灭。此与菩提流支的观点基本一致。

显然，灵泰这里所引，与窥基上述所表，是大同小异的。但是，从这一"小异"的非一致性，可以透显出，后人因理解深奥法义的需要，借助想象和比附，是必不可少的。若如此，那么导致诸种乖离和歧义丛生，已是必然难免。

也许正是这一原因，在不同的文献中，对当现二常错谬的修正均不相同。以下将散见于文献的其他几种观点，集中引述如下。

1. 新罗人元晓所撰的《涅槃宗要》提到：

> 或有说者，当常、现常二果为宗。所谓一切众生悉有佛性，是显当常。如来所证大般涅槃，是明现常；圣行等因，即助显于果，非为正宗；若据佛意，欲使众生各证当果；但当果未非，恐难取信，是故，自说所证，将成物信。以是义故二果为宗。但从现立题，故名涅槃也。①

这里提出以当常果和现常果为宗依。

---

① 《涅槃宗要》卷1，《大正藏》第38册，第240页上。

当常，是指众生皆有佛性；凭此，众生当来（将来）将能证成佛果。谓据恒常之佛性将来定当能成佛果，即是以当常果为依之意。

现常，是指佛现时所证的大般涅槃。凡夫以现常为依，即是以佛的圣行证果为因为信，以此嘉勉，将有助于行者自修而证当来之果。此虽不是成佛宗依的正因，却亦是重要物信。

显然，这与上述所陈的当现二常并不相同，这是从佛陀说法并取信于行者的角度而谓"以当常、现常二果为宗"。

2. 唐朝道暹在《涅槃经疏私记》中也说道：

> 以当、现常者，地人云：涅槃明当常，现常破于无常。亦是待对之法，故同前坏。①

这里的当常和现常义，与上述元晓所表基本相同。据涅槃，即明当常（凡夫有佛性）；据无常，即显现常之功（佛果破无常）。但这里对当现二常的破斥，是重在从中观的立场阐扬，认为凡有相待、对举，必是无常散坏之法。

3. 吉藏（嘉祥）在《百论疏》中，有两处提到"当现二常"，第一处是：

> 十因如论说，但大乘人解出世因果，有当现二常。明生死中已有法身，体用具足，现常义名之，为有、为妄所覆，故不现，名为无果。当常义者，当有于果，名为有义，实时未有，名为无果。②

这里是以"当现二常"来解出世之因和出世之果。

凡夫虽流转生死，已有法身之体用，此称为现常；但此现常法身，被有为妄法遮障而不显，便称为现常无果。

_____

① 《涅槃经疏私记》卷1，《卍新纂续藏经》第37册，第149页下。
② 《百论疏》卷3，《大正藏》第42册，第287页下—第288页上。

凡夫将来当能证果，此称为当常；虽说将来有果，但现时未有，便称为当常无果。

现常、当常，是就凡夫而言的一体两面，二者均是无果。此现常即是当常，当常即是现常。

此外，吉藏在《百论疏》中，还继续提到"当现二常"：

> 北土略论当现二常……。略论二常者：一云定现常，一云定当常。……
>
> 问：佛果内外，当现两常，言有、当有，何过耶？
>
> 答：略明二过。一、进不冥乎实相，二、退失无方之用；伤此体用二义也。
>
> 问：此事云何？
>
> 答：实相何曾当、现？亦当、亦现，非当、非现，四句耶；内外等亦尔。
>
> 退失无方者，诸大乘论，皆明一切诸法，无决定相。佛有无量方便，或说一切实，一切不实，亦实、亦不实，非实、非不实。适缘利物，岂可秉执规矩，以局大方耶？①

定现常和定当常之谓，是对当现二常的存在秉持确凿性的认定。这里明示，提现常和当常之存在，均有过错。

其一，对实相而言，当现二常的提法，全落入现象界的四句内；如此，必远离实相。其二，佛说大乘法，只有方法便利，适缘利物，并不会拘泥于任何确定不移之言说相。这里依然是以中观的立场，破斥现常、当常的确定性执持。

总而言之，以上诸家的解释，尽管各有理则，但是比较起来，玄奘师徒阐述的思想含义，更具贯通、周全和系统性，且更能显出唯识学的深刻意义。

此外，有关玄奘在"启谢"高昌王中所谈到的"大乘不二之宗，

---

① 《百论疏》卷1，《大正藏》第42册，第235页上。

析为南、北两道"，探寻此中缘由，也是因于当现二常谬误的出现而致；但这仅是成因的一个层面，另一层面，尚涉及阿赖耶识与真如的紧密性被不当地二分割裂。有关此点，本人已撰文进行了阐释分析。①

---

① 参见拙作《阿赖耶识与真如及唯识古学今学辨析》，载《吴越佛教》第4卷，九州出版社2009年版。

再论近代唯识学复兴的原因及其本质

沈 庭[*]

摘 要： 从文化人类学的角度来看，玄奘所传的唯识学之所以在近代复兴，深层原因在于近代中国存在一种力图重新编织由西学东渐所破坏的"意义之网"的强烈需求。唯识学的复兴在本质上是近代意义体系的重建，它不仅在本体论层面上对近代世界作出了理性的新阐释，使得其所确立的"世界观"表现为对事物、生活真实状态的"写照"；而且其具有的"精神气质"也激发了寻求社会、文化变革或革命的实践热情。

关键词： 唯识学 近代 世界观 精神气质

主张回归印度佛学之正统是近代佛学的一大新趋势。无论是支那内学院一系代表的居士佛学，还是以武昌佛学院为代表的寺僧佛学，都对流传千余年的中国式佛教提出了或局部，或全面的怀疑。在此新趋势下，断绝已久的唯识学突然迎来了新的"春天"，在僧界、居士界，甚至学界都大有复兴之表现，这成为近代思想史上最值得深思的现象之一。目前，学界对玄奘唯识学在近代复兴的原因和本质已经有了不少成熟的讨论，但这些讨论大多是从思想史、佛教史的角度来考察的，因而

---

* 沈庭（1984—），男，湖南宁乡县人，武汉大学国学院讲师，哲学博士，主要研究中国佛学。本文是 2014 年度教育部哲学社会科学研究重大课题攻关项目"中国现代宗教学术史"阶段性成果，项目批准编号：12J2D034。

本文力图以文化人类学为视角，从近代唯识学兴起的表现出发，进而探讨近代唯识学复兴的原因及其本质，以期在学界已有成果的基础上深化对此论题的学术研究，以求教于方家。

一 表现:近代唯识学的复兴

宋明以后，佛教渐趋衰落，僧徒流品，愈降愈滥，佛学义理上不再有新的发展，而传道手段的花样翻新也几乎殆尽。有清一代，佛教更已成强弩之末，沙门已失昔日精神。欧阳渐曾言："中国内地，僧尼略总在百万之数，其能知大法、办悲智、堪住持称比丘不愧者，诚寡若晨星。其大多数皆游手好闲，晨久坐食，诚国家一大蠹虫，但有无穷之害，而无一毫之利者。"① 然而，到了近代，佛学却通过自我革新而获得了高度的社会认同。佛教革新心性的内在超越精神被视作激励种性、促进道德、净化心灵的积极动力；其对庄严净土的外在超越追求也契合了改革社会积弊，实现人间净土的现实需要，以至于佛学在近代出现了新的转机，颇有复兴之迹象。从如下几个方面可以对此作一管窥。

一、佛教传播媒介的兴盛。随着近代报刊业的出现和发展，社会上涌现了大量宣传佛教文化、探讨佛学义理的佛教刊物。创办最早的佛教类期刊为狄楚青于 1912 年在上海创刊的《佛学丛报》和太虚于1913 年在上海创刊的《佛教月报》，"据不完全统计，仅一九一二至一九四九年，……佛教团体创办的汉文佛教期刊近二百种"②。其中有日报、周刊、旬刊、半月刊、月刊、季刊和年刊，遍及全国各地。办刊时间较长、影响较大的期刊有：《内学》《海潮音》《学衡》《东方杂志》《威音》《微妙声》《世间解》《狮子吼》《新佛教》《佛化新青年》等。佛教期刊的发行促进了佛教思想传播的效率和广度，为佛学研究提供了

① 欧阳竟无:《辨方便与僧制》，载王雷泉编选《欧阳渐文选》，上海远东出版社 2011 年版，第 77 页。

② 参见黄夏年主编《民国佛教期刊文献集成》，全国图书馆文献微缩复制中心 2006 年版。

良好的传播和交流平台，客观上有力地促进了佛教自身的发展，并扩大了其对整个社会、文化的影响力。

除了佛教刊物之外，刻经处的建立使佛教书籍的出版事业也得到了极大的发展。杨仁山居士在南京所创的金陵刻经处是创办较早、影响最大的刻经处。杨仁山皈依佛门以后，广搜亡佚佛典，刻印流通。在他的影响下，长沙、北京、天津、重庆、苏州、杭州、宁波、广州、福州、常州等地，也陆续成立刻经处或佛经流通处。专门编辑、刻印、流通佛教典籍的出版机构也得以成立，上海佛学书局是其中的佼佼者，它于1929 年由上海佛教界发起创办，设有流通、出版、翻印、代办四个部门，是中国近代规模较大的以出版、流通佛教经典为特色的出版机构。此外，尚有功德林佛经流通处、世界佛教居士林佛经流通处、弘化社、大法轮书局、大雄书店、般若书局等。大藏经的刻印也是近代佛教界的一大事，《频伽藏》《碛砂藏》《宋藏遗珍》《普慧大藏经》等先后得以印刷出版。《佛学小辞典》（张祖烈，1919）、《佛学大辞典》（丁福保，1922）、《法相辞典》（朱芾煌，1939）等各种类型的佛学辞书也得以出版发行。① 近代佛教在典籍的流通、发行上呈现出前所未有的繁荣景象。

二、佛教教育机构和研究团体的大量创办。戊戌变法后，社会上涌现了一批专门培养僧伽和佛学人才的教育机构、研究机构或佛学院。其中较为著名的有：湖南僧学堂（1903）、祇洹精舍（1907）、华严大学（1914）、观宗学社（后改名弘法研究社，1914）、法界学院（1917）、支那内学院（1922）、武昌佛学院（1922）、闽南佛学院（1925）、三时学会（1927）、汉藏教理院（1932）等。② 这些佛学院或研究机构培养了大批僧才和佛学研究者。

三、佛教影响的扩大、深入。近代佛学的影响力不再局限于山林寺庙，而是从通经致用、探微索隐的思想进路渗透到近代社会思潮之中。

---

① 关于刻经处、佛书的印刷出版以及佛教刊物的出版，可参见高振农《佛教文化与近代中国》，第 1 章第 1 节"佛教文化复兴的主要标志"和附录"佛学刊物的出版和大藏经的刻印在近代的影响"，上海社会科学院出版社 1992 年版。

② 参见麻天祥《晚清佛学与近代社会思潮》，第 65—69 页。

正如梁任公所言："晚清思想家有一伏流，曰佛学。……故晚清所谓新学家者，殆无一不与佛学有关系"。① 例如，康有为的《大同书》、谭嗣同的《仁学》无不充满佛学思想；梁启超则明确表示："我喜欢研究佛教"②"愿夙好治佛学史"③，不仅在诸多著作中吸取了佛学思想，更专著《佛学研究十八篇》；章太炎因"苏报案"入狱以后，转俗成真，开始研习佛学，他认为搞革命必须"用宗教发起信心，增进国民的道德"④"非说无生，则不能去畏死心；非破我所，则不能去拜金心；非谈平等，则不能去奴隶心；非示众生皆佛，则不能去退屈心；非举三轮清净，则不能去德色心"⑤；熊十力则著《新唯识论》援佛入儒，创立了现代新儒家哲学。可见，近代的部分思想家"以己意进退佛说"，或从佛学中吸取精神力量作为鼓舞人们冲击封建罗网、推动社会革命的理论武器，或以佛学为基础建立自己独特的哲学体系。

正如章太炎所说："自清之季，佛法不在缁衣，而流入长者居士间。"⑥ 近代佛学已经开始由沙门转向居士、学者，由丛林走向社会，而且在学者、居士的努力下，佛学也由纯粹的宗教教义转为科学研究的对象，在近代高等学府的讲台上占有一席之地。邓伯诚首先于北京大学哲学系讲授印度哲学兼及佛学，张克诚、许季平、梁漱溟、汤用彤、熊十力、周叔迦等人接力于后；唐大圆、张化声于武汉大学讲《唯识三十颂》；蒋维乔于东南大学开讲《百法明门论》；景昌极、李政纲于东北大学宣讲唯识论；王恩洋授佛学于成都大学；梁启超也在清华大学等院校开讲佛学思想，宣讲他佛化了的东方人生哲学。总地来说，寺僧佛

---

① 梁启超：《清代学术概论》，中国人民大学出版社2004年版，第219页。

② 梁启超：《佛陀时代及原始佛教教理纲要》，载《佛学研究十八篇》，中华书局1989年版，第45页。

③ 梁启超：《佛家经录在中国目录学之位置》，载《佛学研究十八篇》，中华书局1989年版，第303页。

④ 章太炎：《东京留学生欢迎会演说录》，载姜玢编选《革故鼎新的哲理：章太炎文选》，上海远东出版社1996年版，第142页。

⑤ 章太炎：《建立宗教论》，载《章太炎全集》第4卷，上海人民出版社1985年版，第418页。

⑥ 章太炎：《支那内学院缘起》，载黄夏年主编《章太炎集·杨度集》，中国社会科学出版社1995年版，第133页。

学式微而居士佛学、学者佛学兴盛是近代佛教的一大特点。佛学从山林向社会、文化的各个方面进行了深入的渗透，成为近代思想界极为重要的"一伏流"。

由上可见，与以往相比，近代佛学在文献（文本）、机构和影响（效果）三个方面都有着明显的复兴迹象。

而此中，最为引人注目的事件莫过于唯识学的复兴。自杨仁山居士从日本搜集回古代失传的唯识学典籍，并刻印流通之后，研究唯识之风气便逐渐盛行起来。当时研究唯识最为著名的研究机构有三：南京以欧阳竟无为首的支那内学院、北京韩清净领导的三时学会和太虚法师领导的武昌佛学院。支那内学院以教授、研习法相唯识学而闻名于世，一时名流如吕澂、汤用彤、姚柏年、梁漱溟、陈铭枢、王恩洋、黄树因等皆曾拜投欧阳竟无门下学习唯识，梁启超亦曾听欧阳渐讲学，风雨无阻。支那内学院对法相唯识学推崇备至，对中国化的台禅贤净诸宗则持批判态度，他们认为："我国佛法自奘师一系中绝以来，正统沉沦，经千余载。其间虽有净、密、台、禅继起而盛，然于佛法精神背驰日远，无容讳言。……应知提倡佛法实唯法相一途。"① 在推动唯识学复兴方面，支那内学院贡献最大，影响最深远。三时学会则由韩清净创立，之所以取名"三时"，"系据说《解深密经》佛说第三时真了义中道教义"。三时学会最大的贡献在于对《瑜伽师地论》全本做了深入的研究，撰成鸿篇巨制《瑜伽师地论科句披寻记》一书，学界对此书评价极高。② 三时学会在北京与南京的支那内学院遥相呼应，时人称为"南欧北韩"，二者是居士界研究法相唯识学的重要阵地。在"南欧北韩"的领导下，当时著名的唯识学者还有吕澂、王恩洋、范古农、唐大圆等人。

在教界，推崇唯识最力者莫过于太虚法师。他与欧阳竟无同出于杨文会居士的"祗洹精舍"，是近代佛教革新运动的领袖人物。太虚曾言，唯识学"为欧美人及中国人思想学术之新交易、新倾向上种种需要所推荡催动，崭然濯然发露其精光于现代思潮之顶点，若桃花忽焉红

---

① 吕澂：《法相大学特科开学讲演》，载《内学》第 2 辑，第 224 页。
② 黄夏年：《百年的唯识学研究》，《社会科学动态》2000 年第 1 期。

遍堤上，湖山全景因是一新"①。其虽主张对全体佛学融会贯通，"随机施设而不专承一宗或一派以自碍"②，但是却特别强调法相唯识学的重要性。在《太虚大师全书》中，与唯识学相关的著作占据了五册之多（14—18），凡 50 多篇，其中既有概述法相唯识学义理的，又有专论唯识学某个重要教义的；既有专门讲解唯识典籍的，又有论辩唯识学历史的，涉及唯识学的方方面面。③ 太虚所创办的武昌、闽南、汉藏教理等佛学院皆将唯识学作为必修课程，其所培养的学僧以及太虚门下之弟子中有不少人精通唯识，诸如芝峰、印顺、正果、法尊、福善、法舫、慈航、演培、度寰等。其中，学术成就最高者当属现代佛学泰斗印顺法师。印顺著有《唯识学探源》等书，为近代唯识学研究之力作。

在近代，研究唯识学的名家辈出，研究成果累累，唯识学成为近代佛学最有成就的学问。近代科学思潮以进步、富强之姿态冲击中国传统文化，实证哲学、分析思维风靡一时，中国学者心理为之一变，学术研究也弃空就实，而重逻辑、体系、理性、分析。法相唯识学则大契其机，在哲学领域如日中天。不仅在僧界、居士界成为主流显学，而且对整个近代哲学之转向产生了巨大影响。诸如"有学问的革命家"章太炎在佛教的圣殿中做哲学的沉思，他以法相唯识学作思想基础，先后发表了《建立宗教论》《答铁铮》《人无我论》《国故论衡》《诸子略说》《五无论》《四惑论》《齐物论释》等一系列哲学论文，系统地论述了真如本体论、万法唯识论、以佛释庄的齐物论以及回真向俗的应用哲学。与同时代的思想家相比，章太炎对思辨理性的兴趣最大，而且成绩斐然，贺麟曾评价章氏"是当时革命党主要的哲学代言人，而且可以认作'五四'运动时期新思想的先驱""其对革新思想，和纯学术研究的贡献，其深度远超出当时的今文学派"④。熊十力在章太炎《建立宗教论》等哲学著作之影响下，"益进讨竺坟"（《船山学自记》），开始

---

① 太虚：《新的唯识论》，载《法相唯识学》上册，商务印书馆 2002 年版，第 71 页。
② 太虚：《新与融贯》，载黄夏年主编《太虚集》，中国社会科学出版社 1995 年版，第72 页。
③ 陈兵等：《二十世纪中国佛教》，民族出版社 2000 年版，第 232 页。
④ 贺麟：《五十年来的中国哲学》，商务印书馆 2002 年版，第 5 页。

深入研究法相唯识学。他曾访学于欧阳竟无，在支那内学院钻研唯识；著有《佛家名相通释》《唯识学概论》《新唯识论》等唯识学著作；其代表作《新唯识论》"穷万殊而归一本，要在反之此心，是故以唯识彰名"①，实质上是融会儒佛，辨异观同之作。熊氏为现代新儒家之鼻祖，他通过吸收和批判唯识学而开创出现代新儒家哲学，可见唯识学对中国哲学重建、转型之贡献。

虽然学界大多承认近代佛学有复兴之势，但是，也有学者对此提出质疑。美国著名佛教学者霍姆斯·维慈在《中国佛教的复兴》一书中就提出：

> "中国佛教的复兴"这一说法犯了三重错误。首先，大部分情况不是过去的新生，而是一系列的革新；不是宗教复兴，而是把宗教改为世俗。其次，它决未在整体上影响中国人。……再次，我认为这一说法掩盖了某种趋势，这些趋势如果继续下去，将意味着不是佛教活力的增长，而是一个活生生宗教的最终消亡。②

维慈的观点有一定的合理性，特别是提出近代佛教的复兴不是传统佛教的死灰复燃，而是革新，真是高屋建瓴之见。近代唯识学的复兴绝不是传统唯识学的复活，而是对传统佛学（包括古代唯识学）的一种革新。值得注意的是，维慈所考察的对象主要为制度化的佛教组织。就近代寺僧佛教而言，确实在总体上是趋于式微；但是，就居士佛学和学者佛学而言，佛学对近代思想确有前所未有的影响和渗透。就佛学义理而言，佛学自宋代以后便固步不前，但在近代却又重新迸发出思想活力，特别是唯识学的兴起，在宗教层面、哲学层面以及社会实践层面都对当时的社会文化产生过深刻影响。在这个意义上说，近代佛教确有一定复兴之势。

---

① 熊十力：《新唯识论·全部印行记》，中华书局1985年版，第239页。
② ［美］霍姆斯·维慈：《中国佛教的复兴》，王雷泉等译，上海古籍出版社2006年版，第218页。

二 原因:传统世界图景及自我感知的改变

为什么唯识学会在近代重新兴起？对此，我国学界已经有较为成熟的意见。但是，我们觉得仍有继续探讨的空间。

关于唯识学复兴之原因，学界一般归纳为三大方面：

一、心理机制。西方文化的强势冲击彻底动摇了中国人"天朝上国"的文化自信，对传统中国知识分子而言，这种心理落差正好在佛学中找到了慰藉。现实生活的无常变化、民族国家的风雨飘摇、个人命运的深沉苦难，都为主张人生无常、人生皆苦的佛教打开了信仰市场。

二、明清思想史发展的逻辑必然。近代法相学之兴起是明清学术发展的内在要求。章太炎曾言，法相唯识一术，"以分析名相始，以排遣名相终，从入之途与平生朴学相似，易于契机"①"盖近代学术，渐趋实事求是之途，而用心益复缜密矣。是故法相之学于明代则不宜，于近代则甚宜，由学术所趣然也"②。这表明由朴学而进入法相唯识学，对近代知识分子而言是"易于契机"的逻辑发展。通过考察明清思想史的主题演进，当代学者张志强认为，明清思想史发展到近代面临严峻的挑战，即如何在现实性的基础上重建道德的客观性和超越性；如何在面对现实的此在世界之膨胀对历史性的、经验性的、社会性的知识学的需求时，重建一种面对人心之感情的、创造的、超越之需求的义理学、一种新的性命之学。而近代唯识学的复兴是正面回应这些挑战的结果。③

三、回应西方文化挑战的需求。唯识学以其严密的逻辑思辨性、庞大严谨的体系化和组织化等特征成了一种中国知识分子回应和理解西方哲学和科学的重要思想资源。唐大圆有言："佛教中之有学，且足以纠

---

① 章太炎：《菿汉三言》，虞云国校点，上海书店出版社2011年版，第71页。
② 章太炎：《章太炎全集》第4册，上海人民出版社1985年版，第370页。
③ 张志强：《从"理学别派"到"士人佛学"——由明清思想史的主题演进试论近代唯识学的思想特质》，《哲学研究》2007年第9期。

正今世科学之误，匡西洋哲学之谬而特出者，则莫如唯识。"① 在晚清民初的中国思想世界中，唯识学不仅是理解各种外来新思想的一个途径，② 更是纠正西方科学、哲学之弊端的思想利器。张曼涛在《现代佛学丛刊·唯识学概论（三）》之"编辑旨趣"中对唯识之兴起有一段精彩的概括：

> （在近代中国）而影响思想界最深的，则又可说，只有唯识最为出色。在现代中国几个可数的思想家中，无不跟唯识学发生过关联。主要者如熊十力、梁漱溟、景昌极、梁启超、章太炎等莫不如是。即使是深受西洋哲学影响，而不以东方哲学为意的，如金岳霖、张东荪等，亦对唯识学深表崇意。此原因何在？就在唯识学跟近代西方传来的学术思想，有相当相似的关联，如科学观念、哲学系统，都是有体系、有组织的学问，这与以往中国传统学问中，不重体系、不重组织，完全不同。而在中国，甚至包括印度，能与西方哲学相匹敌，组织化、系统化，从一个观念，而引导出许多连锁观念、系统观念，在整个东方各家学说中，就唯有唯识最具此种精神，因此，西方文化传来的结果，竟不料掀起了一阵唯识研究的高潮。……几乎所有研究佛学的，莫不以唯识为第一研究步骤。③

上述三点理由中，尤以第三点最为重要。因为国人的心理机制和中国自身学术的发展只是为唯识学复兴准备了道路，而真正推动其发生的最为重要的动力因素是西方文化的刺激。总的来说，以上三方面的理由都有其合理处，但是，我们仍然要继续追问的是：唯识学的什么特质符合了时代的需要？能否在更高的理论层次上来解释唯识学复兴这一现象？

---

① 唐大圆：《十五年来中国佛法流行之变相》，载《海潮音》第 16 卷第 1 期。
② 葛兆光：《自家宝藏的失而复得——晚清久佚唯识典籍由日本反传中国之影响》，《史学集刊》2010 年第 1 期。
③ 张曼涛：《唯识学概论（三）》"编辑旨趣"，台北：大乘文化出版社 1978 年版。

我们认为，采用当代美国著名文化人类学家克利福德·格尔兹的宗教学理论来解释此一历史现象会更有说服力。格尔兹认为，宗教即是一种文化体系，而"文化的分析不是一种探索规律的实验科学，而是一种探索意义的阐释性科学"①。按此推论，唯识学的复兴本质上是一种新的意义阐释体系的兴起，其复兴的本根原因在于旧有意义体系所面临的深层危机。

鸦片战争以后，西方的坚船利炮打开了国门，封闭的地理格局被打破，西方文化随之而入，以富强、进步之姿势猛烈地冲击着中国传统文化。近代中国面临着前所未有的巨大危机，不仅是在器物层面和制度层面，更为深刻的是在文化层面，用"天崩地裂"来形容近代中国一点儿都不夸张。故而国人的世界图景和自我感知被大大地改变了。

晚清士大夫宋育仁曾有一段论述，反映了传统世界图景的改变：

> 其（指西学——引者注）用心尤在破中国祖先之言，为以彼教易名教之助，天为无物，地与诸星同为地球，俱由引力相引，则天尊地卑之说为诬，肇造天地之主可信，乾坤不成，两大阴阳，无分贵贱，日月星不为三光，五星不配五行，七曜显于不伦，上祀诬为无理，六经皆虚言，圣人为妄作。据此为本，则人身无上下，推之则家无上下，国无上下，从发源处决去天尊地卑，则一切平等，男女决有自由之权，妇不统于夫，子不制于父，祖性无别，人伦无处立根，举宪天法地，顺阴阳，陈五行诸大义，一扫而空。……如彼学所云，则一部《周易》全无是处，《洪范》五行，《春秋》灾异，皆成蓍说，中国所谓圣人者，亦无知妄人耳，学术日微，为异端所劫。②

---

① ［美］克利福德·格尔兹：《文化的解释》，纳日碧力戈等译，上海人民出版社 1999 年版，第 5 页。

② 宋育仁：《泰西各国采风记》，载钱钟书主编《郭嵩焘等使西记六种》，生活·读书·新知三联书店 1998 年版，第 388 页。

可见，旧有的文化价值、信仰体系在西学东渐的历史洪流中难以为继。① 按西方科学、哲学的说法，"天为无物，地与诸星同为地球，俱由引力相引"，因而天尊地卑之说、阴阳五行说都不可成立，甚至"六经皆虚言，圣人为妄作""人伦无处立根"。传统的意义解释在欧风美雨的无情吹打下"皆成赘说"。新旧文化、中西文化的激烈冲突导致近代文化处于"不新不旧，不中不西，青黄不接"的焦虑状态。黄远生对此有一段文字可作为经典的概括（1916 年）：

> 旧者既已死矣，新者尚未生。吾人往日所奉为权威之宗教、道德、学术、文艺，既已不堪新时代激烈之风潮，犹之往希腊神道之被窜逐然，一一皆即于晦匿，而尚无同等之权威之宗教、道德、学术、文艺而代兴。吾人以一身立于过去遗骸与将来胚胎之间，赤手空拳无一物可把持，徒彷徨于过渡之时期中而已。②

旧的意义解释体系的彻底崩溃呼唤着全新的意义解释体系的建立。既然是全新的体系，那么就必须具有高度普遍性，以至能够对所有新旧事件作出合理解释，否则将无法在本体层面上树立形而上的基石。在近代文化上，最为重要的矛盾便是古今之争、中西之争，如何将古今、中西文化在某一个本体上统一起来，是重建近代文化的核心任务。

这就合理地解释了为什么在 20 世纪中国思想界涌现出一股建构本体论的热潮。正如李维武先生所说，20 世纪中国哲学发展有一个基本特点：三大哲学思潮（引者注：指的是人文主义思潮、科学主义思潮以及马克思主义思潮）在其发展途程中都不可避免地碰到了本体论问题。即使是那些对本体论持否定性态度的人们也不能不对本体论问题作

---

① 李向平曾深刻指出存在与意义的双重迷失是作为"异端"的佛教之所以能够跃向广阔的晚清社会文化领域的时代原因。（参见李向平《救世与救心——中国近代佛教复兴思潮研究》，上海人民出版社 1993 年版，第 2—7 页。）

② 黄远生：《想影录》，载"近代中国史料丛刊"第 3 编，第 21 辑，《黄远生遗著》第 1 卷，台北：文海出版社 1987 年版，第 161 页。

出认真的思考和回答。① 虽然把本体论作为一个重大的哲学问题明确提出并引起中国哲学界广泛关注是在五四时期的科学与玄学论战之中，但是，早在严复、章太炎等人那里以及唯识学的复兴运动之中就已经开始探讨世界的本体了。章太炎说："言哲学创宗教者，无不建立一物以为本体。其所有之实相虽异，其所举之形式是同。"② 他以唯识学三自性理论为基础，积极建构真如本体论，实质上反映了当时知识分子迫切地重建意义体系的一种努力。可以说，热衷于建构本体论不是中国知识分子对西方哲学的简单模仿，而是追寻意义的强烈需求。

就当时的中国而言，新的本体、新文化体系必须能够对西方科学、哲学作出合理的意义解释。正如马克斯·韦伯所言，人是"悬挂在由他们自己编织的意义之网上的动物"③。西方文化的输入破坏了中国原有的"意义之网"，但中国人无法忍受无意义的混乱，因此，必须把外来的西方文化重新编织进中国文化的"意义之网"中。这种努力可以分为两大类：一是"纯宗西洋哲学"，即直接用西洋哲学来构建中国的意义之网；二是"兼宗中西哲学"，即糅合中西两面哲学而组织成意义之网。④ 保守型知识分子以及中国佛教，显然是倾向于后者。

保守型知识分子和佛教徒们普遍的做法是：以本土文化为本位，通过积极推进固有文化的"自我更新"，从而对新的世界图景作出意义解释。唯识学"万法唯识"的一元论主张显然迎合了这种需要，它将一切事物、自我皆纳入心识哲学中，从而编织起一张无所不包的"意义之网"。不仅如此，唯识学注重经验实证、逻辑分析的思维方法以及系统化、理性化的理论品质也与西方科学、哲学相契合。可见，能够在本体论层面上将中西、古今文化融冶于一炉的传统学说，非唯识学莫属。正如大悟在 1935 年总结民国以来"中国佛法之动向"时指出："民国

---

① 李维武：《二十世纪中国哲学本体论问题》，湖南教育出版社 1991 年版，第 60 页。

② 章太炎：《建立宗教论》，载《章太炎全集》第 4 卷，上海人民出版社 1985 年版，第 404 页。

③ 参见［美］克利福德·格尔兹《文化的解释》，纳日碧力戈等译，上海人民出版社 1999 年版，第 5 页。

④ 关于现代中国哲学的划分，参见孙道升《现代中国哲学界之解剖》，《国闻周报》第 12 卷第 45 期，1935 年。

以还，研究佛学之士，多重法相唯识学，盖一切教理，应以法相唯识为基本。……今人研究多重唯识，复有一种意义，即法相唯识学，为佛教中最适于现代思想之佛学，有科学的方法，有哲学的理论，人生宇宙之说明。"① 于是，学者、居士、僧人研习唯识学蔚然成风，这门沉寂已久的古老学问在近代却焕发出异样的光彩。

三　本质：意义体系的重建

按格尔兹的观点，文化就是由符号组成的某个社会公认的、共享的意义背景。如同艺术、常识、政治等，宗教也是一个文化系统。他对宗教的定义为：

（1）一个象征的体系；（2）其目的是确立人类强有力的、普遍的、恒久的情绪与动机（moods and motivation）；（3）其建立的方式是系统阐述关于一般存在秩序的观念；（4）给这些观念披上实在性的外衣；（5）使得这些情绪和动机仿佛具有独特的真实性。②

所谓"象征（符号）"，指的是"概念的可感知的系统表述，是固定于可感知形式的经验抽象，是思想、判断、渴望或信仰的具体体现"③。也就是说，文化模式中的"符号"是能够承载关于思想、判断、渴望或信仰的观念并向他人传达观念的任何事物；并且其深植于我们的可感知形式之中，使得我们能够建构、理解和利用任何观念。

宗教和文化则是"象征符号集（sets）"，它"具有天然的双重性，既按照现实来塑造自身，也按照自身塑造现实，它们以此把意义，即客

---

① 大悟：《十五年来中国佛教之动向》，载《海潮音》第 16 卷第 1 期，第 79 页。

② ［美］克利福德·格尔兹：《文化的解释》，纳日碧力戈等译，上海人民出版社 1999 年版，第 105 页。

③ 同上书，第 106 页。

观的概念形式，赋予社会和心理的现实"①。这种双重性被格尔兹简略地概括成"世界观"和"精神特质"，前者指的是认知的、存在的方面，后者则指特定文化的道德（和审美）方面。二者相互结合、相互作用，共同构成了宗教的核心。"精神气质成为思想上合理的，是因为它看上去代表了一种生活方式，这种生活方式为世界观所描述的事物的真实状态所暗示。世界观则成为情感上可接受的，是因为它被作为一种事物真实状态的图像，这种生活方式是这种状态的真实表现。"② 宗教的本质就在于构建起主观价值与客观存在之间的意义关系，从而为个人解释其经验、组织其行为提供普遍意义。

近代中国佛教作为一种文化体系的特征是很明显的。近代佛学，特别是作为显学的唯识学，其宗教性特征往往被选择性忽视，而其文化特征则得到强调，以至表现出明显的理性化特征——这是近代佛学的一大特点。③"佛教乃智信而非迷信"为近代思想家一再强调。梁启超曾指出，佛教徒西行求法与基督教徒礼拜耶路撒冷、回教徒礼拜麦加有着本质的区别，后二者"纯出于迷信的参拜也"，而"我国人之西行求法，……其动机出于学问——盖不满于西域间接的佛学，不满于一家口说的佛学。譬犹导河必于昆仑，观水必穷溟澥。非自进以探索兹学之发源地而不止也"④。甚至连近代佛学之重镇支那内学院都明确表示，内学院"非宗教性质，是讲学机关"⑤。可见，在近代学者眼中，佛学更偏向于一种理性的"学问"，而非非理性的宗教信仰。

因此，近代佛学，特别是唯识学的复兴在本质上是一种文化体系、意义体系的重建。西学东渐极大地改变了中国人的世界图景和自我感

---

① ［美］克利福德·格尔兹：《文化的解释》，纳日碧力戈等译，上海人民出版社1999年版，第108页。

② 同上书，第148—149页。

③ 关于近代佛学的理性特征，学界已经基本取得共识，代表性研究成果参见麻天祥《科学与理性的佛学百年》，载《佛学百年》论文集，武汉大学出版社2008年版；何建明《佛法观念的近代调适》，广东人民出版社1998年版。

④ 梁启超：《翻译文学与佛典》，载《佛学研究十八篇》，中华书局1989年版，第161页。

⑤ 欧阳竟无：《与章行严书》，载王雷泉编选《欧阳渐文选》，上海远东出版社2011年版，第306页。

知，旧有的文化体系无法对新的世界作出意义解释。例如"天"的观念在中国传统文化中具有非常重要的地位。"天"不仅有自然之天的含义，而且"万物本乎天"（《郊特牲》），"天"是一种具有宗教意味的终极实在，它是一切价值的源泉，也是人间道德和政治的形而上的依据。但是，西方文明，特别是近代天文学的输入从根本上动摇了中国人的"天"观念以及对"天"的认知。"若夫天体，余尝谓苍苍之天，非有形质，亦非有大圜之气。盖日与恒星，皆有地球，其阿屯、以太，上薄无际，其间空气复厚，而人视之苍然，皆众日之余气，固非有天也。"①"天且无物，何论上帝。"② 西方科学、哲学的输入大大改变了中国人所理解的"世界"，旧有的世界观已经失效，那么，就必须重新建构"世界观"。

法相唯识学恰逢其时，它以科学、哲学、理性、实证、分析的姿态迎合了现代性的要求，从而受到知识界的青睐。在近代唯识学者的眼中，系统化、组织化的唯识学理论对近代世界作出了理性的阐释，使得其所确立的"世界观"表现为对事物、生活真实状态的"写照"——这是西方科学、哲学所开辟出来的真实。虽然以现在的眼光来看，万法唯识的世界与科学主义的世界是两种意义完全不同的"真实"，但是，在以唯识学为本位的近代学者、居士和僧人眼中，万法唯识、唯识无境不但与科学、西方哲学相一致，而且甚至比后者更能反映世界的真实状态。

而且唯识学的"世界观"所确立的强有力的、普遍的、恒久的情绪与动机，即"精神气质"，也被视为符合近代社会的时代需求。笼统地说，佛学的否定精神与革新家、革命家的社会批判意识相契合；佛学众生平等的基本主张与民主、平等的现代价值相契合；佛学自贵其心的教义与个性解放意识和意志决定论相契合；普度众生的菩萨行与救亡图

---

① 章太炎：《儒术真论》，载姜玢编选《革故鼎新的哲理：章太炎文选》，上海远东出版社 1996 年版，第 48 页。
② 章太炎：《膏兰室札记》，载《章太炎全集》卷 1，上海人民出版社 1985 年版，第 292 页。

存的使命感相契合；佛学的理性主义与价值重建相契合。① 佛学所确立的世界观被认为忠实地表达了真如、实相，从而为道德和审美的生命力提供了动力源泉。"有力的强制'应当'（ought）生发于理解性的实际'存在'（is），以此，宗教将对人类行为的独特要求根植于人类生存的最普遍的语境当中。"② 反映着存在的真实状态的世界观"有力的强制"着人类的道德行为（和审美的行为），因为精神气质之所以成为思想上合理的，是由于它是世界观所描述的事物的真实状态所暗示的。所以，无常、无我、唯识的世界观又生发出普度众生的菩萨心和众生平等的理念、批判性和否定性的精神、自贵其心的自我意识、大无畏的革命精神、头脑皆可施于人的献身精神……世界观与精神气质的相互配合共同构成了近代佛学思潮的核心。

总之，以唯识学为主体的近代佛学复兴在本质上是意义体系的重建。作为文化体系的近代佛学表现出前所未有的涵化古今、涵化中西的包容性和渗透性，在本体论层面建构起一个庞大的"意义之网"以解决近代的意义危机。正是在这个意义上，我们将近代佛学复兴称作中国佛学的"第二次思想革命"，而唯识学的复兴则是此次革命的开始。

---

① 麻天祥：《晚清佛学与近代社会思潮》，第 76—84 页。
② ［美］克利福德·格尔兹：《文化的解释》，纳日碧力戈等译，上海人民出版社 1999 年版，第 148 页。

翻译、比较中的
佛教与基督教

On the Nestorian Translation of Christian Scriptures: In Comparison with the Buddhist Successful Model

Vincent Shen[*]

Abstract: The Christian Scriptures were first introduced into China by a Nestorian priest named Olopen (or Alopen), who came to Chang An, the capital of Tang Dynasty, in 635 AD. Olopen was welcomed by the Tang government and treated very favorably by Fang Xuanling, the Chinese prime minister of that time. He was accommodated in the royal court, where he translated the scriptures he had brought with him; and later, in 638 AD, the Emperor Taizong issued a royal decree whereby Nestorianism would be disseminated throughout China. Of the early translated Christian texts, *The Sutra of Jesus the Messiah* and *On One God* were among the first to introduce the Christian idea of One God as the creator of the world to the Chinese people. This was a very significant event both in the Chinese history of religion and also the history of philosophy. However, in 845 AD, under the impact of Emperor Tang

* Vincent Shen (沈清松), Professor, Department of Philosophy, University of Toronto, Canada.

Wuzong's persecution of Buddhism, Nestorianism was branded as one of "three foreign (or barbarian) religions" and subsequently banned.

It is interesting to note that Buddhism from India has, together with Confucianism and Daoism, long been accepted as one of the three major teachings (sanjiao) in China; but that Christianity even now, almost 14 centuries after its introduction byOlopen, is still a foreign religion in the eyes of the common Chinese people. I will argue that this state of affairs is related to the different strategies of strangification that were employed by these religions in China.

This paper will analyze some basic ideas in *The Sutra of Jesus the Messiah* and *On One God* and problems arising in the process of translation, and attempt to evaluate the strategies of strangification that were practiced by the Nestorians in China. Strangification, which etymologically means the act of going outside of oneself to multiple others, from one's familiarity to strangeness, to foreigners, will be analyzed through three levels-namely linguistic, pragmatic and ontological-in order to critically evaluate the Nestorians' introduction of Christian monotheism to China. Comparisons with the introduction of Buddhism, a non-theistic religion, will be made in this context.

Key Terms: Nestorianism Monotheism Strangification Buddhism Daoism Religions in Tang dynasty

Introduction

Despite the fact that some Nestorians were already present in China much earlier than the sixth century,[①] the Nestorian version of Christian monotheism

---

① According to the *History of Jin Dynasty*, the ancestors of Mar Sargis, who belonged to a Nestorian family, immigrated from the Western Lands to Lintao in the year 578 AD. See *Jin Shi* 金史 (History of Jin Dynasty), *juan* 124, *Biography of Ma Qingxiang* (*Bainaben Ershiwushi*: 1153).

was officially introduced to the Chinese people by a Nestorian missionary named Olopen (or Alopen) in 635 AD. This could potentially have had a profound influence on this old Eastern civilization, yet to date, almost 14 centuries after its inception, Christianity has significantly failed to become one of the major constitutive elements of Chinese culture. In contrast, Buddhism, introduced into China from India in 2 BC according to the earliest record, has long since become, together with Confucianism and Daoism, one of its three major traditions (*sanjiao* 三教). This state of affairs gives rise to some interesting questions, and a comparative study may teach us a good deal.

In ancient China, there was common belief in a Supreme God on High, named *di* 帝 or *shangdi* 上帝 in Shang Dynasty (1751 – 1112 BC), or *tian* 天 (Heaven) in Zhou Dynasty (1111 – 249 BC), though always within a polytheistic context. In Shang Dynasty, *di* or *shangdi*, which arguably evolved from its cult of ancestry, dominated over a pantheon of divinities comprised of natural powers (like the sun, Yellow River, mountains, etc.), former lords, and pre-dynastic ancestors. In Zhou dynasty, *tian*, which evolved from *shangdi* into a more universal power, as the supreme ruler of both human society and the universe at large, was not independent of the entourage of multiple divinities, such as those of mountains and rivers, those of ancestral spirits, and even those of the stove and the household shrine. ①The concept of *tian* has changed during the course of Chinese intellectual history, from Confucius who still kept its religious meaning as God on High, through the mediation of Zisi 子思, Confucius's grandson, to Mencius, who saw it rather as the highest principle of morality, immanent and therefore accessible to human nature. In the *Zhongyong* 中庸 (Doctrine of the Mean), *cheng* 诚, translated as sincerity on the psychological and ethical level, means also

---

① As evidenced by Wan-shun Jia's dialogue with Confucius: "It is better to pay homage to the spirit of the stove than to the spirits of the household shrine. What does this mean?" The Master replied: "It is not so. A person who offends against *tian* has nowhere to pray" (*Analects* 3. 13, Ames and Rosement: 85).

True Reality on the metaphysical level. For Mencius, if one can succeed in unfolding fully one's own mind/heart, one should be able to understand one's nature, and when one understands one's own nature, one understands Heaven. This is to say there was a humanistic tendency in Confucianism that turned the transcendent God into a principle immanent to and accessible by human subjectivity.

Polytheism has always been present in the tradition of religious Daoism, even if this has a contrasting tendency: on the one hand to see all gods as various manifestations of the same Dao, and on the other hand, to emphasize the cultivation of one's inner body and spiritual resources and therefore to propound the immanence of human subjectivity. We should mention here that in Tang Dynasty, religious Daoism was much cherished by the royal family, who took Laozi as its sacred ancestor. This was without doubt a strategy for subsuming religious power under the control of political leaders, as evidenced by the fact that Emperor Xuanzong annotated the *Laozi* and set up the Daoist Five Scriptures[1] for the purpose of education and state examination.

As to Buddhism, even if there was a tendency in its Indian tradition, according to the Mahasamghikas, to worship Buddha as omnipresent, omnipotent and omniscient and as living endlessly and eternally in the Tusita Heaven, there was also a contrasting humanistic position upheld by the Sthaviras (the Elders), which posited that the human body of Buddha required clothing, food, sleep and medical care when ill, and that only Buddha's Dharmakaya (Spiritual Body) was perfect (Yin Shun: 61 – 63). In its Chinese tradition, despite the fact that there was originally a popular tendency to view Buddha as an omniscient, omnipresent and compassionate divinity, the intellectually more powerful form of Chinese Mahayana Buddhism emphasized

---

[1] The "Daoist Five Scriptures" are the *Laozi*, the *Zhuangzi*, the *Liezi*, the *Wenzi* and the *Gengshangzi*, all canonized as the *Zhengjing* 真经 (True Scriptures). See *Tang Huiyao* 唐会要, juan 卷9, (Taipei: Shijie Book Store, 1960), p. 74.

the non-substantial concept of Mind as the infinite spiritual resources of all sentient-beings. For example, in the early stages of Chinese Buddhism, there was a debate over the existence of a substantial immortal spirit. Against the view of Fan Zhen 范缜 (450 – 515), who, in his *shenmie lun* 神灭论 (On the Perishability of Spirit), posited that the spirit was one with the body and when the body died, the spirit perished too, a counterview was launched by Zheng Xianzhi 郑鲜之, the author of *shenbumie lun* 神不灭论 (On the Immortality of Spirit), along with others, who claimed that the existence of Buddha depended on the immortality of a substantial spirit which, after a process of purification, could finally achieve the intuition of the essence of all things, like a mirror reflecting reality as it is, and thereby became Buddha. In the transformation from ignorance to enlightenment, one was able to return to the original true-thusness of Buddhahood, which was one in all. According to the *Awakening of Faith in the Mahayana*, produced at around the same time, the only existence was the Mind of all sentient beings, the One Mind, which manifested itself in myriad sentient beings. In illusion, myriad sentient beings presumed their individuality; in enlightenment, they were all in the One Mind.

In the burgeoning development of Chinese Mahayana Buddhism, the substantialist vision of immortal spirit was soon replaced by the non-substantialist idea of *kong* 空 (emptiness) in the Sanlun School and the non-substantialist concept of *xin* 心 (Mind) in the Tiantai School, the later Huayan School and the Chan (Zen) School. It later put emphasis on the notion of the infinite resources of the non-substantialist Mind, a concept that reached the peak of its development in Tang Dynasty (618 – 907).

The idea of Christian monotheism-that preached of One God who created the world, and who intervenes in the world by His providence and saves the world from its Fall by incarnating himself in the world-was textually and thereby officially introduced to China by a Nestorian missionary, Olopen (Alopen), who came to Chang An, the capital of Tang Dynasty, in 635

AD. According to the *History of Tang Dynasty* and the Nestorian Inscription that was unearthed in 1625 AD, Olopen was welcomed by Fang Xuanling 房玄龄, the Chinese prime minister at that time, accompanied by guards of honor, sent by the Tang Emperor Taizong 唐太宗, and was then installed in the royal library where he set about translating the Nestorian Scriptures he had brought with him. Later he was invited into the emperor's private apartment to discuss the Way according to the Nestorian Church. In 638 AD, Taizong officially decreed that the teachings of the Church be disseminated throughout China, and ordered the Chinese government to build a Nestorian temple at Yiningfang 义宁坊 and the ordination of 20 Nestorian priests to serve in it. Indeed, never before had a Christian missionary been given such an exceptionally favorable reception. Among the Christian texts translated by Olopen, the *Xuting mishisuo jing* 序听迷诗所经 (*Sutra of Jesus the Messiah*), and the *Yishen lun* 一神论 (*On One God*)[①] were the first to be introduced to the Chinese people. As such, these works are very interesting for understanding how Nestorian monotheism was interpreted in its earliest Chinese version. Nestorianism had in fact existed across China for some two centuries before it was banned, under the impact of Tang Dynasty's persecution of Buddhism, in 845 AD. Together with two other "foreign" religions, namely Zoroastrianism and Manicheanism, Nestorianism was branded as one of the *san yijiao* 三夷教 (three foreign religions).

This paper will proceed to discuss the strategy of strangification practiced by the Nestorian missionaries in China. We will analyze this strangification on three levels-linguistic, pragmatic and ontological-in order to critically evaluate the introduction of Christian monotheism to China. Some comparisons with the introduction of Buddhism, a non-theistic religion, will be made for a bet-

---

① The *Sanwei mengdu zan* 三威蒙度赞 (Hymn to Take Refuge in the Holy Trinity), which contains important prayers for understanding the Nestorian idea of the Trinity, seems to have been translated much later, around 800 AD. See later in this paper.

ter understanding in a comparative context.

Strangification and its Buddhist Model of Great Success

My basic premise is that we can gain some valuable insights by looking at the process by which Christianity was introduced to China. In this age of globalization, people in the world may feel closer to each other, yet at the same time more vulnerable and susceptible to conflicts of all kinds. It is time that we learnt to be more open to multiple others, instead of keeping within our ownself-enclosures. In order to overcome antagonism by appealing to effective dialogue, I have proposed in recent years, on the levels of intercultural interaction and religious dialogue, "strangification"① and "language appropriation" as viable strategies. The term "strangification", a neologism that perhaps seems strange in English but is more understandable in Chinese—*waitui* 外推, means etymologically the act of going beyond oneself to multiple others, or going outside of one's familiarity to strangeness, to strangers. This act presupposes the appropriation of language by which we learn to express our ideas or values in languages understandable to others. In their turn, "strangification" and "language appropriation" presuppose an original generosity toward multiple others, without limiting oneself to the claim of reciprocity, which is quite often presupposed in social relationships and ethical golden rules. Here I use the term "multiple others" or "many others" to replace the post-modern concept of "the Other" proposed by Lacan, Levinas, Derrida, and Deleuze. For me, "the Other" is a mere abstraction. At no moment in our life do we face purely and simply "the Other" . We are all born into multiple others and we grow up among multiple others. It's better for a life of sani-

---

① The term "strangification" was first proposed by F. Wallner, University of Vienna, as an epistemological strategy for interdisciplinary research. This concept was later developed by myself, in combining it with my previous understanding in Confucianism and phenomenology, in the domains of intercultural interaction and religious dialogue.

ty that we keep in our minds the existence of multiple others and our relation with multiple others. In the history of Chinese philosophy and religion, all schools of thought have understood well that we as human beings face multiple others. This is also the case with Buddhism and Christianity. Take the example of Nestorian Christians: from the time of its introduction to China, Nestorianism was aware that it was facing the competition of multiple others, not only the local traditions of Confucianism, Buddhism and Daoism, but also other foreign religions such as Zoroastrianism and Manichaeism, with which it was grouped and branded by the Chinese as *sanyijiao* (three barbarian religions).

As I see it, three approaches of strangification could have been put into practice here.

First, linguistic strangification: If one discourse/value or cultural expression/ religious belief can be translated into a discourse/value/cultural expression/religious belief understandable to another scientific, cultural or religious community, then it has a larger or universalizable validity. Otherwise, its validity is limited only to its own world and reflection must therefore be made on the limit of one's own discourse/value or expression/belief.

Second, pragmatic strangification: If one discourse/value or expression/belief can be drawn out from its original social and pragmatic context and put into other social and pragmatic contexts and remain valid, this means it is more universalizable and has larger validity than being limited only to its own context of origin. Otherwise, reflection must be made on one's discourse/value or expression/belief to see why it's limited only to one's own social and pragmatic context.

Third, ontological strangification: A discourse/ value or expression/belief, when universalizable by a detour of experiencing Reality Itself, for example, a direct experience with Reality Itself, such as other people, Nature, or even the Ultimate Reality, would be very helpful for mutual understanding among different scientific micro-worlds (disciplines or research programs), cultural worlds, and religious worlds.

In the context of Chinese history, Buddhism has been a successful model of strangification in becoming an essential part of Chinese culture. We can therefore take it as a mirror case for the Christian strategy of strangification in China. Buddhism, in its long process of becoming Chinese, has taken different measures of strangification.

First, concerning linguistic strangification, there were successive translations of Buddhist scriptures and intellectual dialogue with Daoism and Confucianism through a process of language appropriation. The translation of Buddhist scriptures was not easy in the beginning, and its quality was poor, as evidenced by Kumārajīva (343 – 413) who commented that translation was like "chewing rice for others, which would not only lose its original taste, but also make people feel like vomiting" (TSD 50: 332). Nevertheless, the translation of Buddhist scriptures proceeded to become a very systematic and rigorous enterprise, with its own institutions, regulations, functions and procedures. In Tang Dynasty, under Taizong's reign, Xuanzang 玄奘 went to India, brought back 657 Buddhist works and translated 75 of them into Chinese. Under his leadership, Chinese Buddhism conducted the largest translation project in Chinese history.

Buddhism made itself understandable through a process of language appropriation, the so-called *geyi* 格义, of Daoist language, such as the Daoist concepts of *dao* 道, *you* 有 (being), *wu* 无 (non-being), *benwu* 本无 (original non-being) ···etc. But, when this kind of language appropriation became misleading for understanding Buddhism, there arose critique of *geyi* Buddhism, and Chinese monks like Sengzhao 僧肇 brought the discourse of being and non-being back to the concept of emptiness, by saying that both being and non-being were unreal, and therefore empty. Since Daosheng 道生, the doctrine that "All sentient beings can become Buddha" made itself congenial with the Confucian doctrine of "Everyone can become Yao and Shun." Later, with Chan Buddhism, the proposition was radicalized into

"All sentient beings are already Buddha. " Translation of Buddhist sutras and appropriation of Daoist and Confucian languages served to make Buddhism understandable to Chinese intellectuals. It also had a great impact on Chinese philosophy, literature, arts, and language.

Concerning pragmatic strangification, it was necessary for Buddhism to be drawn out of the Indian social context and to adapt itself to the Chinese socio-politico-economic context. Anticipating critiques from Chinese elites, Buddhism, in the long history of its conquest of China, adapted itself by taking different measures of strangification. For example, it responded to the critique of anti-filiality by translating or even inventing Buddhist texts on filial piety. ①It also faced the critique that it showed disrespect for the emperor and his officials by distinguishing, as Huiyuan (331 –414) had done in his *Samen bujing wanzhe lun* 沙门不敬王者论 (*On Why Buddhist Monks Don't Pay Respect to Political Leaders*), common believers from monks. It stated that common followers of Buddhism in the secular world should pay respect to and obey the emperor, his officials and social ethics, whereas Buddhist monks should go beyond worldly ethics and rituals so as to concentrate themselves on

---

① The early translated *Liudu Jijing*《六度集经》(*Collected Sutras on Six Pāramitrās*) had already emphasized the importance of filial piety, saying that it was more important than charity. The second part of the Brahma-jāla-sūtra (*Fanwangjing*《梵纲经》), whose translation is attributed to Kumārajīva, also stressed the filial piety of Sākyamuni and combined filial piety with the Buddhist *sīlas* (commandments). The Buddhist scholar QI Song 契嵩 (1011 –1072) in his highly influential *Xiaolun*《孝论》(*On Filial Piety*), said that Buddhism, more than other religions, emphasized filial piety. Qi Song also equated the five Buddhist *sīlas* (*wujie* 五戒) with the Confucian five cardinal virtues: *ren* 仁, *yi* 义, *li* 礼, *zhi* 智, and *xin* 信. In the Tang Dynasty, an invented sutra in Chinese, the *Fumu Enzhong Jing*《父母恩重经》(*Sutra on the Weighty Grace of Parents*) appeared to feature filial piety as a Buddhist value. The *Ullambanapātra-sūtra* (*Yu lan pen jing*《盂兰盆经》), said to have been translated into Chinese by Dhamaraksa 竺法护 (266 –313), is often seen as the *Xiao Jing*《孝经》of Buddhism. In it we find the story of Maudgalyāyana (*Mulian* 目莲), a disciple of Sākyamuni, who enters purgatory to relieve his mother from suffering. This led to the inauguration of the biggest national Buddhist festival—All Souls-which has been held on about the 15th of the seventh moon, from the 6th century until the present day, with the joint participation of Confucianism and Daoism. This festival, together with innumerable Chinese commentaries and related literature, images and dramas, have all transformed Buddhism into a religion of filial piety.

Buddhist truth. Once a monk had perfected his virtue, he saved by the same token not only his family relatives, but also the whole world; therefore his contribution to the welfare of common people was no less-indeed maybe even more-important than showing respect and obedience to Confucians and government officers.

Concerning ontological strangification, with its experience of "emptiness" or *xin* 心 (the Mind) as Ultimate Reality, Buddhists were able to make Buddhism understandable to other endogenous philosophies such as Confucianism and Daoism. The Buddhist experience of emptiness and the Mind, the Daoist experience of *dao* and *wu* (non-being), and the Confucian experience of *ren* 仁 (humanness, humanity, and cosmic interconnectedness) and *cheng* 诚 (sincerity and true reality), though quite different in themselves, still enjoy some sort of similarity and complementarity as experiences of Ultimate Reality. From as early as Mourong's *Lihuolun* (*On the Correction of Doubt*, c. 196 BCE), different versions of complementarity were proposed among these three teachings. Also, by putting forward various versions of the doctrine of the Common Origin of Three Teachings (*sanjiao tongyuan* 三教同源), Buddhism made itself understandable to Chinese intellectuals from different traditions.

With development over time, Buddhism penetrated both the intellectual life and the everyday life of the Chinese people. Chan Buddhism even progressed to becoming immanent to people's everyday life. As the *Platform Sutra* said,

> *If one's heart is even, there is no need of obeying obligations. If one's act is right, there is no need of practicing dhyana. There is gratitude when one is filial and nourishing his parents. There is justice when the superior and the inferior are sympathetic one to another. When one knows how to cede to elders, there is harmony between the noble and the mean; ···Prajna is to be sought in one's heart, there is no need of searching for meta-*

physical truth in the external world. Just to listen, to say and to cultivate one's self in this way, the Western paradise appears just in the present moment. ①

This immanentist attitude had made some basic changes to Indian Buddhism. According to Nāgārjuna and Asanga, the Buddhist way of life should lead to compassion and altruism, to a way of existence for the enlightenment of all sentient beings. By contrast, Chan Buddhism would see it as the enlightenment of one's own heart in everyday life and in everyday virtue. In everything big or small of everydayness there is the *Dao* of enlightenment. If Buddhism became acceptable to the Chinese elites with Dao Sheng's proclamation that "All sentient beings can become Buddha", the Southern Chan Buddhist sects would take it for granted that "all sentient beings are originally Buddha"②, which rendered a philosophical foundation to the affirmation that everyone's everyday practice was the *Dao*. Though this had the merit of instilling Buddhism into the everyday life of the Chinese people, and of unfolding the infinite resource in the human mind, in human subjectivity, by the same token it constrained Chinese life and philosophy in the realm of immanence, so that there was no necessity to be open to the other, to go outside of one's self and go to strangers, to multiple others. This, unfortunately, was the final unexpected consequence of Buddhism's strangification in China. In my view it was exactly at this crucial juncture that Christianity could and should have intervened and done something for the benefit of Chinese culture, in order to enhance it by the dimension of multiple others, by the virtue of generosity toward multiple others, so as to transform Chinese culture, already rich in immanent resources, into an ever-renovating cultural dynamism supported

---

① *Platform Sutra*, Chapter 3 (*Taisho sinshu daizoko*, vol. 48, 352), My translation.

② Such as Huang Po's words: "This Mind/heart is Buddha. Buddha is all sentient beings, all sentient beings are Buddha." (*Taisho sinshu daizoko* 大正新修大藏经, vol. 51, 270).

complementarily by spiritual resources from strangers, from foreign parts of the world.

Christianity's Strangification, Generosity,
and Early Chinese Monotheism

As I see it, Christianity, like Buddhism, is a religion of strangification par excellence,[1] in the sense that it is based on the belief that Jesus Christ died for the salvation of all humankind, that is, for his love of and generosity toward multiple others, even to the extent of sacrificing his own life for them. The existence of the Christian Church, which may at times give rise to human ambition and social conflict, remains meaningful because it can serve as a kind of religious community that assures the realization of Christian ideal values through communitarian life. The spirit of strangification is evident in the doctrine and history of Christianity.

On the doctrinal level, we can see God's creation of the world as a generous act of producing beings other than Himself by going outside of Himself to multiple others, to all things in the cosmos. His providence or his continuous care and participation in the creative process of the universe are his unceasing generosity to the world. Christ's incarnation and his death for the sake of humankind's redemption could be seen as an act of self-sacrifice for the other's cause par excellence. All things, human beings included, are called upon, so it seems, to act accordingly and go outside of themselves to multiple others so as to return eventually to the perfect Being.

On the level of historical dynamism, Christianity's missionary enterprise, first from Judea to Greece and Rome, then to Europe, then to other places in the world such as Africa, America and Asia, could be seen as an unceasing process of strangification, of going outside of itself to mul-

---

[1] Concerning strangification in Buddhism, see Shen 2003.

tiple others to become an integral part of the other's culture, thereby bringing them to the process of self-transcendence. In short, Christianity is a religion of strangification and incarnation. It goes to the other, recontextualizes itself in the other and realizes itself as a constitutive element of that culture and then transcends again any definite form of contextualization and concretization.

In this regard, the introduction of Christianity to China could be seen, not only as a historical moment of its extension and strangification to East Asia under the deep influence of Chinese culture, but also as bringing the vital Christian spirit to Chinese culture that is the virtue of infinite generosity and unlimited altruism realizing itself in the unceasing cyclical process from strangification, to incarnation to strangification again. This Christian spirit par excellence, if it becomes a constitutive element of Chinese culture, could serve to bring more balance to the development of Chinese culture in the contrasting situation of immanence and transcendence, humanness and righteousness, intuition and construction, already contained in Confucianism, Daoism and Buddhism.

All of these religions have their own concept of Ultimate Reality, namely *ren* (humaneness), or *cheng* (sincerity) in classical Confucianism; the *Dao* in Daoism; Buddha, Emptiness or the One Mind in Buddhism, *li* (principle or reason) in Realist neo-Confucianism, and *xin* (Mind) in Idealist Neo-Confucianism; yet none of them retains an irreducible dimension of otherness, such as the Deus Absconditus or Hidden God in Judeo-Christian traditions, that would prevent them from being reduced to the dimension of immanence. For example, the *Dao* in Daoism exists everywhere and is immanent in all things after having given birth to them; Emptiness and Mind in Chinese Mahayana Buddhism have become the infinite resource immanent and accessible to human subjectivity. This was expressed by Sengzhao 僧肇, the first and greatest Chinese Buddhist philosopher, when he said, "Is the Dao far away? Its reality is there when in contact with events; Is the sagehood far away? Live it with innate experience and it becomes marvelous. "① It is similarly expressed in the principle or *li* 理 taken by Zhu Xi 朱熹, a neo-Confucian of the 13th Century, to be the Great Ultimate, which operates within and explains the world and should not be seen as the Ultimate Other.

In its first introduction to China, the idea of an Ultimate Other was shown very clearly in the Chinese translation of scriptures in which terms such as "unthinkable", "incomprehensible" etc., were used to characterize God. However, since Nestorianism appropriated the languages of Buddhism and Daoism to make its doctrine accessible to the Chinese people, its idea of God seems to have been contaminated with a Daoist and Buddhist sense of immanence, although altruistic generosity on the ethical level, as proclaimed by the Lord of Heaven Himself, was preached and practiced. ②*The Sutra of Jesus the Messiah* is the earliest extant text we have of the first Nestorians in China, although in terms of calligraphy, the manuscript style is very similar to that of *On One God*, indicating they were transcribed by the same person. This text consists of two parts: the first deals with Nestorian theology and ethics, while the second tells of the life, words and deeds of Jesus.

The first part, which is this paper's concern, expounds the idea of an invisible, omnipresent God, upon whom the existence of all things, including human beings, is dependent. Because he is omnipresent, His laws are also omnipresent, and this is why people should practice good deeds and avoid doing evil. Those who do good will be able to see God, while those who do evil will be punished in Hell. From these ideas the Ten Vows (*yuan* 愿) or Commandments were derived, starting with three essential obligations: "Of all these three things: the first thing is to obey the Lord of Heaven; the

---

① Sengzhao 僧肇, *Buzhen kong lun* 不真空论 (*Emptiness of the Unreal*) (*Taisho sinshu daizoko*, vol. 45, 153). My translation.

② As evidenced by the third part of the texts contained in *On One God*, titled *The Lord of Heaven's Discourse on Alms-Giving*.

second is to obey the Sage Emperor; the third is to obey father and mother. "[1] These obligations consist in obeying God, the emperor and one's parents. Here we can see the strategic adaptation or recontextualization of Christian dogmatic and ethical theology with Confucian ethics and politics.

In the text of The Sutra of Jesus the Messiah, the terms "*tianzun*" 天尊 (Heaven Honored One, or Lord of Heaven) and "Buddha", were used to translate the concept of One God. This might have been due to the influence of Olopen's Buddhist assistant (s) in the translation process. The beginning of the text, in stating that "All the Buddhas as well as Kinnaras and the super-intending-devas, and arahats can see the Lord of Heaven" (Saeki: 125) seems to give us a hint of its polytheistic context. Here we understand the Sanskrit term "arahat" to mean sages or saints, but the plural form of "Buddha" (Buddhas, *zhufo*) is somewhat misleading. Since angels are referred to as "kinnaras" and "superintending-devas", terms that originally denoted Indian spirits and gods, surely the term "Buddhas" would not also be used to refer to angels. The term *fo* 佛 (Buddha) is used later in the same text to render God. There should be no concept of *zhufo* 诸佛 (All Gods) in a monotheistic theology, except in cases where it denotes the Trinity, that is to say the Holy Father, Holy Son and Holy Spirit, but this is not clear in the text, where the singular term "Buddha" is used to translate "God". This shows that the use of Chinese theological terms in The Sutra of Jesus the Messiah is neither proper nor precise, apart from the fact that it quite often borrows Buddhist terms that are themselves very misleading.

---

[1] See Weng Shaojun: 91. P. Y. Saeki's translation as "Sacred Superior" is misleading, see Saeki: 134. This is due to the fact that, in Chinese tradition, there has been an emphasis on "sage-king" in which *sheng* 圣 is understood as "sage" rather than "Sacred"; therefore, I have corrected the translation of *shengshang* 圣上 to "Sage Emperor". To facilitate the understanding of Western readers, I use Saeki's translation, with my corrections in bold. Sometimes I have retranslated the whole text so as to avoid misunderstanding.

The Sutra of Jesus the Messiah puts more emphasis on the omnipresence of God in the universe, in terms that are dynamic rather than static, in the sense that God operates unceasingly throughout the entire world. As it states, "The Lord of Heaven incessantly going around all over the world, is constantly present everywhere" (Saeki：125). The text suggests that God's work is done by the Holy Spirit in the guise of the Wind, termed in Chinese *feng* 风 (wind) and *liangfeng* 凉风 (cool wind), and corrected as *jingfeng* 净风 (pure wind) in later texts such as *On One God*, *the Nestorian Inscription*, and *Honored Scriptures* etc. In *The Sutra of Jesus the Messiah*, God's omnipresence becomes the main argument in support of the idea of His immanence in the world：that his wind is everywhere, and his law (dharma, *guobao* 果报) is also everywhere. The only transcendent attributes of God seem to be his invisibility, untouchability, and inaccessibility to the human senses; His countenance is invisible, His color is unknown, His residence is beyond apprehension, and so on. Yet all depends on Him in order to exist. The omnipresence of God, in a certain sense, is used to argue theologically that His law is also everywhere, according to which all human beings are to be rewarded or punished according to their good or bad deeds. It is from this that the three most important obligations and ten vows or commandments mentioned above are derived.

It is clear then, that in *The Sutra of Jesus the Messiah*, God was not textually expounded as the Ultimate Other. Even though the text says that God is invisible, it also says that those who have done good will be able to see Him. God's creativity and providence are not conceived in reference to his generous acts, but rather with reference to his act in law-giving. Ethical generosity, such as alms-giving, is therefore considered to be commanded by God's law rather than as coming directly from his infinite generosity.

The second Nestorian scripture translated into Chinese was *Yishen lun* 一神论 (*On One God*), which was misleadingly translated by P. Y. Saeki as *A Discourse on Monotheism.* ①This text contains three sections: the first *On One Heaven*, the second *Metaphors*, and the third *The World Honored One on Alms-giving*. It is very curious that it starts with the second, the *Metaphors*, in which the initial paragraphs explain, through the use of metaphors, the idea of One God and His attributes, and the idea that all beings visible and invisible are created by One God. Then it proceeds to expound the idea of the human being as constituted of body, soul and spirit, and it connects these two discourses, one on man, anther one God, by saying that, "As there is but one master for one house, so is there one soul for one body. If a house has more than one master, then the house can not do any good. If a man's body has more than one soul, then the man can not do good. The soul of a man, therefore, can neither be two, nor three⋯Likewise, there can be only one God in the universe, as there can neither be two nor be three Gods" (Saeki: 165). The text also argues the invisibility of God by the invisibility of the soul: "The One God exists in the universe, but He is invisible, like the soul existing in the body of man is invisible" (Ibid.)

On One God gives us a longer explanation of the idea of the Trinity by using the metaphor of the human body:

> ⋯*heaven and earth are nothing but that which exists by virtue of the One God...Therefore we know that the **marvelous** power of this One God is infinite and **inexhaustible**. Such Divine power of this one God is possessed by no other gods. There truly exists the Only One God from the beginning. Though He himself is invisible, yet there have been*

① This is an incorrect translation based on a misunderstanding of the Chinese. In Tang Dynasty, there was no technical term *yishen lun* 一神论 for Monotheism. The term "*lun*" means "a discourse on", or simply "on"; whereas the term "*yishen*" 一神 means One God. Nevertheless, in the following, I will continue to use Saeki's translation, marking corrections in bold when necessary.

two manifestations. For instance, these may be likened to one's right
and left hands or legs. But there are no such distinctions of before and
after or of upper and lower (between them). There are so alike that
one cannot be distinguished from the other. Likewise, the one Godhead
begot the other one out of one and the same substance and form…Now,
this One God entirely takes the form of One Single Being, and there
can not be, indeed, any second or a third (Saeki: 163 – 164, my cor-
rections in bold). ①

This passage affirms the marvelous and exhaustible power of One God,
who has two manifestations. Therefore the two other persons of God were understood in terms of manifestation, with somewhat Daoist overtones. The metaphor of the body is used here to communicate the idea that three persons own
only one substance between them, like one body. Two terms are used to say
that the Godhead "manifests" (*jian* 见) and "issues" (*chu* 出 or begets)
other persons, without offering any further conceptual precision or explanation. This might give rise to confusion since the same term "manifestation" is
also used to describe God's creation of the world.

The wording of *On One God* suggests to us that the person who assisted
Olopen in translating it into Chinese was more of a Daoist than a Buddhist. This might be indicated by the use of the term "manifestation" to refer
to the "creation" of the world. The idea of creatio ex nihilo is not evident in
the text, and the relation between the manifested and the manifestation is
clear at least on the level of literary meaning. Although it states clearly that

---

① I have changed Saeki's translation "one God" to "One God". Also Saeki's translation of
guzhi yisheng miaoli, *buke qiongjin* 故知一神妙力, 不可穷尽 as "we know that the mysterious power
of this one God is infinite and cannot be understood completely" does not correspond to the meaning of
the Chinese text, in which the term miao 妙 means "marvelous" rather than "mysterious", and *buke*
qiongjin 不可穷尽 means Gos's power itself is "infinite and inexhaustible", rather than the human subjective inability to understand completely, which is contradictory with the beginning of this sentence
which reads "therefore we know".

"It can be known that all things are made by one God", and "There are things visible as well as invisible, which have been all created by the one God" (Saeki: 161), the act of creation is understood in the Daoist sense of manifestation: "Everything that is made, without exception, is like the manifestation thereof" (Ibid.). The identification of the process of manifesting and the manifested surely weakens the sense of God's otherness implied in the use of terms such as "invisible", "infinity" and "eternity".

In *On One God*, it is said that Heaven and earth are made by One God and thereby they manifest God; that all things are in God and are without exception the one God. All things that exist in Heaven and earth are supported by God; otherwise everything will fall into destruction. It reads, "By virtue of the Divine power of the One God, heaven and earth are made neither to crumble nor to fall, and that, because of this Divine power, they will remain steadfast for ever and ever" (Saeki: 163).

As previously discussed, the relation between God and the world is understood in this text as analogous to that of soul and body: "This One God is present everywhere all over the universe in the same manner as the soul of man pervades the whole of his body, indulging to do as he pleases. He dwells in Heaven, but he is not limited in any one place or any period of time" (Saeki: 165: 166). The invisibility of God was argued from the invisibility of the soul. That is to say, God's invisibility was understood and argued through its analogy with the invisibility of the human soul. In a certain sense, we can say that God as described, even metaphorically, in *On One God* is substantial, pantheistic, and somehow anthropomorphic.

In short, the text of *On One God* gives us no strong sense of the Ultimate Otherness of God. God is the Ultimate Reality, but not the Ultimate Other. The Christian spirit of generosity in its Nestorian form is presented and understood on the human ethical level as charity, but not in terms of God's infinitely generous creativity.

Even though *On One God* clearly affirms that there is only One God, not two Gods, nor three Gods, the *Jingjiao Sanwei Mengdu Zan* 景教三威蒙度赞 (Nestorian Hymn to Take Refuge in the Holy Trinity), or the *Sanwei zan jing* 三威赞经 (Sutra of the Hymn to the Trinity), as recorded in the *Zun Jing* 尊经 (The Honored Scriptures), which was written arguably in 800 AD, appeared in the form of prayer to the three persons of God. As a hymn, used mostly in liturgy, of which the first part is taken to be the Nestorian version of *Gloria in Excelsis Deo*, there was no place for theological argumentation or explanation, but its performative language in its use as a prayer, as a statement of faith, would have had both a conscious and unconscious impact on the believers or chanters. The textual value of this hymn consists in the fact that the names of the three persons of the Trinity are made clear: the Tender-hearted Father (*ci fu* 慈父), the Illustrious Son (*ming zi* 明子) or Holy Son (*sheng zi* 圣子), and the Pure Spirit (*jing feng* 净风). The term *shengzi* (Holy Son) is in fact an improvement on the term *feilue* (费略), the Chinese phonetic translation of *filio* adopted by the Jesuits in China in the late 16th Century and early 17th Century. The Chinese text emphasizes, as to the attributes of the Trinity, the "powerfulness", "mercifulness", "incomprehensibility" and "unattainability" (*nanxun wuji* 难寻无及) of the Holy Father, the wisdom and the universal redemption of the Holy Son, and the purity, limpidity and void of the Holy Spirit. The later part of this text reads:

> Thou dwellest from eternity to eternity in the marvelously bright **realm without boundary**; And Thy Brightness and Majesty thoroughly search out the **bordered realm of being**. And yet no mortals have ever been able to see Thee, nor can **they see thy Image in any material** form···O Thou **great holy** and universally honored Messiah! We adore thee, Oh Merciful Father! For thy mercy is as **immense** as the Ocean. Oh thou great Holy Spirit wind **pure and void**, **your limpid and crystal law is unthinkable**

(*Saeki*: 266 – 268, *my corrections in bold*) . ①

We should notice here that the theological terms inherited from Chinese tradition, including Confucianism, Daoism and Buddhism, were not enough to render explicit the Trinity as One God. With its lack of explicit discussion of the idea of "persons" and their relation to one God, and its vague use of terms such as "manifestation" and "issuing", the idea of the Trinity that it presents might appear, in the minds of common believers, to be closer to the religious Daoist deities of the "Three Clarities" who manifest the Original Dao, understood somehow in a polytheistic sense, rather than the Christian idea of One God hidden and transcendent.

We will now proceed to examine more closely the Nestorians' strategies of strangification in China, on linguistic, practical and ontological levels.

Nestorian Linguistic Strangification

First, let us discuss the level of linguistic strangification. The Nestorian missionaries, not being well prepared in Chinese language and belles-lettres, and unfortunately lacking adequate assistance from their Chinese assistants,

---

① My correction in bold. Please note that Saeki's translation of the title of this hymn as "A Nestorian Motwa Hymn in Adoration of the Trinity" is incorrect, and I have subsequently modified it to "Nestorian Hymn to Take Refuge in the Holy Trinity", in which the term "sanwei" should be taken as "Trinity" and "*mengdu*" 蒙度 should be understood as the "*meng yizhi*" 蒙依止 in the main text, that is, "take refuge in", borrowed from Buddhism to express the idea of "salvation". We don't separate "*wei*" 威 from "*san*" 三 to form a unit with "*mengdu*" 蒙度 to become "*weimengdu*" 威蒙度, by which Saeki comes up with the term "Motwa", which in our view is mistaken. In this text, the Chinese term *wupanjie* 无畔界 means "realm without boundary" rather than Saeki's translation as "world of infinity". The following verse, "*fu yi se jian bu ke xiang* 复以色见不可相" should read as 复不可以色相见, which means "nor can they see thy Image in any material form", rather than Saeki's translation "nor can any eye of flesh form Thy (glorious) image". Also *dasheng* 大圣 means "great holy" rather than "most holy", and *qingning fa er busiyi* 清凝法尔不思议 means "your limpid and crystal law is unthinkable", rather than Saeki's translation as "Whose Purity is absolutely embodiment of Law beyond all thought".

produced translations which were frankly not elegant enough to be attractive to the Chinese people, and which were, moreover, overloaded with Daoist and Buddhist terms. We should understand that the Chinese culture was dominated by intellectual elites and men of letters, who would not have been much impressed by the quality of these writings.

This was the case with Nestorian linguistic strangification. Their earlier translations were not conducive to promoting religious faith among the Chinese people, being either too clumsy or too misleading; the name Jesus, for instance, was translated as *yishu* 移鼠, (a moving mouse), Maria as *moyan* 末艳 (the least beautiful), and John as *ruohun* 若昏 (the seemingly confused) ···etc. All these names, in their Chinese connotations, not only lacked any aesthetic beauty, but also provoked disdain or disgust. As such, they invoke Kumārajīva's comment that translation was like "chewing rice for others, which would not only lose its original taste, but also make people feel like vomiting. "

A more serious problem with Nestorian linguistic strangification was that it over appropriated Daoist and Buddhist terms, such as "Buddha", "*Dao*", and "Marvelous *Dao*", to translate "God", which not only misrepresented the Christian message, but also made it indistinguishable from Buddhism or Daoism. For example, even though *On One God* had the merit of introducing monotheism into China through statements such as "in all things we see the operation of one God", and "Myriad of things are created by God", it refers to this one God using Daoist terms such as *yuan yi* 元一, the Original One, and *tian zun* 天尊, the Heavenly Honored One, which makes it somewhat difficult to differentiate Christianity from religious Daoism. Also, the fact that three Nestorian texts, *The Sutra of Jesus the Messiah*, *Hymn to Take Refuge in the Holy Trinity*, and the *Nestorian Inscription* were included in the Buddhist Canon[1] provides textual evidence that they were perceived as

---

[1] For example, in volume 54 of the *Taisho shinshu daizokyo*.

being closely related to Buddhism.

In *The Sutra of Jesus the Messiah*, "God" was translated as "Buddha", "priest" as *sheng* 僧 (sanga), and Buddhist terms were borrowed to translate words related to physical matter and mental states, are easy to confuse in Buddhist terminology, thereby diminishing the communicability of the true Christian message to the Chinese people. When it came to the translation of its most important theological and doctrinal terms, it wavered between the language of Daoism and Buddhism. In a text from a much later date, the *Xuanyuan zhiben jing* 宣元至本经 (Sutra on the Origin of Origins), the use of terms such as "Dao", "Marvelous Dao", "Mysterious Dao", *lingfu* (灵府 Spiritual Mansion), *wu* 无 (non-being), etc., made Nestorian doctrines difficult to differentiate from Daoism (Weng: 159 – 167).

In summary, Nestorian missionaries went directly to strangification without being well prepared in language appropriation and without proper assistance in Chinese belles-lettres, as a consequence of which their translations were not of good quality. Since it is a historical truth that Nestorians all over the world used Syriac texts in their rituals and liturgy, the quality of the Chinese translations seems to have been of little importance to the Nestorian Church itself. But since the translation of its basic terms in the Chinese context led to misconceptions, even to the point of being absorbed by Buddhism or Daoism, the fate of Nestorians was either to suffer persecution alongside Buddhists, or to present themselves as Daoist-Christians in order to survive the religious holocaust against Buddhism that took place in the year 845 AD.

On the level of linguistic strangification, Nestorians would have done well to recruit a community of high intellectual Chinese priests to deliver their true message in good Chinese and to defend them in the Chinese context, in short, to enable them to strangify without losing its own true self. Such had been done in the case of Buddhism, where the monks Daoan 道安, Sengrui 僧叡, Sengzhao 僧肇, Daosheng 道生 etc., had criticized *geyi* (格义)

Buddhism and returned to the true Buddhist doctrine of emptiness after the early Buddhist appropriation of the Daoist language of being and non-being. Unfortunately, Nestorian missionaries didn't have a feasible plan for the recruitment of such priests, and this is one of the reasons why Nestorianism remained one of the three so-called foreign or barbarian religions.

Nestorian Pragmatic Strangification in China

On the ethical level, Nestorians had made great efforts to adapt to Confucian ethics and political norms such as filial piety and loyalty to political leaders, as evidenced by *The Sutra of Jesus the Messiah* which stated: "The most important three things: The first to serve God, the second to serve Emperor, the third to serve parents" (*yizhong xianshi tianzun, di er shishengshang, di shan shifumu* 一种先事天尊, 第二事圣上, 第三事父母) . It justified this by saying that the emperor is born of God, very much like the Son of Heaven was said to have been born of Heaven in ancient China, and that our existence in this life is due to our parents. That's why, besides serving God, one should also respect the emperor as the Son of God and practice filial piety to one's parents.

In the Chinese social context, Christian acts of charity or alms-giving practiced by the Nestorians fitted very well with Buddhist charity work. In the *Nestorian Inscription*, it is mentioned that the Emperor Taizong decreed that the Nestorian Church "is altruistic and benefits people, therefore is suitable for spreading in all Under Heaven (*jiwu liren, yixing tianxia* 济物利人, 宜行天下" Weng: 55) . Such, then, was the reputation of Nestorian charity work, famous even to the point of being known to the Emperor. In *The Sutra of Jesus the Messiah*, it is mentioned, with reference to the *Gospels*, that one should take care of the poor, the weak and the needy etc. , which provides further evidence that Nestorians in China continued the tradition of charity of the early Christians. In practicing altruism and generosity toward the Other, they were indeed showing a true Christian spirit, and thereby exhibiting an ethics of generosity with regard to the Other.

Unfortunately the ethical efforts of the Nestorians did not equip them to deal with the Chinese political abuse of their religion. On the one hand, the Nestorians were politically supported by Tang Empire. Not only was there one temple built for them by the government, but all the "ten provinces" of Tang Empire were full of Nestorian churches, as described by the *Nestorian Inscription*: "Nestorian teaching was spread in all ten provinces, the state was rich and spirit peaceful, Nestorian temples existed in one hundred cities, while every family enjoyed the great blessings realized in Nestorian churches" (Weng: 58, my translation). [1]Unfortunately, on the other hand, the Nestorians were also used and abused politically by Tang Empire. It was common to all religions in Chinese history that they could not avoid being politically used and sometimes abused. This was also the case with Nestorians under Tang's reign, and it is why they could not survive the political persecution after 845 AD unless by presenting themselves as Daoist-Christians. This is evidenced by some archeological discoveries as well as some texts in the *Complete Works of Patriarchal Lu Dongbin* (*Wuwuozi*, volume II, *juan* 22, 7 – 9), in which we find some Daoist chants in Christian prayers. We will return to this a little later.

The Tang royal family, taking Laozi as its holy ancestor, propagated the idea that Nestorianism was resulted from Laozi's going to the West after his retirement from the Zhou court, and that it had now returned in Tang's glorious days. According to the *Nestorian Inscription*, "When Zhou's virtue was in decline, Laozi went to the West, riding on a blue cow; When the Dao of Tang

---

[1] Saiki translates this as "The Law of (Luminous Teaching) spread throughout the ten provinces. Monasteries were built in many cities, whilst every family enjoyed the great blessings (of Salvation)" (Saeki: 59).

Empire is shining brilliantly now, the Nestorian wind spreads back to the East. "① We might suppose that the promotion of the Nestorian Church by the Tang Emperor Taizong was, on the one hand, for the purpose of offering spiritual comfort or religious consolation to foreign armies and merchants and other visitors from Western Lands; and on the other hand, for propagating the glory of Tang Empire in the context of multi-ethnicity and multiculturalism. In 638, immediately after the decree officially recognizing the Nestorian Church, Taizong's gesture in having a huge portrait of himself copied on to the four walls of the Nestorian Temple could be considered as a symbolic act. On this, the text of *Nestorian Inscription* reads: " [Taizong] ordered Immediately the officers to copy the Emperor's portrait on the four walls [of the temple] , so that the Heavenly gesture will spread his glory to shine upon the gate of Nestorian Temple, and His sagely portrait (traces of image) will promote good omen, that will illuminate eternally over all realms of Dharma. "② One can understand, then, that in the high glory of Tang Dynasty, when its foreign policy had opened it to foreigners with intensive multi-ethnic interaction with the Western Lands, the Nestorian Religion was seen by Tang's government as instrumental in calming any anxiety caused by multicultural tension. Then, when an anti-foreign policy took its place, the Nestorian Church would go on to suffer alongside the other three so-called foreign religions when Buddhism was persecuted in 845 AD.

Nestorian Ontological Strangification

As to the Nestorians' ontological strangification in China, the Nestori-

---

① My translation. Saeki's translation was: "The virtue of the honoured House of Zhou has died away; the rider on the black chariot had ascended to the west; But virtue revived and ' The Way' was brilliantly manifested again at the moment when the Great Tang Dynasty began its rule, while the breezes of the Luminous Religion came eastward to fan it" (Saeki: 58) .

② Chinese text see Weng: 55, here is my translation.

an scriptural use of Daoist terms such as "*Dao*", "Marvelous *Dao*", *wu* (non-being), *xuan* 玄 (dark, mysterious), *benwu* 本无 (Original non-being) …etc., was misleading to the extent of confusing the Christian Ultimate Reality with that of Daoism. This confusion was not only unhelpful in religious dialogue, but it could also be quite distorting in its own self-understanding. Nestorianism came to be compounded with Daoist and Buddhist terms with regard to the Ultimate Reality, resulting in a situation of confusion with these religions. Not only were its Chinese terms for the object of worship confounded with Daoism, as was the case in *On One God* where God was called the *Dao*, Marvelous *Dao*, Mysterious *Dao*, *wu* (non-being); and, in the case of *Xuanyuan zhiben jing* 宣元至本经 (Scripture on the Origin of Origins), but, moreover, it also appropriated Buddhist terms of emptiness as well as Daoist terms such as the Original Non-Being, the Dao, Non-Being, …etc. to name the Ultimate Reality. This resulted in ontological confusion instead of ontological strangification. In the *Zhixuan anle jing* 志玄安乐经 (*Sutra on the Mysterious Rest and Joy*), we find Daoist terms such as *xuan* (玄), *xuantong* 玄同, and *wu* 无, and Buddhist terms such as *bianzhao* 遍照, *jiaming* 假名, and great compassion (*daci dabei* 大慈大悲) as well as *xukong* (虚空) used by both Daoism and Buddhism. The ontological confusion thereby produced might have served to prepare for the later integration of the Nestorian survivors, first into Daoism in the time of religious persecution, and later into Buddhism after the latter's recovery from persecution.

The fact that some Chinese Nestorian texts, such as *The Sutra of Jesus the Messiah*, the *Nestorian Hymn to Take Refuge in the Holy Trinity*, and the *Nestorian Inscription* were included in the fifty-fourth volume of the Buddhist Canon, the *Taisho shinshu daizokyo*, was evidence that, because of their similarity in terms of language, they were seen, if not as pure Buddhist texts, then at least as closely related to Buddhist history. Some years ago I personally saw a copy of the Nestorian Inscription housed in *Xilai* 西来 Temple in Los Angeles, which would seem to indicate that it was once seen as a Buddhist object before the temple authority came to understand otherwise and withdrew it.

As to the existence of "Daoist Christians" after the Nestorians were persecuted together with the Buddhists, we find in the *Luzu quanshu* 吕祖全书 (*Complete Works of Patriarchal Lu Dongbin*), attributed to one of the major religious Daoist pioneers, some descriptions of miracles performed by Patriarchal Lu very similar to those performed by Jesus, such as "transforming water into wine", "giving sight to the blind", "curing the lame", and "feeding several hundred priests to full with a handful of flour". [1] Volume 22 of Lu's *Complete Works* contains some chants, titled *zhouwen* (咒文 charms and anathemas) by its editor, for "Salvation from catastrophes and witness of the *Dao*", with some texts written in very elegant Chinese, together with some phonetic Chinese translations of prayers originally either in Sanskrit or in Syriac.

For example, in the *Tianwei* chapter (*tian wei zhang* 天微章 On the Profoundness of Heaven), we read first: "With the head on the ground, Oh Lord of Heaven, we pray thee! Thy original peace pervadeth everywhere. We pray thee, the God of Great Mercy and Sympathy, to save us from all the miseries of life", followed by a line of Chinese translations of texts, read phonetically as "*An cha na li la niu ta chi ma sha ho* 唵刹哪唎啰哞哆瞍嘛娑诃", which, if in Sanskrit, would mean "Oh Three Spirits, May we be awakened to cut ourselves off the momentary pleasure and be saved", but, if in Syriac, would mean "Indeed, Christ is He who goes up to the highest" (*Wuwuozi*, volume II, *juan* 22, 7; . Saeki: 402 – 403, with my correction). [2] The Chi-

---

① These are also mentioned in Saeki: 401.

② Saeki's translation of "*An cha na li la niu ta chi ma sha ho* 唵刹哪唎啰哞哆瞍嘛娑诃", if in Sanskrit, as "O three Spirits! May we be awakened to cut ourselves off the pleasure of a moment and be saved!" and, if Syriac, as "Yes, the Christ did go up to high things!" Basing on Saeki's translations, I refine these to read: "Oh Three Spirits, May we be awakened to cut ourselves off the momentary pleasure and be saved" and "Indeed, Christ is He who goes up to the highest".

nese parts of the rest of this chapter are always followed by some similar chants incomprehensible in Chinese but to be read as phonetically repeating the original prayers（either in Sanskrit or Syriac）：

"Constant Being with Great Divinely Power, thou thoroughly and completely givest the shining Light to the human soul! We pray thee, the God of Great Mercy and Sympathy, to save us from all the miseries of life." An cha na li la niu ta chi ma sha ho.

"Your successive operation endures from the ancient to the present time, to assist universally all sentient beings. We pray thee, to save us from all the miseries of life." An cha na li la niu ta chi ma sha ho.

"Thy Holy wisdom revealth thyself as True Master, forever keep and hold your purity and brightness. We pray thee, to save us from all the miseries of life." An cha na li la niu ta chi ma sha ho. [1]

This kind of prayer, constituted of Chinese prayers and the phonetic rendition of Sanskrit or Syric prayers, continues in the following chapters such as *Dizhen zhang* 地真章（Chapter On the Truth of the Earth）, *Zhengxian zhang* 证仙章（Chapter on the Witness of Immortals）, *Tidao zhang* 体道章（Chapter on Incarnating the Dao）etc. Lack of space limits further dis-

---

[1] These texts, together with further chapters mentioned below, were translated by Saeki（Saeki: 400 – 407）. I use here Dr. Saeki's English translation of the Syriac and Sanskrit chants, correcting in bold his English translation of the Chinese texts. In the Chinese text, changyu dashentong 常有大神通 means "Constant Being with Great Divinely Power" rather than Saeki's wrong understanding as "Ever being in communion with the Great God"; also *dieyun ligujin*, *puji yu zhongsheng* 迭运历今古，普济于众生 should be understood as "Your successive operation endures from the ancient to the present time, to assist universally all sentient beings", rather than Saeki's translation as "At all times and at all places, Thou canst save all the living beings without exception!" Also, the last verse, *shenghui xian zhengzong*, *qingming yong guchi* 圣慧显真宗，清明永固持 should read "Thy Holy wisdom revealed thyself as True Master, forever keep and hold your purity and brightness", in which "revealth thyself as True Master" is indeed much more correct than Saeki's rendition as "revealth the True Religion".

cussion of these; they are mentioned here only to support the existence of Christian Daoists, for whom God is omnipotent, omnipresent, omniscient, savior from the miseries of human life, as shown in these prayers, all in combining Buddhist terms such as *cibei* 慈悲 (compassion), *qingjing xin* 清净心 (pure and clean mind), *yi sheng* 一乘 (One Vehicle), and *juelu* 觉路 (the road to enlightenment), with Daoist terms such as *lingtai* 灵台 (Spiritual Platform), *taixu* 太虚 (Great Void), *xian* 仙 (immortal), *taiji* 太极 (Great Ultimate), and *yin yang* 阴阳…etc.

Conclusions

Based on these traces of historical evidence, we might argue that the Nestorians, having faded out in China after the persecution of Buddhism in 845 AD, made some effort to survive in the form of Daoist-Christians. Later, during the *Yuan* 元 Dynasty (1271 – 1368), the Nestorians returned to China, but this period was less significant in terms of the philosophical and religious dialogue between East and West, Chinese and Christian. All things considered, we should not take the Nestorian experience in China as an example of failure. Just as heroes are not to be judged by the measure of failure or success, neither should we judge the Christian missionaries who generously brought their Christian teachings to a foreign land like China by the secular measure of failure or success. But if religions are seen as living communities and not as historic relics, there should be some lessons that we can draw and learn from the interruption and discontinuity of the Nestorian's first efforts to introduce Christian monotheism to China and to accommodate Christian monotheism with other Chinese religions such as Daoism and Buddhism, and with Chinese culture in general. On this, we can note that:

The shortcomings of the Nestorian's strategy of strangification in China were as follows: first, linguistic strangification was embarked upon without proper preparation with regard to Chinese language and belles-lettres; that is, without adequate language appropriation or assistance from local men of letters. Second, it lost its own subjectivity and authenticity in the process of its pragmatic strangification in the social and political domain. Third, the resultant ontological confusion instead of ontological strangification hindered the transmission of a true understanding of its own religious experience by believers as well as by others. Its ideas of Ultimate Reality and the One God were presented in the form of the Buddhist concepts of emptiness or Buddha and the Daoist Dao or Original non-being, which was an unhappy and misleading confusion that led to it getting absorbed by these two religions and thereby blurring its own Christian monotheism.

The political abuse of the Nestorian Church and the violence of political persecution by Tang Empire: from the very outset, Nestorianism suffered under the political intervention of Tang's state power by which the Emperor used it in his policy for dealing with foreigners in China, a situation that led to political abuse. Finally, Nestorians were subjected to religious persecution along with other foreign religions, which caused the disintegration of the Nestorian Church itself.

The absence of a good policy of localization: Nestorian missionaries failed to root the teachings of their church in the minds and culture of the Chinese people, and, unlike Buddhism, they did not establish a community of Chinese priests that was strong enough on both intellectual and practical levels to be capable of apologetic self-defense and of propagating Nestorian Christianity by more suitable strategies of enculturation. In the absence of such a community, there was no possibility of revival after the era of persecution was over.

As we know, the symbol of Nestorian Christianity as it appeared on the *Nestorian Inscription* was a cross emerging from the base of a huge lotus flower, signifying Christianity's unity with, and promotion of, Buddhism. Unfortunately, in its first encounter with Chinese culture it was unable to purify the lotus by promoting it towards the One God and the Ultimate Other; on the contrary, it suffered from compromise with Buddhism, falling in the political dirt and was obliged to present itself as a form of Daoist-Christianity in order to survive. From the case of Nestorian Christianity, we understand the insufficiency of the virtue of generosity when it comes to the successful realization of the missionary's task. As Jesus said, "Be cunning as snakes and yet as innocent as doves" (*Matthew*, 10: 16, in *The New Jerusalem Bible*: 1158); where "innocent" or "pure" should be understood in terms of the purer essence of Christian doctrines, whereas "cunning" should be understood in terms of the proper discernment and appropriation of the new context, or adequate strategies of recontextualization and strangification.

It should also be noted that in Chinese Mahayana Buddhism, a successful model of strangification in China, it was taught that there should be both *shizhi* (实智 substantial wisdom) and *quanzhi* (权智 expedient wisdom). Substantial wisdom concerns the enlightenment that understands emptiness in seeing all things as arising from interdependent causation and therefore having no substance or self-nature of their own. Nevertheless, one still has to use expedient means, or *fangbian* 方便 (Upāya) to deal properly with the real situations of the world and to spread one's own religious truth in them.

In taking Buddhism as a historic mirror, not only as to its successful strategy of strangification in China whereby it became a member of the family of the Chinese Three Teachings, but also as to its later effect in bringing Chinese thought to the concept of the immanent One Mind, we can see that both China, which is now open to a new world order, and Christianity, which remains a foreign religion to the Chinese people even almost fourteen centuries after its inception, have a lot to learn to incarnate the gospels of unconditional generosity to multiple others, and the true spirit of strangification, to renovate the creative energy in Chinese culture.

Bibliography

Ames. R. , and Rosement H. （tr. ）, 1998, *The Analects of Confucius*, *A Philosophical Translation*, New York: Ballantine Books.

Hage. Wolfgang. 1997. *Syriac Christianity in the East*, Kerala, India: St. Ephrem Ecumenical Research Institue （SEERI）.

Huineng, *Platform Sutra*, in *Taisho sinshu daizoko*, vol. 48, pp. 345 – 365.

New Jerusalem Bible, London: Darton, Longman and Todd, 1998.

Malek R. and Hofrichter P. （editors） 2006. *Jingjao*: *The Church of the East in China and Central Asia*, Sankt Augustin: Institut Monumenta Serica.

Saeki. P. Y. 1951. *The Nestorian Documents and Relics in China*, Tokyo: The Maruzen Co.

Shen V. 1994. *Confucianism*, *Taoism and Constructive Realism*. Vienna: Vienna University Press.

——. 2002. *Duibi*, *waitui yu jiaotan* 对比、外推与交谈（*Contrast*, *Strangification and Dialogue*）, Taipei : Wunan Publishing Company.

——. 1997. "Inter-religious Dialogue Between Buddhism and Christianity Conceived with Strangification and Contrast. " *In The Movement of Constructive Realism*, edited by Thomas Slunecko. Wien: Wilhelm Braumüller.

——. 2003. "Appropriation of the Other and Transformation of Consciousnessinto Wisdom, Some Philosophical Reflections on Chinese Buddhism", in *Dao*: *A Journal of Comparative Philosophy*, December 2003, Vol. III, No. 1, pp. 43 – 62.

Shengzhao, *Buzhen kong lun* （*Emptiness of the Unreal*）, in *Taisho sinshu daizoko*, vol. 45, pp. 152 – 153.

Takakusu and Watanabe （ed. ）, 1924 – 1932, *Taishō shinshū daizōkyō* （Abbreviated as TSD）《大正新修大藏经》, Vols. 1. 30. 38. 45. 48. Tokyo:

Taisho Issaikyo Kankokai.

Tuotuo (Toghto), 1988, *Jin Shi* 金史 (History of Jin Dynasty), in *Bainaben Ershiwushi* 百衲本二十五史, Taipei: Taiwan Commercial Press.

Wallner, Fritz. 1992. *Acht Vorlesungen über den Konstruktiven Realismus.* Vienna: Vienna University Press.

Wang Jing 王静. 2006. *Tangdai jingjiao zai Hua shuailuo zhi wenhua yuanyin shenlun* 唐代景教在华衰落之文化原因深论, in *Xibei gongye daxue xuebao: Sheke ban*/西北工业大学学报社科版 26 (Xi'an 2006) 1, pp. 53 – 59.

Wang Pu 王溥, *Tang Huiyao* 唐会要. Taipei: Shijie Book Store, 1960.

Weng Shaojun 翁绍军 (annotation), 1995. *Hanyu Jingjiao Wendian Quanshi* 《汉语景教文典诠释》. Hong Kong: Institute of Sino-Christian Studies.

Wuwuozi (ed.), 1980. *Luzhu Quanshu* (*Complete Works of Patriarchal Lu Dongbin*), volume II, Taipei: Guanwen Bookstore.

Yin Shun. 1988, *A History of Indian Buddhist Thought*, Taipei: Chengwen Press.

Religious Traditions: Theory to Practice

Fostering a Form of Buddhist and Christian Spirituality that Responds to Social Needs

Thomas Menamparampil *

Abstract: Many thinking people consider religion as a helpless sigh of the oppressed. It is true that religious believers can make of their faith an idle and unproductive force in their lives, if they choose to do so. But, on the contrary, if they so decide, they can make of it the strongest motivating force in the world. A sense of responsibility for the common good which true religious convictions generate and consequent commitment to social betterment is the form of religiosity that would make meaning in our times. This inner urge would help religious believers to make their lives meaningful by addressing the current problems of the world, like the increase of violence and corruption, economic imbalance, aggravation of poverty, ecological disaster, damage to cultures, erosion of ethical values, poor governance, biased media, harassment of minorities, gender bias, and others. Religiously motivated intellectuals will live out their "Spirituality of Responsibility" today in addition by

* Thomas Menamparampil, Professor, Assam Don Bosco University, Guwahati, India.

playing an inspiring and motivating role in a society of fast eroding cultures and values and the absence of ethical principles, by being initiators of reflection in the world of thought and values with an eagerness to reawaken the ethical consciousness in society.

Key Words: Buddhist Christian Value of Religion Spirituality of Responsibility Religious Convictions

1. Religion Marginalized in Modern Times

Jurgen Moltmann would say that the "religion of the market" has taken over the global scene

Materialistic ideologies of one type or the other have been dominating human life and thought for over a century. The inner exploration typical of the Asian peoples finds little space in the economic, political, educational, professional, and recreational spaces of human life. Inner insights and experiences that cannot be verified in the laboratory are marginalized.

The reason is that many thinking people consider religion as the cry of the poor, a helpless sigh of the oppressed, and an obstacle to economic growth. It is true that religious believers can make of their faith an idle and unproductive force in their lives, if they choose to do so. But, on the contrary, if they so decide, they can make of it the strongest motivating force in the world as well. The inner sturdiness they build up supplies the needed energies foran outer commitment. Genuine spirituality transforms the inner world first, and the outer world next.

2. Religion Fosters Human Solidarity and Social Cohesion

"Go you now monks, for the benefit of many, for the welfare of mankind, out of compassion for the world" (*The Buddha*)

If these inner energies are used to harm others in the name of religion, the results can be disastrous as recent experiences have shown is some parts of the world. But if they are made to serve the welfare of humanity with absolute sincerity of purpose and dedication, there is bound to be an enriching of shared human culture and inter-linking of the human family. Religions like **Buddhism and Christianity** have always fostered solidarity and cohesion among human groups and manifested enormous energy in the service of society.

Religious fervour, rightly channelled, manifests itself in extraordinary **dynamism**, in **committed service**, amazing creativity, stunning innovation, and prodigious team-effort towards the common good, which makes of religious spirituality eminently practical. Such a form of spirituality is urgently needed today, which would give sturdiness to the sense of responsibility already existing in individuals to address the most pressing problems of the day.

3. Religion does not Oppose Legitimate Forms of Secular Activities, Only Warns against Exaggerations

"A good person brings good out of the treasure of good things in his heart" (*Jesus in John's Gospel 6: 45*)

What we are suggesting is not a form of religious conviction that despises a secular view of life, but one that enhances it, motivates and energizes its adherents. The social advantages to be derived from **asecular vision** like the recognition of the dignity of the individual and equality of all citizens before the law, right to participation in decision-making, freedom of expression, basic human rights, are too precious to be underestimated. The economic advantages too are evident: the advance of science and technology, division of labour, specialization, mechanization, rationalization, and automation. These processes gave a great impetus to large-scale production and brought cheaper goods to the market, made medical services effective, and made life more comfortable. Such benefits are too many to be ignored.

However, certain exaggerated forms of secularization give rise to a totally materialistic view of life, which identifies social development with economic expansion alone. The mobility of job-seekers as a result of rapid commercial and industrial growth has led to the enfeebling of social bonds which used to benourished by the extended family, the local school, and neighbourhood communities. At the production centres, workers can be reduced to status of production-machines: culture-less, personality-less, individuality-less, humanity-less, soulless. This would evidently be an exaggeration.

In rural areas, whence majority of the workers come, social life has been so transformed as to cause the erosion of cultures where values are generated. This in turn leads to the breakup of families and communities within which ethical convictions are handed down. This has reduced the effectiveness of the traditional patterns of social formation and the **handing on of cultural traditions**, social norms, and religious convictions from one generation to the next. This leads further to the weakening of the codes of moral behaviour, and even more of the handing on of ancestral values and **spiritual motivations**.

4. Revival of Interest in Religious Themes in Our Times, in Spiritual Values

"Change anger, hatred, greed into constructive energy by being aware"
(*Teaching valid in Buddhist and Christian traditions*)

In response these trends, there has been awakening of curiosity about the hidden dimensions of the human 'self' in our times. Young people seem to be greatly attracted to experiences of silent inner search to find a bit of relief amidst the restlessness prevalent in a market-and-ideology-driven society. Books of Confucius, Mencius, Lao Tzu, Sun Tzu, Meitster Eckart, Tauler, Suso and Teilhard de Chardin; classics like the *Mahabharata* and *Ramayana*, *Bhagavadgita* are found in airports and wayside bookshops. History shows that periods of suppression of religion are followed by periods of explosive religious fervour in reaction, at times going to exaggeration, unless guided by wise religious mentors.

Many in the West admire the vibrancy of Eastern spiritual traditions and the amazing religious self-confidence manifest among several Eastern peoples. Religiosity in the East emphasizes **intense inner search**, simplicity of life; it has encouraged a tradition of renunciation and asceticism. Some feel drawn to celibacyand a disciplined form of community life, and develop a sense of call to become the source of wisdom and inspiration among their people. Some of them go further ahead and gain moral authority among their co-believers as propagators of religious teachings in society. These are also typical of both **Buddhist and Christian** traditions.

Even in highly secularized societies, there is growing eagerness to know more about the hidden dimensions of the human person, since these are less-discussed and less held up for public attention; a longing for depth, a thirst for profound and abiding values, and an eagerness to gain insights into the ultimate destiny of the human race. It is during such a search that one discovers **meaning in life and reasons for hope** even amidst the tragic happenings of day-to-day life and the existential agonies that harass human hearts.

One gradually comes to realize that there is an undeniable relationship between the quality of the **inner spiritual resource** that supplies energies and the quality of **an outer commitment** to social welfare.

5. Religious Convictions Should Generate a Sense of Responsibility for the Common Good

"Deep knowledge is to be aware of disturbance before disturbance, to be aware of danger before danger, to be aware of destruction before destruction, to be aware of calamity before calamity... By deep knowledge of principle, one can change disturbance into order, change danger into safety, change destruction into survival, change calamity into fortune. By strong action on the Way, one can bring the body to the realm of longevity, bring the mind to the sphere

of mystery, bring the world to great peace, and bring tasks to great fulfil-
ment" (*Sun Tzu 3*)

A sense of responsibility for the common good which true religious convictions generate and consequent commitment to social betterment is the form
of religiosity that would make meaning in our times. This inner urge would
help religious believers to make their lives meaningful by addressing the current problems of the world, like the increase of **violence and corruption**, e-
conomic imbalance, aggravation of poverty, **ecological disaster**, damage to
cultures, erosion of ethical values, poor governance, biased media, harassment of minorities, gender bias, and others.

Bringing religious beliefs to day-to-day life will mean making ancient
spiritual concepts relevant and meaningful to the people of our times, even to
those who reject religion. Let us take one example. Distancing oneself from
worldly affairs is esteemed as a great value by **Buddhist**, **Christian** and Hindu ascetics. In recent times, those who have reflected deeply have come to
the understanding that this detachment can be expressed equally well by distancing oneself from selfishness, greed, over-ambition, prejudice, and hatred, and that it can be lived to a full measure amidst most challenging life-
situations. This form of religious seriousness is quite intelligible to the Asian
mind. We have an eminent example in Mahatma Gandhi who considered himself a permanent searcher after Ultimate Truth in the midst of his political engagements. He observed days of silence, hours of prayer, and drew inspiration from the Hindu sacred book *Bhagavdgita* in which is presented a serious
discussion on the detached performance of one's duty.

Similarly, the traditional self-emptying and the ' **spirit of sacrifice**' of
the religious person which were calculated to promote his/her personal
growth, can be placed at the service of the needs of under privileged neigh-
bours, classes and communities. The needs of society and the negative trends
in social processes today are calling for new forms of commitment to help people to press with determination towards creating a better world. There have

been great pioneers in our times promoting values and opening out new paths to bring the fruits of religious convictions closer to serve social purposes.

The new trends of **spiritual exhaustion**, **moral collapse**, and non-working systems in our tradition (e. g. neglected social norms, non-functioning dimensions and structures of governance) seem to call for a revival of a "**Spiritual Sense of Responsibility**" and commitment. People are hungering for a new sense of meaning and direction in a chaotic world of clashing ideologies. Here is where we need to a new type of intellectual leadership, of spiritual inspiration, not one of demagoguery and denunciation, not of power and manipulation, but of inviting intelligent reflection, diligent search, and joint exploration towards evolving a consensus on common issues... and of assisting the process in the best way possible.

6. The Mission of Religiously Motivated Intellectuals: Inviting People to Think Responsibly

"*First establish yourself in the good; thereafter you should counsel others. The wise man who acts thus will be above reproach*" (*Dammapada 12, 2*)

Religiously motivated intellectuals will live out their "**Spirituality of Responsibility**" today by playing an inspiring and motivating role in a society of fast eroding cultures and values and of the absence of ethical principles, by being initiators of reflectionin the world of **thought** and **values** with an eagerness to reawaken the ethical consciousness in society. An individual's personal thoughts, both positive and negative, are not just his own secret possession. "Every negative thought I entertain in my head, which I think is my own secret place, actually strengthens the **negative field that sweeps the world**," said Joseph Chilton Pearce. The same would be true with regard to positive thoughts.

Though many socially committed citizens would consider denunciation of the wrong-doer as the chief mission of intellectual leaders, I would consider

inviting people to think with a sense of responsibility and helping them to make intelligent and value-based decisions as the more important challenge today. In these times of contradictory voices inspired by diverse philosophical, ideological, psychological, sociological, and religious convictions, this form of assistance to society has become our most important contribution.

This task does not consist in lecturing to people what they should do or think, nor in denouncing opponents in self-righteous tones so that they feel humiliated and go on the defensive, nor in confronting them in such a way that they are provoked to an angry and aggressive response, nor embarrassing them and crushing their spirit.

Rather it consists in inviting people to reflect on live issues under the light of the principles derived from their own culture and indigenous wisdom and from the common spiritual springs of humanity, whether it be **Buddhist orChristian**. This is the only way that people can be helped to **bring their moral principles and ethical convictions to life**.

7. Religiosity Speaks to the Conscience

"*I neither stood still, nor sat, nor lay down until, pacing to and fro, I had mastered that fear and terror*" (*the Buddha*)

Yudhishtira, the hero of the Indian epic *Mahabharata*, says that *dharma* (uprightness) is hidden in the **cave of one's heart** (Das xliii) . It is the deep religiosity one cultivates in one's heart that generates the ability to identify principles and values that will enrich the ethos of a people. Religiosity speaks directly to the **conscience**, stimulates the convictions of a community, calls for moral transformation, encourages the practice of virtues as members of a loving human family.

Seneca said, becoming good is an art. It is precisely this art that is embedded in the inner being of a person and is intimately linked with his religious convictions and **spiritual depth**. This is the **Spirituality of Responsibility** that we are reflecting on.

Responsibility-based spirituality will take one into new social, cultural and psychological fields; into the world of **ideas**, **attitudes and values**; into **causes like those for peace**, **defence of life**, **probity in society**, protection of weaker communities, promotion of women and children, and good governance; efforts to prevent the erosion of cultures and values, and **damage to environment**.

8. A Responsibility-based Approach

"He who rules by means of virtue may be compared to the pole-star, which keeps its place while all the other stars pay homage to it" (*Confucius*: *Analects 2. 1*).

Speaking too strongly about 'responsibilities' in an era of 'rights' may be considered bad taste. It is not popular to speak of duties in our times. Today the hero is the fighter, fighter for justice (as each one perceives 'justice' in his own way), fighter for rights. A reference to obligations may sound old-fashioned and annoying. But Asia has always emphasized duties. For, the very claim of a right implies someone's duty to respect that right. And since everyone has rights, everyone has the responsibility to recognize those of others. It is in this respect that we fail today, unless responsibility is also given space and importance in our consideration.

Aside from that, looking at real situations in the world today, we realize that when we over-claim our rights, we provoke others to over-claim their rights. When we ask for more than what we deserve, more than what is realistic or possible at a given time, more than what others have or are in a position to claim, we incite others to make counter-claims, often going to an unreasonable extent. This is what is happening today, leading to conflicts and to unresolvable deadlocks. It is here that persons with **a sense of balance** and responsibility can help.

Each citizen within his/her own nation, has a national responsibility. In a globalized world, we have **a global responsibility**. Spiritually inspired citizens cultivate this sense of universal responsibility in themselves and foster it in others. By action or inaction every citizen contributes ill or well to the development and destiny of his/her province, country, the world. If there is violence in the state, if there is chaos in society, if disciplined social habits are forgotten, if healthy social norms are eroded, if inequality increases without limit, if bribery is rampant, if public works fall behind schedule, if trains run late, electricity fails, if slums multiply, if workers are exploited, if universities do not function, if there is national waste, if the environment is being damaged, if children are put to hard labour, if women are taken advantage of, if there is the problem of alcohol, drugs and AIDS, and most of all if elected members do not discharge their duties, every citizen has to be held responsible. This sort of awareness itself is a spiritual perception.

Spirituality must become practical in such contexts. Religious seriousness in action takes one to address the problem of deforestation, bridge repairs, watersupply, drainage diversion, human trafficking, protection of environment, widespread corruption, and social collaboration.

9. Corruption Means Any Form of Unfairness to Others

"Conscience has a 'still small voice' and it 'speaks' to us insistently"
(*Viktor Frankl the psychologist*)

The tragedy in our times is that corrupt practices have risen to the world stage. No one can plead to be totally innocent. That is why all must join hands together in order to wipe out this plague from society. Corruption is not only about the **wrong use of money**, but also about the **wrong use of power**. It is not only about taking bribe in government offices, but also about various forms of manipulation and blackmailing, political arm-twisting, pushing a particular group's interests through underhand ways, unfairness of dominant classes to weaker sections, the imperceptible manner of bulldozing or marginalizing legitimate claims, silencing the voices of the weaker communities, physical elimination of political opponents or commercial competitors, interfering with election processes, using 'strong men' for vacating land or realizing bills, selling drugs. Corruption has also reference to hidden transactions, unpaid salaries, underpaid employees, unfair pressure.

The globalized world has become a hiding place for corrupt business. The global market provides distances, creates anonymity, gives opportunities for dishonest deals, enables one to take advantage of the weak, evade laws, and make an unfair proportion of profit. Let us make a distinction: 1. if greater profits are made through harder work, greater efficiency, more effective customer service or through path-breaking innovation, it is certainly legitimate. 2. But if it is made by underpaying the worker, evading taxes, ignoring safety laws, producing counterfeits, ruining the environment, abusing customer confidence, falsifying accounts or labour figures, double book-keeping, deceptive advertisements, industrial espionage, it is undoubtedly criminal.

Investigative journalism has often highlighted specific cases of dishonesty and unfairness. But media men also can bend to Big Money, and sell their services for an easy bribe: cooking up stories to defame or defend a leader or a business magnate, **distorting facts** to press an argument; presenting allegations as proven truth for minor favours. Plagiarizing, pirating cassettes, and violating intellectual property rights are very common in our days. Those in public service get opportunities to embezzle huge amounts. Doctors are accused of patronizing particular pharmaceutical companies or diagnostic centres, and even dealing in human organs. When citizens are not alert, the mechanisms of accountability and sanction are not activated, and structures of enforcement lie idle. Society remains silent. You and I give a tacit approval.

10. Religious Convictions will Generate Values, Help the Removal of Corruption from Society

"The Master said···. But if even a simple peasant comes in all sincerity and asksme a question, I am ready to thrash the matter out, with all its pros and cons, to the very end" (*Confucius: Analects IX, 7*)

Religiously convinced persons will naturally feel drawn towards committing themselves to create a corruption-free society. Educating civil society in **healthy values** is a service open to every citizen. A religious believer too is a citizen and an initiator of thought in the world of values. Kim Clark, Harvard Business School dean, speaking of principles leadership said, "We need leaders whose behaviour matches and reinforces those values. And that is what I mean by integrity. Integrity is more than being honest, although it certainly means that. It is deeper. It is about the match between what the person says and what he does. Leaders with integrity have **strong values** and standards and principles, and they act on them—consistently, without fail in public and in private. Such leaders inspire trust and confidence in those around them, and the values they espouse become reality in the organization they lead, because people act on them and live them in their organization" (Byron 49 – 50).

Business concerns have discovered that **good ethics is good business**. They are beginning to use a new language: of corporate social responsibility, ethical business behaviour, customer service, social justice, corporate governance, labour relations, ecological concern, community development and lifelong learning. Daniel Kaufman says, "We have also found that the business sector grows significantly faster where corruption is lower and property rights and rule of law is safeguarded". That is why companies appoint **ethical officers**, write inspiring vision and mission statements. They have seen that ethical principles pay in the long run.

Business executives have begun to speak to their employees about the importance of trust, honesty, respect and integrity, for the success of their business. However, it is important to remember that such values are not generated by business concerns, companies, markets, or governments. They are generated within the bosom of a community with its own historical, cultural and religious background. That is why it is right for us to admit that a society's basic ethical rules are rooted in its culture and its religious traditions, **Buddhist or Christian**, or any other. That is why people with **genuine religious convictions** can contribute a great deal to the much needed moral regeneration in our times.

"Conscience is the light of the soul that burns within the chambers of our heart. It is as real as life is. It raises the voice in protest whenever anything is thought of or done contrary to righteousness" says the former President of India Abdul Kalam. For Viktor Frankl the psychologist "Conscience has a 'still small voice' and 'speaks' to us".

11. Do Our Asian Ancestors Have a Message in Such Contexts?

"Let no one deceive anyone else, nor despise anyone anywhere. May no one wish harm to another in anger or ill-will" (*Samyutta Nikaya 146 –8*).

We may take a message from **Buddha's** teachings. The economy had grown brisk in his days: credit, debt, interest and market—everything was in full function. There were rich people going bankrupt and poor people gathering a fortune, honestly and in other ways. A warning against corruption was timely. A passage from early **Buddhist** poetry says, "**Let no one deceive** anyone else, nor despise anyone anywhere. May no one wish harm to another in anger or ill-will" (*Samyutta Nikaya*146 –8).

Similarly, a Taoist teaching says, "When rulers live in splendour and **speculators prosper**, while farmers lose their land and the granaries are emptied; when governments spend money on ostentation and on weapons; when the upper class is extravagant and irresponsible, indulging themselves and possessing more than they can use, while the poor have nowhere to turn. All this is robbery and chaos. It is not in keeping with the *Tao*" (*Tao TeChing* 53) . Are we in such an age? At another place the *Tao Te Ching* says, "The **sage does not accumulate**. The more he does for the people, the more he saves. The more he gives to people, the more he has" (*Tao TeChing 81*) .

In the Confucian tradition, a gentleman is concerned with what is right; the inferior man with profit, with material welfare. Mencius too looked down on the profit motive. Science, technology, and efficient economy have given us good things, but they must be regulated by the norms of wisdom contained in our cultural traditions. Truly, "A gentleman takes as much trouble to discover what is right as lesser men take to discover what will pay" (*Tao TeChing 81*) .

In the West, the first generations of capitalists were models of self-regulation. Their aim was to earn, build up capital, invest, and not to overspend. In fact, Weber and Keynes refer to high accumulation and low consumption (*Sachs* 150) . Today's capitalists on the contrary, and all those who imitate them, tend to profligacy, eager to display: they believe in lavish parties, weddings, anniversaries, election victories. Concentration on fortune-hunting has thrown up a class of super-rich and dumped the weak in dire poverty (*Sachs* 152) .

12. Misuse of the Media

"*Seeing what others do not see is called brilliance, knowing what others do not know is called genius*" (*Sun Tzu 7*) .

Communications have made the greatest contribution to modern age. They have assisted people to come together and co-reflect, and be of assistance to each other. International solidarity has grown in a way that was never considered possible in earlier times.

But these very same instruments of communications can also be misused. They are fast falling into the grip of Big Business and partisan political forces; "**mass media and the politicians are in splendid symbiosis**. The airwaves promote corporate products, consumer values, and the careers of friendly politicians. The politicians promote media deregulation, low taxes, and freedom from scrutiny of performance and public service" (*Sachs 145*). Power slides into the hands of a small number of transnational corporations that are less and less accountable to political structures. Someone has described the tragedy in this manner: humanity is made subject to the market; the corporations control the market subjecting every field of human activity to serve their interests. **Mass media** strengthens this effort by **promoting consumerism** (*Hathaway 16*). Humans are reduced to the level of being mere objects.

Jeremy Sachs is certain that even his own countrymen, living in a free country, are allowing themselves to be **manipulated by corporate propaganda**. What today's commercial media proposes is not serious responsible thinking about the long term good of society; what it proposes are over-consuming, over-borrowing, over-gambling, excessive TV viewing, and other addictions (*Sachs 133*). They are not asking people to sit back and reflect, study the consequences, or plan for the good of humanity, as **Buddhist or Christian** sages would have done. May be that is where reflective people can make their contribution. That remains a challenge for Asia's intellectuals and persons of religious faith.

The technologies of mass persuasion are being used as instruments for **manipulating minds**. Edward Berry, a nephew of Sigmund Freud, used to refer to marketing skills as the skills for '**engineering consent**' with regard to sales. Mass persuasion is also used during elections and military coups. He considered it the art of hidden manipulation of public's unconscious, taking advantage of people's tendency to run in herds. We had been for decades warned about the manipulative power of the TV: George Orwell (1940s), Vance Packard (1950s), John Kenneth Galbraith and Marshall McLuhan (1960s) (*Sachs 137 – 38*). Could we grow a little more conscious of this danger? Nearly all wise teachings of the East spoke of the need for resisting ' **illusions** ' and attaining the ' **truth** '. This is also part of **Buddhist and Christian** teaching. How relevant those teachings seem to us in our times when so many of us spend any length of time in the ' unreal ' (virtual) world of the TV, and in the world of ' illusions ' ?

13. Being Active in Civil Society as Intelligent
and Active Members

"*If anything is to be done, let a man do it, let him attack it vigorously*" (*Dhammapada*)

It is fashionable to blame leaders. It is also citizens that have to accept responsibility for what happens in society. If they remain passive and indifferent, things are bound to go downhill. The consequence can be disastrous. Unfortunately citizens have condoned the un-civic behaviour, partisan proclivity and **self-interest of each other** in exchange for some equally partisan advantage to their own personal or sectarian interests.

If citizens abdicate their responsibility for the general welfare of their society, that nation has no future. They have a duty to **demand a high sense of responsibility** from each other. Unfortunately, many citizens have not learned to insist with the persons with whom they have influence to maintain a sense of dignity about what they say or do, or to demand from them a code of conduct, a style of behaviour, a manner of approach to persons and issues in keeping with that dignity, and expect from them a degree of commitment. This can be done only if the one does so himself/herself is a responsible citizen.

The news-hour (TV) should not be a brief interval for entertainment only, but a moment for self-education and profound reflection. Action would follow.

If, therefore, the environment is being ravaged, globalization injures the local economy, violence raises its ugly head in society; if street children multiply; if the handicapped remain unassisted, every citizen who seeks the good of society and every leader with deep ethical convictions ought to make a positive contribution to handling these problems. For, religious convictions make meaning only when they provide **convincing motivation** for radical commitment to the common good.

14. People with Religious Convictions Contribute to Peace

"Who doth not, when reviled, revile again, a twofold victory wins" (*The Buddha*)

Today, tensions keep mounting right round the world: nation against nation, class against class, ethnic group against ethnic group, majority against minority and vice versa. The strong usually have their way. Those who feel that they are unjustly treated take to violence in response.

There are also enough people to **foster anger** against every perceived injustice, too few people to initiate a helpful dialogue. Even legitimate struggles in the name of culture, ethnicity, minority status, gender, colour, can turn into an **erratic ideology** and go to the point of violence of some sort. Some are happy to have a defined enemy just to be clear about their own identity (*Eco* 1 - 2). All slogans are about 'rights', and every claim of rights seems to be valid until its exaggerations make its limitations evident. Meantime peace keeps eluding the human race.

Not all people who have opted for violence are unteachable. There is a French saying, *to understand is to forgive*. Cynicism or hasty condemnations will not help. If a society **feels a deep sense of injustice**, or is there is gross inequality, there is bound to be a reaction. And when a group of poverty stricken people are brought together, organized and made to feel they are fighting for a good cause, **a radical venture seems to empower them** and help them to discover a new emotional identity (*Lott* 20 – 21) . Many painful happenings in West Asia have to be seen from this perspective. Sometimes religions have been made to serve a wrong cause or adopt a wrong style.

Such situations create contexts for the emergence of **prophets of violence** on either side. After a while it is not clear who is the aggressor and who is the defender. And the earlier victim himself may go to excesses inflicting injury on the aggressor and other groups, reaching to the point of **ethnic cleansing** (*Lott* 43) . Thus, we cannot always believe that the strong are always wrong and that weak always right, that victims of injustice cannot turn unjust themselves.

Vested interests can take ideological and regional fanaticisms to totally irresponsible limits. **Building on emotions**, especially on the smothered anger or unexpressed resentment of deprived groups, justice-fighters can lead matters to such a head that there seems to be no other solution to a problem than violence. The frequent recurrence of violence these days in different parts of the world may be attributed to leaders who make exaggerated claims for their people and exploit their collective anger. To incite people by building on their grievances and rouse their anger in times of their helplessness, and leave them to themselves when the consequences of their reckless activities catch up with them, is the height of irresponsibility.

To bring hope to the disadvantaged and point them a way forward, that is the challenge every upright citizen. This is the mission of religiously motivated people, **Buddhist or Christian**. All need to re-educate themselves in a **Pedagogy of Peace** and by adopting the Path of Persuasion.

15. Healing Memories of Historic Injuries, Missionof Anger-Reduction

"Try to understand the person who caused pain, and have compassion"

(*Buddhist Monk Nhat Hanh 93*) .

One of the greatest hurdles to peace is the memory of historic injuries a community, society, nation or a civilization has received: e. g. colonial exploitation, unequal treaties, exploitation of natural resources by the great powers in West Asia and North Africa; consequent **prejudices**, perception of vested interests on either side.

However, it is good to be humble about these matters. Historically, we have all hurt each other as ethnic groups, nations, or civilizations, whether it be for reasons of religious prejudices, living space, natural resources, gold in the old days, oil or opportunity in our times. It is part of practical spirituality to work in order to **heal the memories of diverse types of historic wounds** at the ethnic, cultural, national and even civilizational levels; and also to deal with emotions built around asymmetries and imbalances in power. But it is not easy. It is a gigantesque task. And yet it is a challenge before practical spirituality.

Collective anger can be terrible. That is why the work of **anger-reduction** has become central to the creation of social harmony. If collective emotions are not healed, violence recurs again. Every Citizen ought to make his/her small contribution to this sort of healing and the rebuilding of relationships.

Negative memories of the past can harden. But they can also be changed. What is most important is to cultivate **sensitivity in sensitive matters**. **ErnestRenan** used to say that nations must forget the past, forgive each other, and move forward. Religious and ethnic groups today must do precisely that. Representatives of every section of the global society must make it possible; intellectuals, media men, politicians, business leaders, religious personnel, students, associations, all must help. Arnold Toynbee in his voluminous *Study of History* argues that the collective violence of a society (nation, civilizational block) in one direction is a response to an earlier violence in the opposite direction. We must put more energy into promoting **religious, cultural and ethical sensitivities** among people and spending some time on self-examination whether we are promoting our own collective interest at the expense of others.

Immanuel Kant's assessment over a century ago was that societies had become so interdependent economically and in other ways, that violence (war) would be damaging to the aggressor himself. Normal Angell brought the idea forward insisting, "The day for progress by force has passed," he said, "it will be **progress by ideas** or not at all. " (*Morris* 235) . "Progress by Ideas" is what Amartya Sen, the Nobel Prizewinner, would call "**Public Reasoning**. " Such a secular message can serve as a thought-provoker for all, whether they be political stalwarts and religious champions, **Buddhist or Christian**.

A creative and religiously inspired approach is greatly required. First of all, we need to explore the **psycho-social reasons** for the emergence of this terrible phenomenon of violence in modern times, observe the **emotional content** of what is being said and done, remove causes within possibility, and engage people in a **dialogue** once the emotions are down. We need today persons who can demolish walls of prejudice and **build bridges** of dialogue (*Kung* 2007 : *xxiv*) .

16. Religiously Motivated People in Defence of Vanishing Values

"*Indeed, to be able to do something before it exists, sense something before it becomes active, see something before it sprouts, are three abilities that develop interdependently*" (*Sun Tzu 4*) .

In an increasingly consumeristic world, what we notice today is a steady erosion of cultures and values. Consequently, it has emerged as a core concern for religiously motivated persons, **Buddhist or Christian** equally, to defend cultural heritages of communities that are under threat and restore those that have been lost. It has become extremely important to come to the rescue of **vanishing values like** concern for others, mutuality, altruism, forgiveness, peace, family and community relationships, honesty, probity in public life, protection of the environment, promotion of good governance, freedom of religion, and ethics in the media.

In times of trouble, everyone instinctively falls back on his/her own culture for inspiration and guidance. However, no culture is self-sufficient in itself. We all need to profit from the cultural heritages of other communities in our search for relevant values. It is in the context of a **dialogue of cultures** that new ways open for building a common future for all the people of the world.

It is said that all religious traditions are under threat today; but so are all rigid forms of comprehensive philosophical explanations of reality and ideologies, which are often called *metanarratives*. Religions have always withstood storms, since they have roots in the deepest psyche of human persons. Secular (political, economical, social) concerns, of course, need to be addressed and their voices heard. They are of great importance to human life. Every form of social self-assertion and criticism, even when radical, serves as a thought-provoker. But when everything is said and done and the dust has settled over the storm, what is right will show itself right again; what is true true, and what is beautiful beautiful.

If a community perceives that its collective personality, its inner identity, its selfhood, is threatened, it goes on the defensive. It is very difficult to draw it forth again from that position. But if the community feels its SELF-HOOD affirmed and senses that it may be further enhanced through its association with an enlightened and spiritually inspired leader, a door gradually opens out. And an unspoken dialogue begins.

17. Dialoguing with the Thinking Element in a Community

"The Helper. . . will teach you everything and make you remember all that

I have told you" (*Jesus in John's Gospel 14: 26*)

In this context, I would like to emphasize the strategic importance of one more category of people: I am referring to those who influence public thinking and take the rising generations towards new horizons. In this list I would put **thinkers, writers, poets, artists, educators** and speakers of special ability who give a self-understanding and self-pride to their society and provide a living philosophy for the social movements of the day. If you wish to exert influence in society, you need to keep close to such persons, learn from the positive contribution they make, and initiate a dialogue with them, suggesting correctives where they are required. Those with vested interests like opportunistic politicians and self-serving media men belong to another category.

Even if this dialogue does not evoke an immediate response, a day comes when the seeds planted bear fruit in abundance and the dreams fostered come to reality. If one consistently seeks to be **objective, balanced**, measured in words, sincere in purpose, eager to take every aspect of the issue into consideration and be seriously committed to the good of all persons and communities concerned, one is bound to win a hearing and exert a healthy influence all around.

As we have said earlier, our task does not consist in lecturing to people what they should do or think, nor in denouncing opponents in self-righteous tones, nor in confronting them in such a way that they are provoked to an angry and aggressive response.

Rather it consists in inviting people to reflect on live issues under the light of the principles derived from their own culture and indigenous wisdom and from the common spiritual springs of humanity. This is the only way that people can be helped to **bring their moral principles and ethical convictions to life**. This alone will ensure a future to humanity. Both **Buddhist and Christian** heritages provide enough resources towards this purpose.

References

Byron, William J., The Power of Principles, Orbis Books, New York, 2006

Confucius, Analects

Das, Gurucharan, The Difficulty of Being Good, Allen Lane (Penguin), New Delhi 2009 Dhammapada

Eco, Umberto, Inventing the Enemy, Vintage Books, London, 2013

Hathaway, Mark & Boff, Leonardo, The Tao of Liberation, Orbis Books, New York, 2009

John's Gospel

Kung, Hans, Islam, One World Publications, Oxford, 2007

Lott, Eric, Religious Faith, Human Identity, Asian Trading Corporation, Bangalore, 2005

Morris, Ian, War-What Is It Good For, Profile Books, London, 2014

Nhat Hanh, Thich, Being Peace, Parallax Press, Berkeley, 1987

Sachs, Jeremy, The Price of Civilization, The Bodley Head, London, 2011

Sun Tzu, Tr. Cleary, Thomas Cleary, The Art of War, Rupa, New Delhi, 1999

心与道的差异

——《心经》对话《约翰福音》

谢劲松[*]

摘　要：《心经》是佛经中最短、最核心的经，也是大乘了义经典，所有佛经的法义都可以从这部经中得到诠释。《约翰福音》是神学福音，代表了圣经教义和思想的核心内容。本文比较了两种最具代表性的经典在核心义理上的差异，用《心经》之心和空是指第八识之义解《约翰福音》中的神，反之则不能。

关键词：心　空　第八识　神　道

《心经》[①]是佛经中最短然而又是核心了义经典，《约翰福音》是《新约圣经》中的神学福音。两经代表了两教的思想核心，比较此两经中的核心义理可以发现两教的差别，并可加深对各自经典乃至教理的理解。

《心经》中的"心"要理解为第八识，亦即能生眼耳鼻舌身意和末那识七识、能生又能摄万法的真心，是"三界唯心""万法唯识"之心与识。在佛经中第八识有众多别名：我、空、常、自性、法身、本际、

　＊　谢劲松，副教授，华中科技大学马克思主义学院。

　①　《心经》全名《般若波罗蜜多心经》，本文用玄奘译文，《大正藏》第 8 册，第 251 号经。另有鸠摩罗什、法月、般若、利言、智慧轮、法成、施护等译文。

如来、如来藏、阿赖耶识、藏识、无垢识等。这个心是第一因，是真正的缘起。祂自身无相，"于相离相"，既以万法之相为相，又是真正的空相，其体能藏又显空性。如果从形而上学的意义上讲，祂是存在、本体、第一因，但不是西方意义上唯一本体，而是多重本体，每一有情都有此一本体，也是真正的主体。从真谛讲，"一真法界"，唯有此本体之"常、乐、我、净"。这是真正的了义法，究竟法，事实真相。描述事实真相之经典的思想应与形而上学思想有结构上的一致性，而基督教的思想结构乃是形而上学的同构，因此可认为基督教是柏拉图主义，柏拉图主义是精致的基督教。

作为神学福音的《约翰福音》，与其他福音之不同在于，它除了宣示教义，还在教义之外更多地宣示了教理，这个教理的核心就是"道成肉身"，这个道就是《旧约》中隐秘不显的神显现为有肉身的耶稣。一个既是神又是人的人格化的神降临于世，一方面是直接将神的爱带给人，化解《旧约》中由神对人的惩罚而带来的人对神的怨恨；另一方面也是显示唯有通过对神的信仰，才能到天国去与神、父相遇。耶稣说："我就是道路、真理、生命。若不借着我，没人能到父那里去。"（约翰 14：6）信、望、爱成为《新约》的基本主题，而爱成为《新约》的核心主题。

以上是对两种宗教核心义理的简单描述。

一　佛经的区分与解经原则

佛陀证悟后直至入灭，讲法四十九年，所说皆集结为佛经。按五时说法[1]，第一时为华严时，佛陀为十方三世诸菩萨讲《华严经》，其中涵盖了以后所讲佛法之全部、刚要、框架；第二时是十二年阿含时，佛

---

[1] "二教五时"说，参见吉藏《三论玄义校译》，韩廷杰校译，中华书局1987年版，第102页，第105页。又见李四龙《天台智者研究》，北京大学出版社2003年版，第55页；李尚全《简明中国佛教史》，上海社会科学院出版社2011年版，第38页。董群认为吉藏否定五时教，参见董群《三论宗通史》，江苏凤凰出版社2008年版，第237—239页。

陀为声闻者讲声闻法，为缘觉者讲缘觉法，最早结集为四《阿含经》；其后是八年的方等时，代表经典有《楞严经》《胜鬘经》《维摩诘所说经》《净土十三经》；第四时是二十二年般若时，佛陀讲《大般若经》等，《金刚经》《心经》都是这个时期所讲；最后八年的法华时，佛陀说《妙法莲华经》，并于入灭前一天一夜说《涅槃经》。以阿含经典为小乘，方等时的经典为兼顾大小乘，其他时的经典为大乘，这可看成是按照法义的目标来区分，亦即按照证果的不同来区分。如果按照经典的法义来区分，那么小乘是声闻缘觉法，大乘是菩萨法、成佛法。按照法义，全部佛法可称为三乘菩提：声闻菩提、缘觉菩提和佛菩提。按照法义之究竟与否可区分为了义法和不了义法，亦即了义说和方便说。用来描述其法义区分的词还有俗谛和真谛、有为法与无为法、世间法与出世间法、世出世间法、渐教法与顿教法、生灭法与不生不灭法等。如此区分，我们便可以在理解佛经时知道佛如此宣教之目的何在，不至于把不了义法当做了义法来看待，这就容易做到佛陀在《涅槃经》中所讲的"四依法"。

一般说来，阿含之后的经典是大乘经，大乘经是说成佛之法，讲究竟真相，说了义法，但其中也有方便说，不了义说。《阿含经》虽然是说声闻法、缘觉法，是破外道法，破常见断见及各种邪思邪见，断我见证声闻菩提和缘觉菩提，是小乘法，但其中也隐藏着大乘法。如此说来，小乘经典的主要目的是证五阴非我与六见处法，但其前提是要承认有个"我"，如果没有这个"我"，非我就失去了依据。此外，如果没有一个常住的我，酬偿因果就不可能；如果一切都是虚空意义上的空和无，那因果法则就不成立；如果因果法则不成立，那与可观察的因果事实就不符。佛陀在《杂阿含经》中讲色蕴"非我，不异我，不相在"[①]，这个"我"是真我，第八识。讲第八识的法是大乘法，实证第八识的真实，发现祂的作用，就是禅宗讲的破参。

佛法分有为法与无为法。有为法是有生灭之法，凡与有生有灭的事情相关的就是有为法，凡与不生不灭的第八识相关的就是无为法。不生

---

① 《杂阿含经》，《大正藏》第2册，第5页上。

不灭指第八识心体，有生灭的都是有为法。"一切有为法，如梦幻泡影，如露亦如电，应作如是观"。

佛陀在入灭前一天一夜讲《涅槃经》，其中有四依法："依法不依人，依义不依语，依智不依识，依了义经不依不了义经。"① 《瑜伽师地论》讲"一法是依，非数取趣。二义是依，非文。三了义经是依，非不了义经。四智是依，非识"②。此四依四不依明确奠定了读经解经之原则。"依法不依人"就是说任何一个人所讲都未必全对，佛陀自己也告诫人，对他的话不能理解和接受的可以存疑，这就是提倡一种理性精神来平等对话和探讨究竟真相，不陷入盲目的个人崇拜。法指事实真相，包括佛陀所讲的教法。佛陀教法之法义，具体可以理解为三乘菩提，再狭隘的理解可为《法华经》所讲之"一佛乘"的成佛之法。这个事实真相是应该依止于"常住不变"之"法"的，也就是《心经》所讲的"不生不灭"的"心"，也就是"如来""法性""第八识"。"依法者，即是如来大般涅槃。一切佛法即是法性，是法性者即是如来，是故如来常住不变。"③

"依义不依语"之"义"可理解为含义、意义，相当于英语的"meaning"，"语"相当于英语"language"，即语言文字。"依义不依语者，义者名曰觉了，觉了义者名不羸劣，不羸劣者名曰满足，满足义者名曰如来常住不变，如来常住不变义者即是法常，法常义者即是僧常，是名依义不依语也。"④这里仍然是强调"如来常住不变"义，"语"指世俗言辞，欲望、工具性之语。这就是说一切不是讲第八识常住法的话语都可不依止。

按照《涅槃经》讲法，"所言智者即是如来"，而识则是声闻法之知见以及一切不是第八识的有为法。智是了知"如来即是法身"，亦即

---

① 《大般涅槃经》卷6，《大正藏》第12册，第401页中。
② 《瑜伽师地论》卷11，《大正藏》第30册，第332页中。
③ 《大般涅槃经》卷6，《大正藏》第12册，第401页下。
④ 《大般涅槃经》卷6，《大正藏》第12册，第401页下。觉了，意思是懂得语言文字的意义。不羸劣，就是不瘦弱。不瘦弱就是满足，也就是说，要是完全懂得了佛说的语言文字，一定会知道如来常住不变才是佛所要传达给我们的义理。

实证第八识，发现其作用，亦即对第八识有现量。识包括了错误的见解和言论，如说如来有五蕴身，就是不知法身不是五蕴，哪怕经中这样说也是识，不能依。在如来是法身这个角度讲，即使知道，而没有实证，也还是识不是智，只是听闻、思维，或以此起修，还不是现量，也只是可作为闻思修的参考，而不是发现第八识真相后的解脱。

了义经是讲第八识真谛，是大乘法，"了义者名为菩萨，真实智慧"是"无上大乘"，"言如来常住不变""入法性""证知菩萨所说"。"不了义经者谓声闻乘，闻佛如来深密藏处悉生疑怪"①，即使证知声闻法也是不了义。

这个常住法，是佛教正法最简明的依据。如果认为佛教没有这个常住法，那就不是真正的佛法，就不能认为是正法。佛陀在最后的遗教《大般涅槃经》中反复说到这个常住法，说到"常、乐、我、净"涅槃四德。因此，佛法之正法就是常住法，常住法就是佛法正法。这个常住法也是无为法，也是第八识如来藏心体。一切外于祂而说的法，都是生灭法、有为法，因此为外道法。"外于真相而说的法即为外道法。"②

二 《心经》实义

《般若波罗蜜多心经》③的核心语词就是"般若""心"和"空"，此三词都是指第八识、如来藏、真心。般若非一般世俗智慧，而是实证第八识生起的实相智慧。"照见五蕴皆空"中的"照见"就是观照般若，就是发现真心如来藏，"三世诸佛，依般若波罗蜜多故，得阿耨多罗三藐三菩提"就是实相般若。"五蕴皆空""色不异空""诸法空相"和"空中无色"等语句中的"空"都是指代第八识，用第八识来解《心经》中的空，语义可贯通全经。第一句：

① 《大般涅槃经》卷6，《大正藏》第12册，第402页上。
② 谢劲松：《禅宗心性论》，湖北人民出版社2015年版，第33页。
③ 《般若波罗蜜多心经》，《大正藏》第8册，第251号经。

观自在菩萨，行深般若波罗蜜多时，照见五蕴皆空，度一切苦厄。①

这句话的意思是：一个观察到自己的第八识之自在体性的菩萨，他的观行深入到了发现真心生起般若智慧的现量境界，此时他能现观自己的五蕴都是第八识出生的，这个时候，他就是一个消除了一切苦厄的菩萨了。"照见五蕴皆空"之"空"不能理解为一般意义上的虚假、非真，如果仅是这个道理，那么《阿含经》早就说过了；更为重要的是，这个道理不需"观自在"，也不需"行深般若"就能知道，声闻道的断我见，一个初果人就能证到，它是声闻见道的标志，无须是菩萨之后才明白。"五蕴皆空"之真实义是五蕴都是由空所生，这里的空是第八识真心，亦即五蕴是由第八识出生的。正因为第八识恒常存在，相对于此，五蕴自然是假有、有生灭。

"观自在"，就是观察自己，就是观行，在明白有个恒常存在的如来藏真心之后，观察五蕴十八界的虚幻，确证我见的断除。不仅如此，还要达到"行深般若波罗蜜"，能做到这一点的是能够现量观察到第八识的菩萨，对第八识有了现量，发现了第八识的真实存在，也看到了其自在性。所谓自在即从来就在，从没出生过，也从没消失过。祂不依靠任何其他一法而存在，祂是自足的。但第八识自身又不能"观自在"，能观的是妄心、意识心，第八识自身不能观察自身，也不能观察妄心，不能观察由祂所出生的身口意行。由于真妄和合，第八识与七转识和合为一，第七识末那识总是自以为是，自以为是"一"。观行就是要断尽我见，明心就是从八识中区分出第八识来。如果能这样，"一切苦厄"就消失、菩萨就解脱烦恼了。

第二句：

色不异空，空不异色，色即是空，空即是色。受想行识，亦复

---

① 《般若波罗蜜多心经》，《大正藏》第8册，第251号经，第848页下。

如是。①

　　五蕴不仅是第八识（空）所生，而且与第八识不相异，即彼此不能分离，也就是彼此不是两个，故说"色""空"不异，甚至于可以把色就看成是第八识而说"色即是空"，把第八识就看成是色而说"空即是色"。色不是第八识，但又离不开第八识；色就是第八识的相，色就是第八识，因为第八识无相，以万物之相为相。受不异空，空不异受，受即是第八识，第八识即是受；行不异第八识，第八识不离行，行就是第八识，第八识就是行；识不离第八识，第八识不离眼耳鼻舌身五识，同时此五识就是第八识，第八识就是五识；这些都是同样的事实，都是一个道理。五蕴都是如此与第八识彼此"不一不异"，既不是一个，又不是可分离的两个。"不一"与"不异"必须同时讲，如同《杂阿含》讲的"非我、不异我、不相在"②主要是讲"不一"，《心经》在此主要讲"不异"。

　　至于"诸法空相"，是说一切万法都是第八识出生的相，"不生不灭，不垢不净，不增不减"是讲第八识的体性。诸法是生灭法，有为法，有相甚至有形，但第八识（空）是不生灭法，其相是无相。诸法之相也是生灭相、变异相，相对于第八识心体之不变异，诸法是虚幻相。不是把"空相"作为一个语词，而是把"空"和"相"各作为一个语词。"诸法空相"为"诸法'空'相"，就是说诸法是第八识出生的相。空相也是无相，第八识自身无相，但以万法之相为相。万法在第八识中显现，第八识就在万法中。正如《起信论》讲真妄和合一样，诸法之相与第八识之无相也是合一的。"诸法"是第八识生出的相，这样说的前提是"诸法有相"，其相是第八识所生，第八识是诸法的根源。

　　第四句从"空中无色"，一连讲了十三个"无"：

---

① 《般若波罗蜜多心经》，《大正藏》第 8 册，第 251 号经，第 848 页下。
② 《杂阿含经》，《大正藏》第 2 册，第 5 页上。

是故空中无色，无受想行识，无眼耳鼻舌身意，无色声香味触法，无眼界，乃至无意识界，无无明，亦无无明尽，乃至无老死，亦无老死尽，无苦集灭道，无智亦无得。①

这样讲都是站在第八识的角度上讲，亦即从真谛上讲，"空中"就是说在第八识中，就是从胜义谛看，从第八识自身讲。这十三个"无"中的前六个分别否定的是六识六根六尘，亦即十八界法。这个否定是说第八识不是、不在十八界法，亦即远离三界万法及其法相。无明、老死、苦集灭道和智慧得失是俗谛，亦是有为法，从第八识胜义谛讲，也是不存在的，存在的仅仅是一真法界，是第八识如来藏界而已。因为智慧是觉知心，有觉知心才有智，有智就会观察和分别——分别善恶、真假、美丑、法与非法、明与无明、真谛与俗谛、了义法与不了义法等，这都是智慧分别，都是俗谛才有的分别，从胜义谛来看就无有分别了。大乘见道者见证第八识的存在所具有的般若智慧，是正智。正智只在世俗谛上作分别，在胜义谛上则不分别。大乘见道者于世俗谛的分别和于胜义谛的不分别是同时存在的，他虽然处于胜义谛中，但日常生活中该有的分别行为仍然具有，在世俗人的眼中他仍然是正常人。他安住在自性清净涅槃中，却又与世人一样的行住坐卧、工作和生活。他虽然已超凡入圣，是见道位的圣者，但这也是从俗谛才如此说，从胜义谛讲，"心佛及众生，是三无差别"②，所见者通通是一真法界，都是第八识。自性清净涅槃也是从俗谛讲的。从真谛讲无十八界万法和无明可说，也没有开悟和明心乃至成佛可说，没有破一念无明和无始无明之说，也就没有无明可以除尽，没有智慧可求或失去。总之，所有列举的"无"，都是从第八识这个真谛上讲。这就是究竟的大乘了义法，就是般若波罗蜜。所以说：

菩提萨埵，依般若波罗蜜多故，心无罣碍。无罣碍故，无有恐

① 《般若波罗蜜多心经》，《大正藏》第 8 册，第 251 号经，第 848 页下。
② 《华严经》卷 10，《大正藏》第 9 册，第 465 页下。

怖，远离颠倒梦想，究竟涅槃。三世诸佛，依般若波罗蜜多故，得阿耨多罗三藐三菩提。①

无有恐怖，是真正的解脱。恐怖和畏惧，都是意识觉知心生起的。② 第八识远离觉知，因此，祂无有恐怖。实证了第八识的菩萨，不仅无有恐怖，也能远离颠倒梦想，因为发现了第八识这个事实真相的菩萨不会把意识觉知心的五蕴之我当作不生灭的真我。"心无罣碍"之"心"是指第八识真心没有罣碍、没有恐怖梦想，同时也可指意识心缘在第八识体性上，不仅可以没有罣碍和恐怖、梦想，也可以实证第八识，也可最后得到无上的正等正觉，成佛而证究竟涅槃，亦即无住处涅槃。③ 过去佛、现在佛和未来佛，包括一切众生都可如此走上成佛之道。

三　对比《约翰福音》

《约翰福音》作为神学福音宣讲了神自身的本性、人与神的关系，人如何走向神。

> 太初有道，道与神同在，道就是神。（约翰 1：1）

从文本语词讲，这里的"道"是希腊文的"logos"和英文"Word"的译文。"logos"在希腊文中有许多种含义，主要的含义有语言、言说、关系、性质、现象、理性等。赫拉克利特说世界的本源是

---

① 《般若波罗蜜多心经》，《大正藏》第 8 册，第 251 号经，第 848 页下。
② 死亡是有情最大的恐惧。海德格尔在《存在与时间》中区分了怕与畏。怕是有对象的，畏是无对象的。在此意义上畏惧轮回是怕，但轮回既不是具体的对象，也不是完全无对象，因此畏惧轮回也同样有海德格尔意义上的畏。
③ 涅槃分为有余涅槃、无余涅槃、自性清净涅槃和无住处涅槃四种涅槃。究竟涅槃就是断尽分段生死和变异生死，四种涅槃全部证得，出生了无住处涅槃，这是佛地不可思议的境界。涅槃自身无实体，只是境界和名，是假名施设。第八识才有体，是唯一真实。

火，火的燃烧和熄灭遵循着逻各斯。逻各斯在古希腊作为理论理性就是要探讨永恒。形而上学的永恒中心就是逻各斯。德里达把形而上学描述为逻各斯中心主义。逻各斯在中世纪就变成了上帝，亦即在《圣经》中的神的话语。《旧约》是神间接向人说话，这个说话的耶和华隐而不显；《新约》是神直接向人说话，亦即耶稣直接向门徒和世人说话。在《圣经》中，逻各斯作为神的话语，即是真理。《约翰福音》不同于奇迹福音，其内容不是神秘信仰而是理性的话语。这里的理性就是逻各斯，亦即上帝之道，上帝就是逻各斯。道、神、逻各斯同一。

"太初"一词表明，神是最先、最高的存在，是第一因。上帝就其词义讲是最高的善，就其存在讲是最高的真，就其显现讲是最高的美。相对于人的欲望之言，道作为神言是真理的言说。此真理区别于人言，人言是谎言。正因为如此，读经解经就是从《圣经》中找相关话语来理解、证明，而不是首先从经文外找理解的根据和可能，包括自己的理解也不优先于神的话语。而且读经前祷告神，便是已经相信了一个活着的神就在眼前，祂将通过经书来给予启示。这是以经解经的原则。与假定《圣经》的绝对正确和权威不同，虽然佛经经典被看成是正教量，但现量优先于正教量和比量；与现量、比量、正教量三量互证不同，以及与四依四不依相比，后者多了许多维度，更接近实证科学和理性。从佛经的解经原则讲，以经解经的原则仅是在语言语义上寻找根据和启示。

"太初有道"，从英文看也可译为"太初是道"。译为"是道"避免了还有道之外的其他存在。道就是太初，就是开始，亦即肯定逻各斯的原初性，"道与神同在"则也表明了神的原初性。为什么不直接说"太初有神"？道和神是两个，同时又是一个，是二而一，一而二。如此表明神就是神的逻各斯，亦即神就是神的言说。神的言说就是耶稣的话语。道和神的二而一的关系，也隐含地表明了神和耶稣的关系，世间的父和子本是二，但"道成了肉身"①，二也是一。如此一个《旧约》中隐秘的神变成了一个活生生的人神合一的耶稣：

---

① 既然"道就是神"，为什么不直接讲"神成肉身"？这问有意义吗？

道成了肉身、住在我们中间、充充满满的有恩典有真理。我们
也见过他的荣光、正是父独生子的荣光。(约翰 1：14)

耶稣的人神合一，神显现为人，这是基督教被黑格尔看成是高级宗
教的原因，因为其他宗教信仰的神都是不能直接显现的。从《心经》
之心是第八识而第八识无相上讲，任何个人都是五蕴的聚合，五蕴之相
非第八识之相；从"色不异空"上讲，五蕴也是第八识的显现，第八
识"于相离相"，即自身无相却以万法之相为相。如此说，如果耶稣是
神，那么每一个人和有情都是神，因为"心佛众生三无差别"，亦即都
有第八识不生灭的心体。第八识和五蕴身是"不一不异"的，对于一
个有五蕴身的耶稣也不例外。因此从佛法上讲，只能说耶稣和其他人都
有第八识，第八识的心体是没有差异的。

基督教将有肉身的耶稣当神，这在佛教看来，既对又不对。对在有
肉身的耶稣也是一有情，也有第八识，在"心佛众生三无差别"上讲
也是佛，其心体也是第一因，但不是佛陀意义上无上正等正觉的佛，而
是有待走向无上正等正觉的有情。其不对在于不能把五蕴构成的肉身耶
稣当成《旧约》中隐而不显的神，哪怕有三位一体说也不能，这点犹
太教比基督教，特别是基督新教高明。基督教是启示的宗教，以信仰为
根本特征，以祷告作为人与神沟通的途径，亦即以语言为媒介，不仅如
此，神就是神的言说，人则聆听神言并照此指引而生活。

从了义法上讲，佛教不是宗教，特别不是西方基督教意义上的宗
教，而是实证，亦即发现事实真相的行为科学。从内在经验讲，两教都
有内在经验，基督教的内在经验是语言构成的话语，佛教的内在经验则
超越语言，所谓"言语道断"，如《金刚经》所言可概括为"说 A，非
A，是名为 A"① 的语言模式和禅宗公案中不知所言的奇怪言说，这是
因为用来指称第八识的语言文字并不是第八识自身。

---

① 典型表达在《金刚经》："须菩提，说法者，无法可说，是名说法。""须菩提！所言
一切法者，即非一切法，是故名一切法。""如来说第一波罗蜜，非第一波
罗蜜，是名第一波罗蜜。"(参见谢劲松《禅宗心性论》，湖北人民出版社 2015 年版，第 9、134—136 页。)

第八识与《约翰福音》所说的道之不同在于，第八识远离语言文字，也无知无觉，自身不可能言说。从第八识能生万法来讲，《圣经》之言是神说，可理解为《圣经》之言都是第八识所生出，《旧约》的间接言说并未明示其言说是如何可能的，《新约》的直接言说则需在《圣经》自身的诠释系统中才成立。这个神的"直接说"，亦即耶稣作为神的言说，在佛法看来也是耶稣的第八识流注种子所现起的功能差别，在功能的实现上其真相与其他人讲话没有不同，只是话语内容有区别。话语及其内容相对于第八识来讲也是妄想，也是业力的作用。不过从真谛讲，亦即从一真法界，不取相分别讲，神言即是神，无所谓神言，神就是第八识，只有第八识，没有其他，也无第八识之所生万法。在此真谛意义上来理解人神合一，已经不是基督教所理解的"三位一体"，而是从佛法了义法上所理解的"不二"。佛法能理解和解释基督教及《约翰福音》，反之则难。这也表明了基督教的一神教之排他性，彰显了佛法的圆融性——圆融不是没有或放弃原则，而是因为了解事实真相而具有解释力。

黑格尔说其他宗教的神不直接显现，佛法中所说的第八识不是任何其他宗教意义上的神，但可以认为是第一因，因此是第一义谛。第八识并不是不显现，而是时时刻刻在显现，祂自身无相，却以万法之相为相。如此也只是一种知识性的观念，禅的直指人心就是现观第八识，禅宗公案记载的就是禅师们当下指认第八识。第八识时刻在显现，但只有破参、明心、开悟的大乘见道者当下能发现，未到此种境界，其他任何人还是不能明白。

第八识与《约翰福音》的道和神都有能生性，都可看成是万物出生的第一因，是本源、本体。《约翰福音》也区分了生就的和造就的不同，"这等人……乃是从神生的"（约翰1：13），耶稣是神生就的，万物是被造的。生就的与能生的在本性上是一致的，神作为父与独生子耶稣是人神合一。第八识之能生万法，不仅仅指胎生，而是指变现，指显现出来的一切。《约翰福音》讲父出生子，而不讲母出生子，虽然可成为女权主义者的一个话柄，但这样说，是把生与造区分开来，是为了说明耶稣是神人合一。

"万物是借着他造的。凡被造的，没有一样不是借着他造的。"
（约翰 1：3）

此说表明了神的创造性，但这个创造并没有表明其时间性，没有表明是不是每时每刻的事物都是借着祂被创造，也没有说明这个"借着"是何意。在最低限度上讲，可认为"借着"是因为有祂，而且必须有祂。如果耶稣是人神合一，那也可说耶稣造了万物，虽然耶稣也行了神迹，但此神迹仍然是个别性的，即使无宗教信仰的人也会经历具有神秘性的奇异之事。此外，"异教"也有奇迹，如果奇迹或神迹是神存在和起作用的根据，那就无法解释和否定被基督教命名的异教和被佛教命名的外道都有奇异的现象了。如果只有耶稣行的神迹才能表明祂是神、祂正在创造万物，那其他非神迹的万物，亦即一切现象难道就不是神在创造？把耶稣看成是人神合一的，神造就万物就应该也可看成耶稣在造就万物。被钉十字架的耶稣虽然是祂的大能与无能的合一，但却表现出了事实上的和说法的逻辑上的悖论。佛法虽然不否定第八识时时刻刻的能生性，但每一有情都有第八识，是所有的无数个第八识共同在变现万法，万法之为万法，是所有参与的有情的妄想与业力共同作用的结果，如果无业力与妄想，就没有万法和万物了。神创了世界，但世界却不认识神（约翰 1：10），也不认识耶稣就是神。耶稣为了让人信他的话，行了许多神迹，用中性一点的词表达是奇迹。奇迹也可用佛经中的"神通"一词来看待甚至替换，佛陀一般不让人用神通来达到某种目的，因为神通逃避不了因果。那些得到耶稣神迹的恩惠的人，也是和他有缘的人，成为其门徒乃至又出卖耶稣，用佛理来看也是业力和因果的表现，耶稣说这些都是神所安排的，这个神和安排可以看成是业力、因果的结果。

在此，《约翰福音》讲的道和神是唯一的，耶稣只有一个；而佛教中的第八识是无数的，"不增不减"在表达上就表明了不止一个。因此在存在论上讲，基督教的本体是一，佛法讲的本体是多。

神与万物的关系是造和被造的关系，世界聚集了万物，但世界却不认识神，亦即拒绝神，这是对人与神的关系的描述。

> 生命在他里头。这生命就是人的光。（约翰 1：4）
> 光照在黑暗里，黑暗却不接受光。（约翰 1：5）
> 他在世界，世界也是借着他造的，世界却不认识他。（约翰 1：10）

光在佛经中，即使是指佛光普照的光，只要肉眼可见，那也是属于色的范畴，也在生灭中。从"色不异空"上讲，也是第八识现起的功能差别，色与第八识也是"不一不异"的关系。在《约翰福音》中，神与光的关系，虽然不是同一，但光却是神对人、对世界的指引，这光不是物理之光，而是上帝之光。"神说，要有光，就有了光。"（旧 1：3）《旧约》中的光是神造的，包括了物理之光；《新约》中的光作为真光，是指引人生活的光，是比喻和象征。

> 那光是真光，照亮一切生在世上的人。（约翰 1：9）

真光只是比喻性的说法，是为区别于物理之光。"黑暗却不接受光"说明此光非物理性的可照亮黑暗的光，因为物理之光会驱逐黑暗，也可理解为黑暗接受了光。"生命是人的光"，而"生命在他里头"意味着人的生命离不开神，但此生命并非肉体生命，而是属灵的生命，指的是相信神的人，意即相信耶稣是神的人才有灵性生命。不过，此光是真光"照亮世上一切的人"，包括了不信耶稣是神的人。然而"黑暗却不接受光""世界却不认识他"都表明他遭遇到了拒绝，也预示着最后耶稣被钉十字架，此拒绝达到了高峰。从佛法角度讲，拒绝和认识是五蕴中想、行、识三者共同作用的结果，五蕴是变化无常的，更不能把五蕴当成第八识真我和真心，如此连断我见证初果都不能。耶稣是人格化的神，所谓人格化即有人的形象，也就是以五蕴身显现。从了义佛法讲，人格"神"耶稣也是生灭无常的，非不灭的法身，耶稣在五蕴构成上讲与其他任何人无异，在其心体不生不灭以及"三无差别"的意义上也可把他看成佛，但作为佛的并非是其五蕴，而是其心体。同时把此心体看成一个主体，由祂变现出耶稣，乃至在天国又变现为另一形象，如父，乃至死而后生的可被摸到的身体，乃至后又有圣灵在，在了义的佛法上讲都是可理解的。父子灵三位一体之"体"可理解为同一个第八识的不同变现而非不同五蕴结合为一。

从第八识看《约翰福音》中的神，并非是那个符合事实真相的能生万法创造万物的神。换个说法，《约翰福音》中的神在道成肉身、人神合一的意义上指耶稣，但至少在耶稣出现之前，神是无所指、无指称的，甚至可说其所指是虚无的，而第八识虽然无相却是有所指可实证的真实存在。如果要问一个无所指不存在的专名是否或为什么会有意义和价值，其理如望梅可止渴，也如分析哲学讲命题的含义不是来自所指①，也如德里达讲能指的差异构成了意义②。德里达讲能指在其游戏和文本之外无他物，这就切断了语言和实在的联系，由此取消了实在和所指的真实。说"道就是神"，如果按照弗雷格在《意义与指称》一文说若"a＝b"，则 a、b 的指称同一时等式才成立，如果所指不同则等式不成立。③ 形式上只能把道和神分别看成是 a 和 b，耶稣则只能命名为 c，如果耶稣就是神，若要 a＝b＝c，则 a、b、c 的指称必须是同一的。如果等式成立，则《约翰福音》的第一句为什么不说"太初有耶稣"？至少在说了太初有（是）逻各斯、太初有（是）言、太初有（是）道、太初有（是）神之后，按照《约翰福音》道成肉身说，同时按照弗雷格《意义与指称》等式成立说，耶稣的肉身与太初的神必

---

① 如"'离地球最远的天体'这一说法，它有含义，但它是否也有一个所指，则十分可疑。"（转引自张庆熊等《二十世纪英美哲学》，人民出版社 2005 年版，第 44 页。）弗雷格明确指出"句子的意义是它的思想，句子的意谓是它的真值，即真和假。这是他的一个最基本最重要的思想"。（参见王路《弗雷格思想研究》，社会科学文献出版社 1996 年版，第 150 页。）"意谓（Bedeutung）也就是意义，并不是所指赋予的，并不是指称的对象赋予的。"（参见谢劲松《20 世纪的西方哲学》，武汉大学出版社 2009 年版，第 281 页。）含义、意义、意谓都是意思之意，都可用意思一词代之。

② 索绪尔也讲符号的任意性原则，即所指和能指的联系是任意的。德里达对此进行了解构并赋予了新义。

③ 参见韩震等编《现代西方哲学经典著作选读》（英文版），北京师范大学出版社 2008 年版，第 3—4 页。

须是同一指称；可耶稣又是神的独生子，是神生的，在时间上父与子有先后，父和子也有不同肉身，即使这个父是无肉身的，由于子晚生，子的肉身就不可能与父有同一指称了。如此若说"太初有耶稣"则不可能。当然，从分析哲学的思路讲，可能就另一篇文章了。不过《心经》的"色即是空"之空是指第八识，第八识不仅有明确具体的所指，而且可讲明并讲通耶稣就是神，但耶稣的独特性则没有了。同样，"诸法空相"之理也可讲明人神合一，不过《心经》意义上的神是第八识而非《约翰福音》中的耶稣。

四 结语

无论读佛经还是《新约》，都可以感到其话语的温柔、亲切，体会到佛陀的慈悲智慧和耶稣对身边人的爱与关怀。以上比较是将《心经》之心理解为第八识，第八识具有形而上学本体的含义，这就与《约翰福音》中的道和神具有结构和功能上的相似性，但《约翰福音》中的道和神之特性不如佛经中讲的可发现的第八识之特性那般丰富和全面，而第八识则包含了《约翰福音》乃至《圣经》中神与耶稣的特性。耶稣是人神合一的说法从第八识与五蕴是"不异"关系，"色即是空"上讲是可讲通的，但所有有情都是"人""神"合一，并非独耶稣如此，甚至在此意义上就是"与神同在"，这与信仰没有关系，而是事实真相。从佛理看耶稣和基督教，也不可能认为耶稣说出了创造万物的"神"——第八识这个事实真相。第八识心体的不生不灭性就是永恒。如此用佛理解《圣经》，用一本或多本佛经解释一本《圣经》，是想跳出以经解经的传统，给《圣经》一个新的诠释角度，同时也展示出佛经所具有的真义和解释力。

跨文化哲学
理论探讨

The Project of Intercultural Philosophy and Intercultural Communication

William Sweet [*]

Abstract: Some scholars have argued that while intercultural communication is possible, it is only about particular matters of fact or at a superficial level, and that there are significant challenges to dialogue and exchange at a deeper level – on matters of religion, philosophy, and cultural beliefs, values, and traditions. In this paper, I argue, however, that it is possible to engage in dialogue and exchange at a deeper level. To show this, I focus on the possibility of the project of intercultural philosophy. I conclude that the project of an intercultural philosophy provides an example of, and a model for, intercultural communication.

Key words: dialogue intercultural communication intercultural philosophy

The possibility of intercultural communication would seem to be unques-

* Vice President, Council for Research in Values and Philosophy, Professor of Philosophy, St Francis Xavier University, 2329 Notre Dame Avenue, Antigonish, NS B2G 2W5 Canada e-mail: wcpsweet@ gmail. com OR wsweet@ stfx. ca

tionable; the fact that we are here today, with scholars from Asia and the West, would surely establish that intercultural communication is possible. Yet some scholars have suggested that while intercultural communication is possible about particular matters of fact or at a superficial level, there are significant challenges to dialogue and exchange at a deeper level – on matters of religion, philosophy, and cultural beliefs, values, and traditions.

In this paper, I want to look at this issue of intercultural communication by focusing on the project of intercultural philosophy. I begin with some examples of challenges to whether there can be intercultural communication and intercultural philosophy at this 'deeper' level. I then turn to the example of Giulio Aleni (1582 – 1649), one of the early Jesuit missionaries to China, and outline briefly some of his strategies in introducing European philosophical ideas to China. Yet, one may well ask whether Aleni's methods – and those of his Jesuit colleagues, such as Matteo Ricci – are a model for today. Thus, I introduce a more recent approach, that of the German-British-South African philosopher of the early 20th century, R. F. A. Hoernlé. Hoernlé – who instantiates several different cultures in his writings – offers strategies and a model for 'intercultural philosophy.' Based on the examples of Aleni and Hoernlé, I extrapolate a number of principles that we can draw on to find a basis for communication between Western and Asian cultures. [1]

Challenges to intercultural communication and to intercultural philosophy

Intercultural communication, the exchange of ideas, and intercultural and international cooperation are, for many, unproblematic and uncontrover-

---

[1] This paper includes extracts from my "Intercultural Philosophy and the Phenomenon of Migrating Texts and Traditions," in *Comparative and Intercultural Philosophy*, ed. Hans Lenk (Berlin: LIT Verlag, 2009), pp. 39 –58, pp. 40 –41, 45 –50, 53 –56, though the order here is different and there is new material.

sial. Nevertheless, there are some scholars who would disagree. They do not deny that there has been some kind of encounter of the texts, ideas, and traditions of various cultures with one another, but they challenge how far or how deep this encounter goes – and they suggest that the appropriation, or even the actual engagement, of texts and traditions bearing on distinctive values, beliefs, and culture, are more apparent than real. Thus, recent efforts at developing a philosophy across cultures – an intercultural philosophy – are viewed with deep suspicion.

What reasons might sceptics appeal to in order to justify their claims about intercultural philosophy and, more broadly, intercultural communication on matters of culture and value?

A first reason derives its force from a claim about philosophy and its relation to culture. A number of philosophers today argue that philosophies and philosophical traditions are deeply marked by the cultures in which they arise, and that this precludes not only any direct engagement, but any attempt at comparison. Philosophy is embedded in culture. It is not just that it has its source in its culture of origin, but it can never break free of that source.

The reasons for this are fairly easy to surmise.

Our language and values are rooted in our culture, and it is within this context that we find the specific sorts of problems and questions that philosophers pursue. Indeed, it is from one's culture that we learn what counts as philosophy (as distinct from literature, science, history, or religion), and how to distinguish philosophy from the religious, the scientific, and the literary. One's culture influences in what 'language' philosophical questions are expressed and answered – and evenwhat counts as a satisfactory answer. ① It is

---

① We see this in the way that classical Greek culture influenced Greek philosophy, that Christianity influenced mediaeval Western philosophy, that French culture influenced a range of philosophies in France from Cartesianism to post-modernism, and so on.

because of this that, for some time in the West, the work of figures such as Laozi, Confucius, or Sankara, or the traditions of thought in Asia or Africa or of American aboriginal tribes, were regarded by many as not being philosophy, but, at best, religions or 'social practices' or 'worldviews'.

As an illustration of this, some point to cases where one tradition or culture lacks the terminology, or concepts, or even the syntax to permit problems or concepts of other traditions to be intelligible – or where a language can 'tilt' a discussion in a way that makes the expression of philosophical issues from one culture awkward or irrelevant. ① This has been a concern of some African philosophers, particularly on matters related to ontology. For, if there are, as some African philosophers report, three or four constituent principles of human being, rather than the traditional two of Western thought (i. e. , mind or soul and body), then such issues as mind/body dualism, or the nature of death as the radical separation of soul and body, are not only not translatable, but arguably irrelevant to African thought. ②

Second, the thesis of 'communication' across (philosophical) cultural traditions is challenged by an account of (the nature of) philosophy itself. R. G. Collingwood writes of philosophy as involving a method of 'question and answer' – of "asking questions and answering them." ③ And so, in order to understand what exactly a philosopher said or meant, we need to know

---

① For more on this, see my "Culture and Pluralism in Philosophy," in William Sweet (ed.), *Philosophy, Culture, and Pluralism* (Aylmer, QC: Editions du scribe, 2002), pp. v – xxi. It has been claimed that some philosophers may simply not understand the views of philosophers from other cultures (because their own philosophical views are so culturally laden that they cannot recognise the propositions and conceptual structures of other cultures; or because they are so immersed in their own approach that they cannot recognize that they have an approach) .

② See, for example, Chibueze Udeani, "The Body-Mind-Spirit Relationship within the African World-View," in *Philosophy, Culture, and Traditions*, Vol. 2 (2003), pp. 57 – 62.

③ R. G. Collingwood, *New Leviathan* [1942], rev. edn. , ed. D. Boucher (Oxford: Oxford University Press, 1992), p. 74. It is interesting that Hans-Georg Gadamer finds a link with Collingwood in Gadamer's own logic of question and answer, which he develops in *Wahrheit und Methode*; See Gadamer, *Truth and Method* (New York: Seabury Press, 1975, p. 333.) .

the question that she or he sought to answer. ①If this is so, then how to engage philosophies and philosophers from different cultures — and how a text from another context can be understood in one's own — are, at the very least, rather complicated. Prior to engaging a philosophy from another culture as possibly providing an answer to one's problems, we must, presumably, engage in a 'mini history of philosophy' in order to discern the questions that gave rise to that philosophical view or system in the first place. But if we do not or cannot know the questions that gave rise to it, then there can be no real engagement at all.

Third, the thesis that philosophical concepts from one culture can be understood within and possibly assimilated into philosophical traditions of another culture, seems also to be challenged by a claim found in Alasdair MacIntyre, concerning the nature and role of terms and concepts in relation to traditions. ②MacIntyre notes, for example, that in our contemporary philosophical — and, particularly, ethical — vocabulary, we have terms and concepts coming from a range of texts and traditions, but without any particular coherence or consistency. Now, when people share a language or live together, they may believe that they share a broader overall culture and tradition — and so they may think that they can understand one another quite well, and that there is no problem in communicating with each other and working together on philosophical problems. But, MacIntyre writes, this flies in the face of experience; for example, "... nothing is more striking in the contemporary university than the extent of the apparently ineliminable continuing divisions

---

① Collingwood writes that "every statement that anybody ever makes is made in answer to a question" [Collingwood, *An Essay on Metaphysics* (Oxford: Clarendon Press, 1940), p. 23], and that "In order to find out [a philosopher's] meaning you must also know what the question was... to which the thing he [or she] has said or written was meant as an answer" (Collingwood, *Autobiography* [Oxford: Clarendon Press, 1939], p. 31) .

② Nothing in what follows hinges on whether MacIntyre himself would accept this reading, but a follower of MacIntyre may have to.

and conflicts within all humanistic enquiry. "① For MacIntyre, moral beliefs and practices are constituted or formed by the traditions in which they are found. Each tradition has " its own standards of rational justification... [and] its set of authoritative texts. "② With different traditions – and the corresponding beliefs and epistemic and moral practices – we will have different standards of reasonableness, or justification, or proof. And so, when discussion "between fundamentally opposed standpoints does occur... it is inevitably inconclusive. Each warring position characteristically appears irrefutable to its own adherents; indeed in its own terms and by its own standards of argument it is in practice irrefutable. "③ Efforts at dialogue, on this model, will not get us very far. This is not to say that there cannot be any communication across traditions; but MacIntyre would insist that it is much more challenging than many realise. Fruitful contact and integration are far from automatic and, when they do occur, this is the result of a good deal of discernment by a person of 'practical wisdom. ' In many if not most cases, then, MacIntyre's argument suggests that efforts at intercultural philosophy are problematic.

The preceding objections and concerns are clearly forceful. Nevertheless, it is also clear that there seems to have been some communication and exchange, particularly in cases where we find the 'migration' of philosophical and religious texts and traditions from one culture to another – for example, the presence of Buddhist philosophy in China, Korea, and Japan, and, more recently, in North America and Europe. Thus, from an 'original' Buddhism in India, there has been a 'migration' – the development of 'schools' of Buddhism in different cultures: Mahayana, predominantly in north and

---

① Alasdair MacIntyre, *Three Rival Versions of Moral Enquiry* (London: Duckworth, 1990), p. 6.

② Alasdair MacIntyre, *Whose Justice? Which Rationality?* (Notre Dame: University of Notre Dame Press, 1988), p. 345.

③ Alasdair MacIntyre, *Three Rival Versions of Moral Enquiry*, p. 7. MacIntyre provides a series of caveats, however, starting on p. 5.

north east Asia; Theravada in south east Asia (Cambodia, Laos, Sri Lanka, Thailand, and Burma), and a number of further developments (within Mahayana) in Tibet, in Japan and China (including Pure Land and Chan/ Zen), and in Korea (Seon).

Similarly, many philosophies originating in the West seem to have 'migrated' east and south; they have been introduced, and, it would seem, have often been integrated and appropriated, into non-Western cultures and traditions (e. g., in Africa, in the Indian sub-continent, and in China and Japan). As examples here we can think of the introduction of British philosophy (e. g., empiricism, utilitarianism, but also idealism) into India in the 19th and 20th centuries and the exchanges that resulted, and the introduction of hermeneutics and postmodern thought into Asia. Today, a number of Asian scholars adopt phenomenology and hermeneutics in their work on Asian thought, and there is a steady market for the translation of texts by H. - G. Gadamer and others – e. g., J. Derrida, G. Deleuze, and M. Foucault – into various Asian languages, particularly Chinese.

What kinds of methods might underlie these examples of migration of philosophical and religious texts, and traditions related to culture and values?

Missionaries, philosophy, and method

Consider, for example, the communication of Western philosophy and theology to China in the 17th century by Jesuit missionaries and philosophers.

Perhaps the most famous of these men is Matteo Ricci (Li Madou, 1552—1610). [1] Ricci is generally known for his efforts to propagate faith through science; he did this through, for example, the translation of Western scientific texts, such as *The First Six Books of Euclid* (1607), and his

---

[1] See, for example, the discussion by John W. O'Malley in *The Jesuits II: Cultures, Sciences, and the Arts*, 1540 – 1773 (Toronto: University of Toronto Press, 1999), p. 659.

research in, and teaching of the sciences, including astronomy and geography, in China. As well, Ricci and his fellow Jesuits made efforts to translate and introduce texts dealing with the study of nature, human nature, and ethics.

But such efforts would likely have not gone very far had Ricci not also adopted social methods of cultural accommodation in his work and in his own deportment. We can see cultural accommodation in at least two respects: first, he adopted social customs (in attire, in hospitality, in adopting a 'Chinese name', and the like), which led to developing friendships and building confidences. Second, he made a great effort to provide an understanding and an acknowledgement (and not just an 'accommodation') of Chinese practice and belief in the presentation of the Christian religious view.

A third element of Ricci's methods is found in what we may see as the moral dimension of his methods – and that is the demonstration of one's own moral character, one's concern for the well-being of others, and the exhibition of tact. ①

Throughout, the objective of Ricci, and of his fellow Jesuits, was acquiring a genuine understanding of those to whom they were sent to mission, but also – and this is the key part – the building of mutual respect.

Yet the Jesuits, such as Ricci, also sought to carry out their engagement at a broad intellectual level – at the level of values and culture. The task of engaging Chinese thought through writing or translating texts into Chinese was carried out by several Jesuits, such as Giulio Aleni and Francisco Sambiasi. ②

How did this occur? First, Aleni and others recognised the need to find

---

① See, Katharine Louise Renich, *The Life and Methods of Matteo Ricci, Jesuit missionary to China*, 1582 – 1610. Thesis (M. A.) University of Illinois, 1914.

② Here, I draw from an example provided by Vincent Shen, in his "The Migration of Aristotelian Philosophy to China in the 17th Century," in William Sweet (ed.), *Migrating Texts and Traditions* (Ottawa: University of Ottawa Press, 2012).

ways to make Western philosophical ideas less 'foreign' to the Chinese. Their solution was to attempt to find suitable texts − and they focused on the work of Aristotle. Specifically, the method they took was to begin by presenting Aristotle the person − telling the story of Aristotle (e. g. , identifying him as a sage) − and then introducing elements of his philosophy that reflected Chinese interests.

One of Aleni's better known philosophical works was the *Xingxue Cushu* (*Introduction to the Study of Human Nature*, 1621), which was a translation and paraphrase of the *De Anima*, along with books related to it. Aleni and his confreres, then, produced Chinese translations of certain of Aristotle's works (or, to be more precise, summaries of and introductions to them in Chinese, sometimes in the form of a dialogue). Francisco Sambiasi (Bi Fangji, 1582 – 1649), together with Xu Guangqi, completed a brief summary/translation of the opening chapters of Aristotle's *In tres libros De anima*, as *Lingyan Lishao* ("A Spoonful of Words on the Soul"). Alfonso Vagnone (Gao Yizhi, 1568 – 1640), was the author of *Xiushen Xixue* (*Western Knowledge on Personal Cultivation*) which drew from material in Aristotle's *Nicomachean ethics*. ①

By focusing on areas such as the philosophy of human nature, moral philosophy, and ethical values; by adopting a literary style that was congenial to their readers; by presenting themselves and their work in a way suited to their audience − in short, by trying as far as possible to enter into the life-world of those with whom they wished to be in dialogue, Jesuits such as Aleni were then able to present Aristotle's philosophy of nature and theory of soul in Chinese terms. In this way, Aristotelian thought was 'introduced' and, in some degree, appropriated into a Chinese context.

But does this method still hold today?

---

① See the discussion in *The Discovery of Chinese Logic*, by Joachim Kurtz (Leiden: Brill, 2011), p. 45.

Another method

The examples of migrating texts and traditions, and the specific example of Matteo Ricci, Giulio Aleni, and his compatriots, suggest to us that some kind of intercultural communication of philosophical ideas is possible.

How might this help to engage in such a philosophy today? To help, here, let me briefly outline the method of the German-British-South African philosopher, R. F. A. Hoernlé,① whose life history and philosophical career might be a testament to philosophy across cultures and an intercultural philosophy.

R. F. A. Hoernlé was a man of many cultures. Born in Germany, his early childhood years were spent in India where his Indian-born father (and, therefore, a British subject), A. F. R. Hoernlé, was a leading Sanskrit scholar. The dominant language of the household in R. F. A. 's early years was Hindi; he was next sent to school in Germany and later studied in England, before going on to teach in Scotland, and subsequently moving on to Professorships in England (Newcastle-upon-Tyne), the United States (Harvard), and South Africa (Cape Town and Witwatersrand) .

In a number of his later writings, Hoernlé employs what he calls the ‘synoptic method. ’ For Hoernlé, a synoptic philosophy is simply one that “seeks to achieve a coherent world-view”② “or. . . an integration [by the individual] of the various [conflicting or disparate] aspects of. . . culture. ” It “rests on the assumption that truth has many sides, and that to the whole truth on any subject every point of view has some contri-

---

① See my entry on ‘Hoernlé, (Reinhold Friedrich) Alfred (1880 – 1943) ’, in *Oxford Dictionary of National Biography*, online edn, first published May 2006.

② See Hoernlé, “Philosophy of Religion in the Context of a Synoptic Philosophy,” p. 1 [in the Hoernlé papers, Witwatersrand University Archives, Johannesburg, South Africa] .

bution to make. "① But achieving this coherence requires at least "a desire to enter into [the life around one], and to share it from the inside, rather than to stand outside as a mere spectator or even to reject it as foreign to [one] self. "② In short, then, the synoptic method is an attitude and an ideal – an ideal of comprehensiveness and inclusiveness. ③

For Hoernlé, knowledge of other cultures and traditions than one's own was necessary, because all cultures and traditions were reflections of human responses to the world, and each of these reflections said something that was, at least partly, true about the world. At the same time, the divisions, tensions, conflicts, and the like, that one finds in a culture, and in the world, needed to be brought into some measure of coherence and consistency. This approach held that no culture or tradition was complete – nor could it be, so long as there was new experience to be encountered and engaged.

Such an approach was not just a method of intercultural communication, but offered a way to carry out an intercultural philosophy. Hoernlé was not offering a particular content to philosophy – though he would hold that philosophy (and, indeed, all knowledge) was broadly coherent, that this coherence was a demand of (what one might call) 'rationality,' and that the reality one sought to know had to be ultimately coherent. To know what a thing is, is to know it in its relations to other things.

For Hoernlé, philosophy was effectively what we might call intercultural philosophy. He insisted on the openness of philosophy and to philosophies of different cultures, though he clearly thought that the kind of method he offered, which was the result of an idealism developed in the West, was to be preferred.

---

① See I. D. MacCrone, "Introduction," to Hoernlé's *Race and Reason: Being Mainly a Selection of Contributions to the Race Problem*, ed. I. D. MacCrone (Johannesburg: Witwatersrand University Press, 1945), p. xvi.

② MacCrone, "Introduction," *Race and Reason*, p. xvi.

③ Ibid.

Responding to the challenges

How, and how far, do the preceding examples and remarks help to address the challenges to intercultural philosophy presented at the beginning of this paper?

First, recall the claim, noted earlier, that philosophy is so culturally embedded that an intercultural philosophy is difficult, if not altogether presumptuous.

This challenge, however, seems to presuppose a rather rigid view of what constitutes the migration, exchange, and engagement of philosophies of different cultures. If we expect the meaning and use of a term or concept or a philosophy to be univocal in its use in different cultures, then we are certain to be disappointed. But this is not obviously what the encounter of different philosophical traditions requires. Terms can be refined and even redefined after initial exchange. They can broaden, or narrow, in meaning. There can be an 'integrity' in the meaning of a term without an 'identity.' To assess the challenge that philosophical terms and ideas cannot break free of their cultural sources, perhaps all that we need do is to see how the terms in question are ultimately used and how claims are accepted and judged within different philosophical traditions.

This leads to the second challenge noted earlier. Recall the 'Collingwoodian' point that an 'answer' – and, by extension, a philosophical claim or tradition – can be understood only if we know the question (s) that gave rise to it. This is even more demanding if we are seeking not only an answer to a problem, but an answer coming from another tradition altogether. This would require a 'mini history of philosophy' of the source culture before one can begin to make sense of that 'answer.'

Such a challenge may be forceful in those cases where one has a very specific, perhaps idiosyncratic, question in mind. But if the issue is broader, and not just an isolated claim, Collingwood's own solution may not be so problematic after all. Carrying out a 'mini philosophical history' on the issue, or of the insight, is precisely what any good historian of philosophy would do – and, in this way, one may be able to determine not only the meaning but also the relevance of the answer – and the relevance or helpfulness of a different philosophical tradition.

A third challenge, derived from a view found in Alasdair MacIntyre, states that turning to another culture or philosophy for illumination on an issue or an answer is often not just unenlightening but problematic. Yet the possibility of looking outside one's culture and traditions, and finding resources in another to respond to the crises within one's own tradition, is clearly part of MacIntyre's own view. MacIntyre points out that traditions may experience 'epistemological crisis' – times when practices or the tradition as a whole seems to run into a dead end. And even though we are all rooted in a specific tradition, should we ever be confronted with certain grave problems or limitations, he writes, we might find ourselves turning to another outlook or tradition for help. When we do this, it is not because this other view possesses some sort of transcendental truth or objective validity, but simply because it enables us to address problems in our own view, "and so constitutes an advance on it, in relative but not absolute terms. "

Such a move is not arbitrary. Indeed, according to MacIntyre, it is 'rational' – something that a practically wise person would see – and the notion of rationality, here, can remain that of the tradition from which one comes. It is in this way that MacIntyre believes one can talk about 'rationality' and 'progress' in ethics, – and, one might argue, about rationality and progress in philosophy in general.

MacIntyre's warning, then, is not that people cannot go outside their philosophical traditions or engage with other traditions, but that they should be extremely careful in doing this. For, in order to be of help or of relevance, the insights of 'other' traditions cannot remain entirely 'other. '

Finally, it is important to remind ourselves that the encounter of cultures, and the effects of cultures on one another, are far from unknown. What encounter brings, when one culture has contact with another, is novelty – and it is very rare that any culture can control this phenomenon of novelty for very long. At best, what a culture can do is attempt to control the way in which it deals with the novelty. Thus, a culture cannot ignore new ideas altogether, and its response will often lead to some change in the culture. But this is not obviously something negative. Change is a property of anything that develops and flourishes; what does not change, can neither develop nor flourish. A culture that seeks to respond in a positive way, does so such that that culture retains a certain integrity through the change. What the project of intercultural philosophy brings to philosophies characteristic of particular cultures and traditions, then, is simply novelty – novelty that incites development.

There remain, of course, a number of other challenges concerning the possibility of intercultural philosophy. Some may ask whether there are many genuine examples of intercultural philosophy in the past, or whether they have simply involved the appropriation of another's ideas without mutuality or dialogue. One may ask, as well, whether all philosophical traditions can, in fact, enter into such an intercultural exchange – and, further, whether there are any philosophies that should not be engaged at all.

Nevertheless, the challenges to intercultural communication on issues of culture and value – what an intercultural philosophy proposes to address – may not be as great as initially suggested. Still, one might well ask, more concretely, what method such a philosophy might follow.

Principles for intercultural comm, unication

The preceding examples and the 'alternative' model offered by Hoernlé are, by themselves, only suggestive, but they provide more evidence for the claim that not only has there been a 'migration' of philosophical ideas, but an integration, and that a kind of 'intercultural philosophy', or better, perhaps, intercultural philosophizing, has occurred.

So what do the examples enumerated above tell us about the prospects for – and perhaps the character of – an intercultural philosophy and, by extension, intercultural communication?

First, some general comments: Intercultural philosophy is a method; it is not simply a history of ideas. It might best be seen as a kind of conversation, but not a mere idle one; intercultural philosophy has a purpose.

Second, from the accounts of Hoernlé and the practice of Aleni, several features would seem to characterize (and perhaps are required for) intercultural philosophizing.

1. The philosophers or the traditions involved must be open to some change or to the integration of new insights – i. e. , are not resistant to change. Only then can the beliefs, values, texts, and cultural traditions migrate or be appropriated or contribute to 'new' philosophies, or to philosophizing across cultures or interculturally.

2. Intercultural philosophizing may occur if philosophers are able to engage one another because (or to the extent that) there are related traditions or philosophical schools or histories that are already present in the 'recipient' culture. Some philosophical traditions (e. g. , rationalism, realism, and idealism) seem to be found, independently, in a range of cultures, and so engagement of cognate traditions is possible. (For example, it has been claimed that parallels between Aristotelian and Chinese Mohist logic allow not only a comparison between them but, for each of these traditions, the possibility of drawing on the resources of the other tradition. ①) And some philosophical traditions – e. g. , those that emphasize 'the empirical' – may pro-

---

① Fenrong Liu and Jialong Zhang, "New Perspectives on Moist Logic," *Journal of Chinese Philosophy*, 37 (2010): 605 –21; Gregor Paul, 1993, "Equivalent Axioms of Aristotelian, or Traditional European, and Later Mohist Logic," in Hans Lenk and Gregor Paul, eds. , *Epistemological Issues in Classical Chinese Philosophy* (Albany: SUNY Press, 1993), pp. 119 – 136.

vide more initial 'access points' and be more likely to bridge (and therefore to migrate into) traditions and cultures.

3. Again, philosophical traditions from different cultures may be able to learn from one another and exchange because (or to the extent that) there are underlying concepts – or, at least, concepts that are cognate – (such as 'community,' 'duty,' or 'sacred') that are already present in the 'recipient' culture.

4. Further, philosophical traditions from different cultures may be able to learn from and engage with one another because (or to the extent that) they are responses to underlying questions that are also present in the recipient cultures or traditions. Engagements of traditions are successful to the extent that what frames and provides the context of the exchange in one culture is (at least to some extent) that of another culture.

5. There needs to be (what I might call) a methodological openness, adaptiveness, and even a humility. (The examples of Aleni and Hoernlé are particularly instructive here.) Exchange and mutual development may be facilitated to the extent that the interlocutors can talk about the respective traditions in a way that reflects one of the above features, or using aspects of the methodologies of the tradition one wishes to engage.

6. When there is a (deep) familiarity with at least one other culture or philosophical tradition, the possibility of communication across or among cultures is facilitated.

7. Finally, it would seem that a combination of as many of the preceding features as possible would indicate or lead to a genuine mutual engagement of ideas and philosophies.

Let me note two caveats.

First, this account is not to deny the political or sociological background to philosophical encounters or exchanges – e. g. , the results of invasions, evangelization, etc. But this, by itself, I would claim, is not sufficient to explain what, exactly, it is about a philosophical tradition that enables it to enter into exchange, and why it does. There must also be at least some of the epistemological points indicated above. Second, not all 'exchange' is a case of intercultural philosophizing – and I would say that the mere presence of concepts and terms from one tradition in another is not sufficient evidence of a genuine encounter. (By way of example, consider those cases where a philosophical text from one culture seems to be simply that which occasions a philosophical insight or practice or discussion in another. Here, ideas are not really exchanged, but simply have a presence.)

Conclusion

In light of the preceding comments in this paper, what can we say concerning the project of intercultural philosophy and, more broadly, concerning intercultural communication about deep issues of culture, belief, value, and tradition?

We should have confidence in the project of an intercultural philosophy. If, as some hold, that philosophy is rooted in, and inseparable from culture – i. e. , if it cannot genuinely 'emigrate' beyond its culture of origin – it is difficult to see how philosophies can be compared or even regarded as incompatible.

We should also have confidence that skepticism and perspectivism do not undermine the project. From the examples and instances enumerated above, there is little doubt that there has been contact and migration of ideas on culture, value, philosophy, and religion. In different ways, at different times, and to lesser and greater degrees, texts and traditions have been introduced into 'other' cultures (e. g. , as shown through the coining of new terms or the freeing of familiar terms from old meanings, and the development of new philosophies) .

This issue is not simply a matter of historical interest.

Understanding the nature and conditions of intercultural philosophy bears on how, today, new ideas may be brought into contact with traditions from another culture – and give rise to new philosophies, or to lead to doing 'local' philosophy differently, or to lead to a return to sources, or to reaffirm local philosophies.

This also reminds us of the importance of being open to experience; that truth can be uncovered or more deeply understood, and that philosophy is truth-seeking and not just truth-transmitting.

Above all, the project of an intercultural philosophy is an example of, and a model for communication between and among Western and Asian cultures.

From the Imitation of Nature to a Meeting between Cultures

Wojciech Golubiewski[*]

Abstract: In my paper, I would like to elucidate some aspects of Thomas Aquinas's doctrine of the imitation of nature, as implicitly present in the teachings of Matteo Ricci. I intend to highlight especially those aspects of Aquinas's account of the imitation of nature that I find pertinent to a more thorough understanding of Ricci's paradigm of communication and meeting between the cultures.

Key words: imitation of nature Thomas Aquinas Matteo Ricci Western and Chinese cultures

In my paper, I would like to elucidate some aspects of Thomas Aquinas's doctrine of the imitation of nature, as implicitly present in the teachings of Matteo Ricci.

Firstly I will explain briefly what Aquinas's doctrine of the imitation of nature consists of, and why in my view it is pertinent for understanding the Ricci's method. Secondly I will illustrate how Matteo Ricci draws on the imita-

---

* Wojciech Golubiewski Ph. D. , Fv Jen Catholic University, Post-doctoral Fellow, Academia Catholica.

tion of nature in two sample texts of his masterpiece, *Tianzhu Shiyi* (天主实义, *the True Meaning of the Lord of Heaven*). Finally, I will aim to show how the doctrine of the imitation of nature has contributed to the meeting between Western and Chinese cultures, and how today communication between these cultures could benefit from this aspect of Ricci's paradigm today.

Thomas Aquinas and Matteo Ricci

Alasdair MacIntyre and Charles Taylor who in recent decades sought to respond to challenges of the contemporary Western secular culture, respectively pointed out the importance of Thomas Aquinas (MacIntyre) and Matteo Ricci (Taylor), as two historical figures able to integrate distant cultural and philosophical traditions. ① Although Taylor and MacIntyre differ in their approaches in various respects, Ricci's account cannot be utterly detached from that of Aquinas. The thoughtful openness of Aquinas and Ricci to varying and distant cultures, particularly evident in the case of Ricci's heritage shaped by the meeting with the Chinese "other", had a common source in their appreciation of the sapiential capacities of natural reason. ②

I believe that the doctrine of the imitation of nature can help us see why

---

① See *A Catholic Modernity? Charles Taylor's Marianist Award Lecture*, edited by L. Heft, New York/Oxford: Oxford University Press, 1999; Alasdair MacIntyre, *Three Rival Versions of Moral Enquiry: Encyclopedia, Genealogy, and Tradition*, Notre Dames: University of Notre Dames Press, 1990.

② For an account of how the Chinese "other" shaped the method and accomplishments of Matteo Ricci, see Nicolas Standaert, "Matteo Ricci Shaped by the Chinese" *in Scienza, ragione e fede*: il genio di p. Matteo Ricci, Claudio Giuliodori C. and Sani R. (eds.), Macerata: Edizioni Universita di Macerata, 2012, pp. 149 – 166; for an interpretation of the sapiential and natural reason in works of Matteo Ricci's, see also Antonio Olmi, "Ragione naturale e ragione sapienziale nel pensiero di P. Matteo Ricci" *in Scienza, ragione e fede*: il genio di p. Matteo Ricci, Claudio Giuliodori C. and Sani R. (eds.), Macerata: Edizioni Universita di Macerata, 2012, pp. 259 – 287; for some account of "Thomism" in the doctrine of Matteo Ricci, see Michele Ferrero, *The Cultivation of Virtue in Matteo Ricci's* "The True Meaning of the Lord of Heaven" (天主实义), Taipei: Fu Jen Catholic University Press, 2004, especially pp. 150 – 151; 161 – 176.

both authors' rigorous respect for natural reason did not impede but rather helped them assume various elements of other cultures into their own philosophical accounts. It may also serve as a promising tool of communication between distant cultures in spite of the reservations raised against the actuality of this concept. ①

Imitation of nature-more than a copy

The history of the idea of imitation (mimesis) is probably as long as the history of Western philosophy. It should be made clear however, that neither the Aristotelian nor the Neo-Platonist account, both of which Aquinas assumes and somehow refines in his own doctrine of the imitation of nature, entail a mere copying of physical nature. In Aquinas's view the imitation of nature is certainly not a simple mimicry either. It rather implies following certain teleological patterns of sensible nature (Aristotle), manifest in various modes of its mimetic semblance to the very first principle of the cosmos (Plotinus). ② Stephen Halliwell in his book *The Aesthetics of Mimesis* makes an important observation regarding Neo-Platonist defense of the mimetic character of art:

---

① Stephen Halliwell pertinently observes that some authors consider the very concept of mimesis, close to that of imitation, a relic of a past classical period: "In an age when talk of representation has become increasingly subject to both ideological and epistemological suspicion, mimesis is, for many philosophers and critics, little more than a broken column surviving from a long-dilapidated classical edifice, a sadly obsolete relic of former certainties" in Stephen Halliwell, *The Aesthetics of Mimesis*: *Ancient Texts and Modern Problems*, Princeton/Oxford: Princeton University Press, 2002, 344.

② Ibid. , 153; 314; cf. Thomas Aquinas, *Sententia libri Politicorum* pr. 1. : Sicut philosophus docet in secundo physicorum, ars imitatur naturam. Cuius ratio est, quia sicut se habent principia adinvicem, ita proportionabiliter se habent operationes et effectus. Principium autem eorum quae secundum artem fiunt est intellectus humanus, qui secundum similitudinem quamdam derivatur ab intellectu divino, qui est principium rerum naturalium. Unde necesse est, quod et operationes artis imitentur operationes naturae; et ea quae sunt secundum artem, imitentur ea quae sunt in natura.

Plotinus brings together three points in compound defense of the mimetic arts against the implied slur that they are mere semblances or simulacra of mimetic nature: one, that mimesis itself is a pervasive principle of reality (so that to be mimetic is not per se to fall away from the real); two, that art can reach beyond the appearances to the underlying principles of nature (and in that respect emulate the mimetic activity of nature itself); three, that art can enhance or improve on the beauty of nature. ①

I think that this account of Plotinus' understanding of mimetic arts is close to Aquinas's understanding of the mimetic character of human culture in general. Aquinas's doctrine of the imitation of nature in this sense includes moral and political aspects of human culture, and consists of enhancing the beauty and goodness of human virtuous life. The imitation of nature constitutes a congruence of culture with the all-pervasive wisdom somehow common to the whole universe, and manifest in natural movement and changes of sensible things. I will now proceed to explain more in detail some aspects of what I understand by Aquinas's doctrine of the imitation of nature. ②

Aquinas's doctrine of the imitation of nature

In light of Aquinas's doctrine of the imitation of nature, all humans share some kind of wisdom, which can be considered natural in three ways. Firstly, wisdom is natural according to its very metaphysical aspect, inasmuch as it applies to a quite universal range of things, from inanimate things of nature entirely immersed in matter, to purely spiritual immaterial

---

① Halliwell, op. cit., 317.

② I give a more thorough account and textual analysis of Aquinas's doctrine of the imitation of nature with respect to moral aspects of human action in my paper on the Imitation of Nature and the Way of Moral Wisdom (CRVP, Shanghai, 2013).

natures. ① The former are determined in the ways of attaining their natural ends through the material modes of their natures, while the latter attain their proper ends by free acts of intellect and will. ② The latter need therefore to share and conform with the natural wisdom through their intellects while the former spontaneously follow the wisdom as if it was instilled in their natures inclining them to their due ends. ③

In another sense the wisdom is natural, inasmuch as it is manifest and accessible to human natural reason through the intelligible order of natural movements and changes of sensible things. ④ This is an epistemological aspect of natural wisdom. Due to the weakness of human intellect it needs to "feed on" natures of sensible things to acquire any knowledge. ⑤ Human acts remain within the scope of natural wisdom as long as the human intellect follows the sapiential lights, whose terms reason gathers from the sensible things, the blind "bearers" of wisdom instilled in their natures. ⑥ All human acts ordered to and directed by reason are congruent with the natural ways of wisdom inasmuch as they are in harmony with the intelligible order manifest in unimpeded

---

① Cf. Thomas Aquimas, *Summa Theologiae* I q. 60 a. 5.

② On universal aspects of practical wisdom applying to all natures and by imitation of nature to the order of human agency, see esp. Stephen L. Brock, "The Primacy of the Common Good and the Foundations of Natural Law in St. Thomas," in *Ressourcement Thomism*, Hütter, R. and Levering, M. [eds.], Washington, D. C: The Catholic University of America Press, 2010, 234–255.

③ Cf. Thomas Aquinas, *Summa contra Gentiles* lib. 3 cap. 24 n. 4. : operationes naturae inveniuntur ordinate procedere ad finem, sicut operationes sapientis; idem, *Summa Theologiae* I q. 103 a. 1 ad 1. : aliquid movetur vel peratur propter finem dupliciter. Uno modo, sicut agens seipsum in finem, ut homo et aliae creaturae rationales, et talium est cognoscere rationem finis, et eorum quae sunt ad finem. Aliquid autem dicitur moveri vel operari propter finem, quasi ab alio actum vel directum in finem, sicut sagitta movetur ad signum directa a sagittante, qui cognoscit finem, non autem sagitta.

④ E. g. ibid. , II – II q. 26 a. 6 co. Videmus autem in naturalibus quod inclinatio naturalis proportionatur actui vel motui qui convenit naturae uniuscuiusque, sicut terra habet maiorem inclinationem gravitatis quam aqua, quia competit ei esse sub aqua.

⑤ Ibid. , I q. 55 a. 2 co. : inferiores substantiae intellectivae, scilicet animae humanae, habent potentiam intellectivam non completam naturaliter; sed completur in eis successive, per hoc quod accipiunt species intelligibiles a rebus.

⑥ Cf. Lawrence Dewan, O. P. , *Wisdom, Law, and Virtue. Essays in Thomistic Ethics*, New York: Fordham University Press, 2008, 199–212.

spontaneous movement of sensible natures.

Finally, wisdom is natural with respect to properly human free actions, through the natural seeds of intellectual and moral virtues instilled in reason, which are a sort of application of natural wisdom to the specific human nature of rational animal. The dependence on the natural seeds of virtues entails a specifically human share in the natural wisdom, which needs to be enhanced towards the beauty of virtuous human life by free human acts.

All three senses of natural wisdom: metaphysical, epistemological, and concerning properly human actions are therefore constitutive of a virtuous humanity. A wise man, either pondering on the highest causes of nature (*sapientia simipliciter*), or in a qualified sense of wisdom directing human actions to the good of human life (*sapientia viro*), shares some greater wisdom, which constitutes things in their natures and directs them to their proper operations congruent with these natures. ①

For Aquinas, a virtuous way of human being imitates nature by intellectual and moral virtues' congruence with natural wisdom and its order manifest in spontaneous operations of sensible things. This congruence implies an application of the universal patterns of natural wisdom shaping myriads of natural things' movements and changes to the properly human ways of thought and action ordered to reason.

Thus, in Aquinas's view there are some rules of the natural wisdom shaping the beauty and harmony of things, which become immediately known as soon as human intellect is "nourished" by the intelligibility of sensible things' natures. ② Inasmuch as they concern human actions Aquinas calls them the

---

① Cfr. Thomas Aquinas, *Summa contra Gentiles* lib. 1 cap. 1 n. 3. ; *Summa Theologiae* II – II q. 47 a. 2 ad 1; *Commentaria in octo libros Physicorum Aristotelis* II, lect. 4, n. 171; lect. 14, n. 268. The citations of Aquinas's commentaries on Aristotle's *Physics* and *Metaphysics*, as well as of *Summa contra Gentiles* follow the subdivisions of Marietti's editions.

② Cf. Idem, *Summa Theologiae* I – II q. 51 a. 1 co.

common principles of natural law. ① Some secondary rules of natural wisdom of human actions may require deeper intellectual insight into the nature of things, which is proper for the wise. ② Accordingly, the principles of human intellect, also the practical ones, require the attuning of reason with the natural wisdom manifest in the movements and changes of sensible things.

Human natural reason is right and operates well according to its principles, in so far as it imitates nature, or more precisely in so far as it imitates the wisdom, which shapes also the intelligible principles of sensible nature. ③ For Aquinas, the principles of human intellect on which all properly human acts depend, are therefore applications of the all-pervasive wisdom, whose intelligible effects are manifest through the natural operations of sensible things. Abandoning the principles of intellect entails detachment from the harmony of nature and leaving the scope of natural wisdom manifest through the movement and changes of things.

Natural reason and the imitation of nature
in the doctrine of Matteo Ricci

The rule of imitation of nature seems to be relevant not only for Aquinas but also for Matteo Ricci. So too, Matteo Ricci does not hesitate to endorse the principles of intellect as having validity over any kind of opinion:

Man, then transcends all other creatures since he is endowed with a spiritual soul within, and the ability to observe the principles of things without. By examining the outcome of things he is able to know their origins, and by observing their existence he can know that by which they

---

① Cf. Ibid. , q. 93 a. 2 co. ; q. 94 a. 4 co.
② Cf. Ibid. , q. 100 a. 1 co.
③ Cf. Idem, *Sententia libri Politicorum* pr. 1.

exist. Thus, without leaving this world of toil, he can devote himself to the cultivation of the Way and prepare himself for an eternity of peace and joy following his death. That which is brought to light by the intellect cannot forcibly be made to comply with that which is untrue. Everything which reason shows to be true I must acknowledge as true, and everything which reason shows to be false I must acknowledge as false. Reason stands in relation to a man as the sun to the world, shedding its light everywhere. To abandon the principles affirmed by the intellect and to comply with the opinion of others is like shutting out the light of the sun and searching for an object with the lantern. [①]

It seems that in Ricci's view, the principles affirmed by the intellect bring into light and verify every opinion formed within any cultural context whatsoever. Inasmuch as principles of human intellect share the natural wisdom they can verify any cultural proposal. I think that both Aquinas and Ricci would agree that the seeds of human virtues, which may be cultivated in various ways and shape different cultures, belong firstly to the natural wisdom manifest in operations of sensible things, congruent with the very nature of humanity, and formed by a wisdom greater than merely human wisdom. Just as seeds of human virtues naturally underpin the unique personality of someone acquiring mature virtuous dispositions through education and his own free actions, so every culture may imitate wisdom manifest in nature in various ways, by developing from the common natural seeds of humanity and

---

① 人则超拔万类，内禀神灵，外睹物理，察其末而知其本，视其固然而知其所以然，故能不辞今世之苦劳，以专精修道，图身后万世之安乐也。灵才所显，不能强之以殉夫不真者。凡理所真是，我不能不以为真是；理所伪诞，不能不以为伪诞。斯于人身，犹太阳于世间，普遍光明。舍灵才所是之理，而殉他人之所传，无异乎寻觅物，方遮日光而持灯烛也。The original text and the translations after Matteo Ricci, S. J., *The True Meaning of the Lord of Heaven* (*T'ien-chu Shih-i*), Translated with Introduction and Notes by Douglas Lancashire and Peter Hu Kuo-chen, S. J.; a Chinese English Edition edited by Edward J. Malatesta, S. J., St. Louis/Taipei: The Institute of Jesuit Sources, 1985, nn. 24 – 25, pp. 68 – 69.

gradually maturing within and shaping the context of each specific cultural heritage.

The sapiential lights of human intellect congruent with natural wisdom open therefore a vast horizon of possible personal and cultural development, not limited to one particular mode of virtuous cultivation. The seeds of natural wisdom instilled in the human nature underpin wisdom of every culture, but ways of their mimetic cultivation are manifold, and cannot be narrowed to one cultural manifestation only.

Consequently, what different cultures seem to have in common, are the seeds of humanity congruent with and somehow received from a higher wisdom through its self-manifestation in natures' of sensible things. Ways of cultivation of wisdom vary among peoples and cultures, but their "natural strength", in light of Aquinas's account, seems to lie in the imitation of nature, by which they grow and enhance the harmony with natural seeds of virtuous humanity gathered from the natural wisdom manifest in sensible nature.

The common seeds of virtuous humanity congruent with the natural wisdom manifest in harmony of movement and changes of nature (tangible and visible things of basic human experience) enable communication between great cultures, which never remain utterly incommensurable. Moreover, cultures that derive from natural wisdom may somehow share with one another and verify one another in their different ways of cultivation of natural wisdom. In this way Matteo Ricci seems to be convinced that the Chinese, especially the Confucian tradition, as well as the heritage of the Western classical and medieval thought, share the same source of wisdom, conveyed and expressed through different cultural contexts and languages. In my view therefore, his recognition of the treasures of the Chinese culture is based on the conviction that natural wisdom is greater than any of its particular cultural expressions.

I will now address the imitation of nature in the context of natural theology firstly to Aquinas and then to Matteo Ricci.

Natural theology of the imitation of nature in
Thomas Aquinas and Matteo Ricci

According to Aquinas, following rather closely Aristotle's Physics, spontaneous movements of visible and tangible natural things, insofar as they are congruent with their material natures, bear a trace of harmony and goodness as if shaped by an Intelligence. [1] For Aquinas, this natural harmony or congruence, by which sensible things spontaneously move according to their intrinsic virtuous dispositions, resemble the effects of art. Works of art become perfect and complete when they fulfill the specific purpose for which they were produced. [2] Moreover, in Aquinas's view, sensible things are not only like the works of art, but they actually are works of divine art, by which each thing naturally moves to its proper end. [3] Aquinas gives therefore an explanation of the intelligible order of nature, which goes somewhat further than the explanation of Aristotle. The imitation of nature not only consists in the congruence of human actions with the intelligible order manifest in the natural agency of sensible things, it amounts to the imitation of the very source of natural order: the divine mind. [4] In this sense Aquinas gets closer to the

---

[1] Thomas Aquinas, *Commentaria in octo libros Physicorum Aristotelis*, II, lect. 4, n. 171: res naturales imitabiles sunt per artem, quia ab aliquo principio intellectivo tota natura ordinatur ad finem suum, ut sic opus naturae videatur esse opus intelligentiae, dum per determinata media ad certos fines procedit: quod etiam in operando ars imitatur.

[2] Idem, *Summa Theologiae* I q. 91 a. 3 co.: Quilibet autem artifex intendit suo operi dispositionem optimam inducere, non simpliciter, sed per comparationem ad finem. Et si talis dispositio habet secum adiunctum aliquem defectum, artifex non curat. Sicut artifex qui facit serram ad secandum, facit eam ex ferro, ut sit idonea ad secandum; nec curat eam facere ex vitro, quae est pulchrior materia, quia talis pulchritudo esset impedimentum finis. Sic igitur Deus unicuique rei naturali dedit optimam dispositionem, non quidem simpliciter, sed secundum ordinem ad proprium finem.

[3] Idem, *Commentaria in octo libros Physicorum Aristotelis*, lect. 14, n. 268: natura nihil est aliud quam ratio cuiusdam artis, scilicet divinae, indita rebus, qua ipsae res moventur ad finem determinatum.

[4] Brock, op. cit., 242.

Neo-Platonist account of the imitation of nature as imitation of the one principle of the cosmos. ① Aquinas's account of the imitation of nature as imitation
of the divine mind is not, however, an immediate and self-evident consequence of the human natural knowledge of sensible things. ② It is a result of
his refined natural theology, which is also one of the main components of
Ricci's *True Meaning of the Lord of Heaven.* ③ The source of movement and
rest belongs intrinsically to each thing through its sensible nature, but Aquinas provides an ultimate metaphysical account of sensible nature as an effect
of divine generation by causality of art. ④ Since, as Aquinas states, all works
of art reveal somehow the mind of the artist, the intelligible order of nature
can be conceived as a remote trace of the divine wisdom itself. ⑤ Imitation of
nature becomes therefore like an apprenticeship under a greater master, who
reveals effects of his own art in the natural wisdom manifest to the mind of the
apprentice through the natural operations of sensible things. ⑥ Sensible nature
plays therefore a rudimentary educative role for the human mind, and resem-
bles somehow the educative role of mimetic arts in general. In light of

---

① Halliwell, op. cit., 313 – 323.

② Thomas Aquinas, *Summa Theologiae* I q. 1 a. 1 co.: veritas de Deo, per rationem investiga-
ta, a paucis, et per longum tempus, et cum admixtione multorum errorum, homini proveniret.

③ Cf. Ibid. q. 2 a. 3 co.; Nicolas Standaert explains in the *Handbook of Christianity in China*
that Ricci's 天主实义 "is a typical example of the use of natural theology as a way to approach Chinese
literati." (Nicolas Standaert, *Handbook of Christianity in China.* T. 1. Boston: Brill, 2001, 612).
Natural theology, as Standaert puts it, was considered at Ricci's time "the knowledge that humans can
have of the existence and nature of God by means of reason" (ibid. 608 – 609).

④ Thomas Aquinas, *Sententia super Metaphysicam*, VII, lect. 6, n. 1381.

⑤ Idem, *De operationibus occultis naturae*: invenitur in naturae operibus quod determinatis vi-
is ad determinatos fines ordine et modo congruissimo procedunt, sicut et ea quae fiunt ab arte: ita
quod totum opus naturae videtur esse opus cuiusdam sapientis, propter quod natura dicitur sagaciter
operari.

⑥ Cf. idem, *Sententia libri Politicorum* pr. 1: Si enim aliquis instructor alicuius artis opus artis
efficeret; oporteret discipulum, qui ab eo artem suscepisset, ad opus illius attendere, ut ad eius similitudinem et ipse operaretur. Et ideo intellectus humanus ad quem intelligibile lumen ab intellectu divino derivatur, necesse habet in his quae facit informari ex inspectione eorum quae sunt naturaliter fac-
ta, ut similiter operetur.

Aquinas's texts, especially of the *Summa Theologica*, human art and reason are best when they imitate nature, because in this way they imitate also the very source of all natural wisdom manifest in sensible nature.

There are three texts, one of Aquinas and two of Matteo Ricci, which in my view show that the doctrine of the imitation of nature is present also in the writings of Matteo Ricci. The first text comes from an Aquinas's opusculum, *On Kingship*, *to the King of Cyprus* (*De regno ad regem Cypri*), a pedagogical and moral work addressed to a prince. [1] Aquinas writes to him:

> Whatever is in accord with nature is best, for in all things nature does what is best. Now, every natural governance is governance by one. In the multitude of bodily members there is one which is the principal mover, namely, the heart; and among the powers of the soul one power presides as chief, namely, the reason. Among bees there is one 'king bee' and in the whole universe there is One God, Maker and Ruler of all things. And there is a reason for this. Every multitude is derived from unity. Wherefore, if artificial things are an imitation of natural things (ea quae sunt secundum artem, imitantur ea quae sunt secundum naturam) and a work of art is better according as it attains a closer likeness to what is in nature, it follows that it is best for a human multitude to be ruled by one person. [2]

---

[1] Jean-Pierre Torrell O. P. , *Saint Thomas Aquinas*, vol. 1. , *The Person and His Work*, rev. edition; transl. by R. Royal, Washington D. C. : Catholic University Press, 2005, 350.

[2] Thomas Aquinas, *De regno ad regem Cypri*, lib. 1 cap. 3 co. : Adhuc: ea, quae sunt ad naturam, optime se habent: in singulis enim operatur natura, quod optimum est. Omne autem naturale regimen ab uno est. In membrorum enim multitudine unum est quod omnia movet, scilicet cor; et in partibus animae una vis principaliter praesidet, scilicet ratio. Est etiam apibus unus rex, et in toto universo unus Deus factor omnium et rector. Et hoc rationabiliter. Omnis enim multitudo derivatur ab uno. Quare si ea quae sunt secundum artem, imitantur ea quae sunt secundum naturam, et tanto magis opus artis est melius, quanto magis assequitur similitudinem eius quod est in natura, necesse est quod in humana multitudine optimum sit quod per unum regatur.

In light of the preceding section of this paper, it could be said that whatever nature does, it follows and manifests some kind of natural wisdom directing things to what is best for each. Since the natural wisdom makes things do what is their best, whatever closely follows the natural wisdom manifest in nature is also the best (optimum). One of the practical principles of that natural wisdom, which Aquinas distinguishes here, is "governance by one" (regimen ab uno). Aquinas illustrates this natural rule of wisdom on examples concerning various multitudes of members deriving somehow from one. The examples he gives cover a metaphysical range of different multitudes, the heart among members of a living body, reason as principal among the parts of human soul, the king of bees among the bees, and one God as maker and ruler of the universe. All these examples are analogical applications of the same metaphysical rule of nature that every multitude derives from one (omnis multitudo derivatur ab uno). The way that reason arrives at this rule is bottom-up rather than top-down. In other words, although Aquinas mentions here the uniqueness of the divine government over the whole universe, he gives it as an example of application of a general metaphysical rule to which, according to him, human natural reason can arrive through knowledge of sensible natures. Metaphysical understanding of nature allows Aquinas to consider the "governance by one" to be a rule of natural wisdom. In his letter to the King of Cyprus Aquinas suggests therefore that the rule of natural wisdom applies also to the political science as a kind of art, which is best when it imitates nature, by drawing on the rule of "government by one". The more the kingship of the King imitates the natural rule of "government by one", Aquinas says, and the greater likeness to nature it attains, the better it becomes. That seems to be the best, which is congruent by imitation with the natural wisdom manifest in nature. The imitation of nature seems to entail here an application of the metaphysical order of nature to human affairs, which include political and therefore moral science as well. ①

I want to show now some parallels between Aquinas's doctrine of the imitation of nature in the above passage of *De Regno*, and the very beginning of Matteo Ricci's *the True Meaning of the Lord of Heaven*. In the opening text of 天主实义 (*Tianzhu Shiyi*) Mateo Ricci states:

> All doctrines about making the whole world peaceful and governing a country rightly are focused on the principle of uniqueness (or oneness). Therefore, worthies and sages have always advised the ministers to be loyal, that is, not to have a second [lord in their mind]. Among the Five Human Relationships the most important is that regarding the king, and the first of the Three Bonds in Human Relations is that between the king and the minister. A just man must understand this and act accordingly. ②

Here Matteo Ricci strongly affirms the principle of oneness as a guarantee of peaceful government, referring to the authority of "all doctrines" and of "worthies and sages". He does not seem to give any immediate "rational" or "natural" argument for this due way of government, at least not at this point. Instead, he immediately shows the principle of oneness in light of the Confucian doctrine of Five Human Relationships and of the Three Bonds. What seems striking here is that Ricci explains the optimal rule of

---

① Cf. Thomas Aquinas, *Sententia libri Politicorum*, pr. 6. : Rursumque cum ratio quaedam operetur per modum factionis operatione in exteriorem materiam transeunte, quod proprie ad artes pertinet, quae mechanicae vocantur, utpote fabrilis et navifactiva et similes: quaedam vero operetur per modum actionis operatione manente in eo qui operatur, sicut est consiliari, eligere, velle et hujusmodi quae ad moralem scientiam pertinent: manifestum est politicam scientiam, quae de hominum considerat ordinatione, non contineri sub factivis scientiis, quae sunt artes mechanicae, sed sub activis quae sunt scientiae morales.

② 平治庸理，唯竟于一，故圣贤劝臣以忠。忠也者，无二之谓也。五伦甲乎君，君臣为三纲之首，夫正义之士此明此行。(n. 1, pp. 56 - 57).

"government by one", as an aspect of the traditional Chinese political and moral wisdom. Only after acknowledging this, Ricci draws some further theological conclusions from his argument, saying that as there is one lord uniting one country so there is also one lord uniting heaven and earth. ①

I think that Ricci applies here the principle of oneness (of "government by one"), which in light of Aquinas's doctrine of the imitation of nature is one of the rules of natural wisdom in political and moral science. However, Ricci presents this principle as expressed in a unique way of genuine cultivation of natural wisdom of the Chinese culture. He further aims to show that some insights of natural theology, to which the Western philosophical tradition arrives in its own terms of wisdom, are in perfect harmony with the Chinese way of cultivation of the same natural wisdom. Ricci does not therefore develop theological aspects of his doctrine in terms of the Western philosophy only. He is rather at pains to point out that natural wisdom, conceived by him in terms of the Western philosophical tradition, underpins the Chinese Way of its cultivation. I think therefore that Ricci steps back from the Western formulation of the metaphysical wisdom discovered in the movement and changes of natural things, to what he considers the very phenomenal manifestations of that wisdom both in nature and in mimetic arts drawing on the patterns of nature, as the basic data of every culture's harmonious imitation of nature in congruence with its natural wisdom. He then applies this method in formulations of his natural theology.

Further, the things in this world are exceedingly numerous, and if there were no supreme lord to keep and maintain order among them, they would inevitably disperse and be destroyed. It is like a musical performance: even though the musicians might wish to make music, with-

---

① See ibid. n. 3: 国统以一, 天地有二主乎? 故乾坤之原、造化之宗, 君子不可不识而仰思焉。

out a maestro, there would be no music. Therefore, each family has but one head, and each nation has but one sovereign. Should there be two a nation will find itself in a state of anarchy. A man has only one body; a body has only one head. If it had two heads the man would be a freak. We know therefore, that although there are many kinds of spiritual beings in the universe, there is only one Lord of Heaven who is the first creator of heaven and earth, mankind and all phenomena and who constantly controls and sustains them. What room is there for doubt?[1]

Ricci seems therefore to justify the wisdom of Chinese culture, or to discuss some of its aspects, by direct reference to the phenomena of natural things constitutive of the Western (Aquinas's) arriving at natural wisdom, rather than to the Western philosophical formulations of that wisdom. Clearly, he does not entirely abandon these Western formulations of natural wisdom, because they help him to bring forward the meaning of natural phenomena, which he presents as constitutive also of the Chinese Way of wisdom.

Conclusions

I think that for Ricci, as well as for Aquinas, the imitation of nature manifesting a higher wisdom as source of the harmony of movement and changes of things might have served as a kind of bridge between quite distant cultures. Metaphysical reflection on natural wisdom may still help to find points of congruence between the Chinese and Western cultures, especially considered in their classical pre-modern periods, seen as ways of cultivation of natural wisdom by imitation of nature. Consequently, a rigorous metaphysical account

---

① Ibid. n. 50, pp. 88 – 89: 且天下之物，极多极盛，苟无一尊，维持调护，不免散坏：如作乐大成，苟无太师集众小成，完音亦几绝响。是故一家止有一长，一国止有一君，有二，则国家乱矣；一人止有一身，一身止有一首；有二，则怪异甚矣。吾因是知乾坤之内，虽有鬼神多品，独有一天主始制作天、地、人、物，而时主宰存安之。子何疑乎？

of nature, taking into consideration Aquinas's and Ricci's interpretations of natural theology, could be a "natural ally" in mutual understanding between the two cultures.

Aquinas admits that not only virtue, but also grace imitates nature, since they all derive from the same source of divine wisdom. [1] One can rightly reflect upon the intelligibility of divine action by grace, and about virtue disposed to a good action, in so far as one's own reason also imitates operations of nature, in congruence with natural wisdom. In the accounts of both Aquinas and Ricci, natural reason is neither constrained by the material modes of nature, nor limited to the context of one particular cultural heritage. The doctrine of the imitation of nature by human reason opens it to various ways of cultivation of natural wisdom and to possible fruitful dialogue between different cultures, in so far as they share the common seeds of wisdom and virtuous humanity. In this sense the doctrine of the imitation of nature of Thomas Aquinas might have been an important factor in the so-called "method of Matteo Ricci" in his approach to the meeting between cultures.

The doctrine of the imitation of nature could become a source of common (congruent) theology of East and West insofar as the intelligible dynamics of nature, interpreted by Western or Chinese culture, render the divine action of grace intelligible within the very different cultural contexts. The heritage of Aquinas and Ricci might encourage the development of properly Chinese theology as a unique cultural expression of the natural wisdom harmonious with the Heavenly Dao, of which all things and cultures are somehow but imitations.

---

[1] Thomas Aquinas, *Summa Theologiae* II – II q. 31 a. 3 co. : gratia et virtus imitantur naturae ordinem, qui est exspace divina sapientia institutus.

Lost in Translation?

Peter Jonkers [*]

Abstract: Translating sacred scriptures is not only a praxis that is crucial for the fruitful, i. e. non-distorted and unbiased dialogue between different religious traditions, but also raises some fundamental theoretical questions when it comes to translating the sacred texts of the religious other or understanding her ideas correctly. This paper focuses in particular on the question what a hermeneutic understanding of the religious other and her sacred scriptures presupposes and, more importantly, what this implies for the dialogue between various religious and secular traditions. In order to answer this question the second section opposes a contextualist and a hermeneutic view on translation and understanding, as exemplified by the philosophies of Richard Rorty and Jürgen Habermas respectively. I will argue that the contextualist view leads to an impasse, since it reduces intercultural understanding and dialogue to assimilating the other in the light of one's own standards. Habermas's hermeneutic view on translating the sacred texts of other religions raises a fundamental problem too, since it presupposes that translation and understanding the religious other take place in a homogeneous universe of

* Peter Jonkers, Professor, Tilburg University, the Netherlands.

discourse. On the basis of these negative results I explore, in the third section, Paul Ricoeur's views on the problems of translation. He shows that translation can only aim at a supposed equivalence between the original text and its translation, not founded on a demonstrable identity of meaning. Moreover, this view is not only paradigmatic for translation in the narrow sense, but also for a hermeneutic understanding of the religious other. This leads to the idea of linguistic hospitality, which can also serve as a model for interreligious dialogue.

Key Words: Translation   Hermeneutic Understanding   Dialogue

1. Introduction

While preparing my paper for this conference on translation, ① the film ' Lost in Translation ' immediately came to mind. ② The film shows two Ameri-

---

① This paper was presented at a conference on "Hermeneutic Understanding of Translation of Early Buddhist and Christian Scriptures: Theories and Praxis", organized by Wuhan University on July 7 - 8, 2016.

② Sofia Coppola's film *Lost in Translation*, released in 2003 tells the story of Bob, an aging American movie star, arriving in Tokyo to film an advertisement for whisky. Charlotte, a young college graduate, is left in her hotel room by her husband, a celebrity photographer on assignment in Tokyo. She is unsure of her future with her husband, feeling detached from his lifestyle and dispassionate about their relationship. Bob's own 25 - year marriage is tired as he goes through a midlife crisis. Each day Bob and Charlotte encounter each other in the hotel, and finally meet at the hotel bar one night when neither can sleep. Eventually Charlotte invites Bob to meet with some local friends of hers. The two bond through a memorable night in Tokyo, welcomed without prejudice by Charlotte's friends and experiencing Japanese nightlife and culture. In the days that follow, Bob and Charlotte's platonic relationship develops as they spend more time together. One night, each unable to sleep, the two share an intimate conversation about Charlotte's personal troubles and Bob's married life. On the penultimate night of his stay, Bob sleeps with the hotel bar's female jazz singer. The next morning Charlotte arrives at his room to invite him for lunch and overhears the woman in his room, leading to an argument over lunch. Later that night, during a fire alarm at the hotel, Bob and Charlotte reconcile and express how they will miss each other as they make a final visit to the hotel bar. The following morning, Bob is set to return to the United States. He tells Charlotte goodbye at the hotel lobby and watches her walk back to the elevator. In a taxi to the airport, Bob sees Charlotte on a crowded street. He gets out, embraces the tearful Charlotte and whispers something in her ear. The two share a kiss, say goodbye and Bob departs.

cans, who are in Tokyo for professional reasons. In the course of their stay, they feel more and more 'lost in translation', not only because the meaning and detail of the communication is lost in the translation from Japanese into English and vice versa, but also because they feel lost in the Japanese culture, which is completely alien to them. Finally yet importantly, although the two main characters try hard to communicate with each other, they feel lost in translation as well, and this because of their difference in age and, hence, their stage of life. Thus, the film shows that translation and, by extension, understanding are essential, because they are the only ways for us to communicate with each other, but, at the same time, that they seem to be impossible. This is not only the case when people speak two completely different languages, but also when they are confronted with socio-cultural strangeness, even within their own linguistic community. Apparently, an unbridgeable rift separates our language and cultural world from that of the other. And yet, again, everyone knows that there *is* translation and understanding of the other: although we live in a world characterized by linguistic and cultural diversity, a world 'after Babel', ① we never give up trying to find our way in the labyrinth of meanings, however deficient and clumsy the result of our translations and understanding may turn out to be.

These observations hint at the general theme of this paper. It does not so much intend to discuss the specific theories and praxis that guide the translation of early Buddhist and Christian scriptures, but rather aims at discussing an underlying problem, namely to examine 'the paradigm of translation'②, in other words the rules that govern the practices of translating and understanding the language and culture of the other. My approach rests on the assumption that translation from one linguistic community into another is closely

---

① George Steiner, *After Babel. Aspects of Language and Translation.* Oxford: Oxford University Press, 1975, p. 507.

② See: Paul Ricoeur, *On Translation.* Abingdon: Routledge, 2006, 11 – 29.

connected to understanding within the same linguistic community, because to understand is to translate. ① Hence, translating a text of from one linguistic community into another raises the same problems as understanding it within the same linguistic community.

This paper starts with a philosophical analysis of the opposed views of the impossibility and the factuality of translation and understanding, thereby making use of the discussion between Richard Rorty and Jürgen Habermas. The former stands for a radically contextualist approach, arguing that communicating with the linguistical and cultural other that goes beyond assimilating her, is impossible. The latter defends a hermeneutical approach, holding that a symmetric intercultural communication is possible if certain conditions are met. In the section thereafter, I will examine to what extent Paul Ricoeur's views on translation help us to take this discussion a step further. In essence, he holds a plea for linguistic hospitality, which can serve as a model for intercultural dialogue.

2. A contextualist versus a hermeneutic idea of translation

Let us first return to the above example in order to examine the consequences of Richard Rorty's radical contextualism for our translation and understanding of the cultural (and religious) other. The main reason why the protagonists of the film feel lost in translation is that they lead completely different lives and coincidentally meet in a country, whose language and culture they do not understand at all. What they are lacking is a shared universe of discourse that would enable them to understand the linguistical and cultural other. From a Rortyan perspective, the film illustrates our postmodern condition, in particular our problems to deal with the effects of linguistic and socio-cultural diversity in a globalized world. Modernity still believed that all

---

① Ricoeur, *On Translation*, 24.

different cultures and languages referred to or were grounded in a common
meta-vocabulary, namely (scientific) reason as the universal language that
could depict reality objectively. From a modern perspective, this meta-vocabulary could serve as a common ground for the translation and the understanding of all specific vocabularies. However, in our postmodern condition, this
faith in a common meta-vocabulary has lost its plausibility. Nowadays, the
dominant conviction is that there is only a wide variety of individual linguistic
and cultural vocabularies, spoken by just as many local communities, which
are incommensurable with regard to each other. Hence, if an outsider wants
to translate or understand the vocabularies of the (religious) other correctly,
she is doomed to fail, since speaking and understanding has become a parochial matter, confined to the persons or local communities sharing a specific
vocabulary. Every communication with the other that goes beyond the superficial 'airport communication' runs up against a brick wall. All cultures are
nothing but contingent social constructions, available only on the local market, so that understanding the linguistical or cultural other in her own right is
impossible.

However, such a radical linguistic and cultural perspectivism would,
according to Rorty, create a pathological feeling of irony among the users of
this or that vocabulary, since, if every vocabulary is contingent, people
would be in permanent doubt about whether another vocabulary might be more
attractive than their own. ①In order to avoid such a pathology he holds that we
are entitled on psychological, rather than rational grounds, to privilege the
interpretative horizon of our own linguistic community. This view inevitably
leads to a kind of ethnocentrism, according to which "there is nothing to be

---

① Richard Rorty, *Contingency, Irony, Solidarity*. Cambridge: Cambridge University Press,
1989, 73f. I discussed this aspect of Rorty's position in more detail in: Peter Jonkers, Contingent Religions, Contingent Truths? In: D. M. Grube and P. Jonkers (ed.), *Religions Challenged by Contingency. Theological and Philosophical Perspectives to the Problem of Contingency*. (Star-series) Leiden:
Brill, 2008, 169f.

said about either truth or rationality apart from descriptions of the familiar procedures of justification which a given society-*ours* -uses in one or another area
of enquiry. "① In other words, instead of trying to engage in a process of
proper translating and understanding the linguistic and cultural other, people
are entitled to devote themselves to the vocabulary with which they are familiar, declaring that there are limits to what they can take seriously. ②The overall conclusion is that, from this radically contextualist perspective, translation and understanding of the linguistic, cultural, and religious other are impossible, so that every attempt to intercultural and interreligious understanding and dialogue results in assimilating the other in the light of our own standards.

Jürgen Habermas, by contrast, takes a hermeneutic perspective on
translation and intercultural understanding by asking for the meaning of these
practices, starting from their factuality. He has set himself the task to understand the underlying normative rules that guide all forms of human interaction
and make it fruitful and fair. In particular, he examines the conditions that
have to be fulfilled in order to interact with the linguistic, cultural, and religious other in a symmetric way, so that the pitfall of an assimilation of the
other's ideas and behaviors by the self is averted. His position on this matter
can be summarized as follows: "The unity of reason only remains perceptible
in the plurality of its voices—as the possibility in principle of passing from
one language into another—a passage that, no matter how occasional, is still
comprehensible. "③ This means that Habermas, just like Rorty, has given
up the modern idea that reason could serve as a universal meta-vocabulary,
the common point of reference and foundation of all individual vocabularies. In

---

① Richard Rorty, *Objectivity, Relativism and Truth*. Cambridge: Cambridge University Press,
1991, 23.

② Rorty, *Objectivity, Relativism and Truth*, 187f.

③ Jürgen Habermas, The Unity of Reason in the Diversity of Its Voices. In: Idem, *Postmeta-
physical Thinking*. Cambridge MA: MIT Press, 1992, 117.

our times, we only perceive a plurality of the voices of reason, not only in the shape of individual national languages, cultures, and religious traditions, but also in that of conflicting standards of rationality. However, in contrast to Rorty, Habermas believes in the possibility, however occasional it may be, of linguistic and cultural interaction, of passing from one language to another. Such an interaction is essentially a symmetric one, goes beyond reducing our understanding of what is alien to us to an assimilative incorporation into our own world and an interpretation of this strangeness by our own standards. Hence, the question arises how such a symmetric interaction can be comprehended.

Habermas criticizes what he calls Rorty's defeatist concept of reason and understanding: If "the reflexive activity of mind always remained caught in the grammatical limits of various particular worlds that were linguistically constituted, reason would necessarily disintegrate kaleidoscopically into a multiplicity of incommensurable embodiments."① For Habermas, such a conclusion runs counter to our experience that linguistic and cultural interaction really has the power of breaking open our familiar ideas and changing our common practices, thus enabling us to see things from the perspective of the other. Furthermore, the problematic consequence of Rorty's radical contextualism is that it is impossible to making a distinction between properly transferring the meaning of a text into a different language and manipulating this meaning ideologically, just like between a true and a distorted understanding of the other. In sum, Habermas asks: "Can we explain the possibility of the critique and self-critique of established practices of justification at all if we do not take the idea of the expansion of our interpretative horizon seriously *as an idea*, and if we do not connect this idea with the intersubjectivity of an agreement that allows precisely for the distinction between what is current 'for us'

---

① Habermas, The Unity of Reason, 134f.

and what is current 'for them'?"①

So, in contrast to Rorty, Habermas argues that one of the most fundamental normative rules for every interaction is that there is a *symmetrical* relationship between all participants in the dialogue. This means that, in a situation of profound disagreement, it is not only necessary for 'them' to try to
understand things from 'our' perspective, but also that 'we' try in the same
manner to grasp things from 'their' perspective. In other words, only if the
interaction is symmetric, it is possible to distinguish translation and interpretation from assimilation and appropriation. Ideally, this approach results in a
'merging of interpretative horizons' (Gadamer), which Habermas interprets
as "a convergence, steered through learning, of 'our' perspective *and*
'their' perspective—no matter whether 'they' or 'we' or both sides have to
reformulate established practices of justification to a greater or lesser extent. For learning itself belongs neither to us nor to them; both sides are
caught up in it in this same way. Even in the most difficult processes of reaching understanding, all parties appeal to the common reference point of a
possible consensus, even if this reference point is projected in each case from
within their own contexts. For, although they may be interpreted in various
ways and applied according to different criteria, concepts like truth, rationality, or justification play the *same* grammatical role in *every* linguistic community."②

In sum, symmetry in participant perspectives and the willingness to engage in mutual learning-processes are normative rules for translation, as well
as for intercultural and interreligious understanding. These rules allow Habermas to make the distinction between a good translation and a bad one, between understanding someone correctly and misunderstanding her, between
what is true and what we only hold to be true. Because these rules are inter-

---

① Habermas, The Unity of Reason, 137.
② Ibid., 138.

subjective or post-metaphysical, there is no need to have recourse to the fallacy of the objectivism of metaphysical truth, or to the fantasy of an ideal language that is context-free and appears in the singular. Especially in a situation of intercultural and interreligious dialogue, such a seemingly objective and ideal position is actually nothing else than privileging a Western perspective. The overall result is the concept of a situated reason: insofar as it is 'situated', this reason is dependent on the languages and cultures in which it expresses itself, but insofar as it is 'reason', it is a regulative idea that can orientate us when we criticize existing translations and intercultural understanding. ①

In my view, Habermas's approach offers a good explanation of the meaning of translation, as well as of intercultural and interreligious understanding, and defines some basic normative rules for their correct development, thus avoiding the impasse of Rorty's view. Nevertheless, I think that Habermas underestimates the problems of translation that arise in a situation, where there is no common reference point and, hence, no regulative idea of what a correct translation and a symmetric intercultural communication are. He assumes too easily that a merging of interpretative horizons is possible, which then can serve as the common basis of all translation and understanding. Indeed, he may be right in arguing that concepts like truth, rationality, or justification play the same grammatical role in every linguistic community, but this common basis is limited to the syntactical level and does not include the (semantic) meaning of these concepts in different linguistic and cultural contexts. Hence, the unity of reason is a formal concept and its regulative function is confined to the procedural rules that have to be followed to criticize existing translations fairly and to reach symmetric intercultural under-

---

① Habermas, The Unity of Reason, 139.

standing. ①Consequently, Habermas cannot explain how translation and understanding succeed in transposing the semantic substance of texts or other cultural contents in such a way that facilitate a mutual intercultural and interreligious learning process, especially when the linguistic, cultural, and religious differences are so great that there is no common interpretative framework. ②Furthermore, Habermas reduces translation and understanding to rephrasing the cognitive content of a text in a different idiom, thereby underplaying the importance of conveying its connotation and the inspiration to the reader or listener. He tries to solve these shortcomings by referring to a concept of reason that attends to the lifeworld, thus focusing on the practical meaning of the idea of the unity of reason. This results in "a weak but not defeatist concept of linguistically embodied reason", ③ but Habermas admits that this concept of the lifeworld crumbles the moment it is thematized.

The conclusion of this analysis of Habermas's discussion with Rorty is that linguistic and interpretational symmetry are essential formal conditions to ensure that translation and understanding result in a mutual learning process of the linguistic, cultural, and religious other and to prevent these processes from degenerating into an assimilation of the other. Nevertheless, this symmetry is not enough to result in a common understanding of the semantics of a text that is translated or of the substantial meaning of the culture of the other.

①　For the procedural character of the unconditionality that is preserved in these discursive concepts see: Habermas, The Unity of Reason, 144.

②　Maeve Cook, Translating Truth. In: *Philosophy and Social Criticism* 37 (4), 2011, 480f. In her article, Cook gives an example of the absence and presence of common interpretative frameworks (see Idem, 485f). Habermas himself also realizes that his purely procedural definition of the act of translation does not do justice to the semantic problem of transposing the contents of one interpretative framework into another. See: Habermas, Religion in the Public Sphere, 132, footnote 37.

③　Habermas, The Unity of Reason, 142.

3. A plea for linguistic hospitality

In order to find a better solution to the problem of being lost in translation than the ones proposed by Rorty and Habermas, I want to start from a term that Ricoeur introduced in his book *On Translation*. ① As said, the term translation not only refers to transferring meaning from one language to another, but also includes explaining oneself to others or the interpretation of one human self by another. Moreover, the need for interpretation not only applies to the other, but also to ourselves; as Hölderlin remarked, what is our own has to be learned just as much as what is foreign. ② Since others perceive us from perspectives that differ from our own, they may lay bare traits that remain hidden to our self-understanding. In order to grasp the intellectual and ethical challenges posed by the practices of translation and understanding Ricoeur introduces the catchword 'linguistic hospitality': it carries the double duty "to expropriate oneself from oneself as one appropriates the other to oneself. "③ By fulfilling this duty linguistic hospitality offers a pragmatic way out of the ruinous alternative of complete untranslatability and non-communication versus perfect translatability and complete understanding. With such a pragmatic approach Ricoeur makes clear that he gives priority to the factuality of translation and interpretation over the meta-questions about its possibility, in other words over translatability. ④But replacing this ruinous alternative by

---

① For an excellent introduction to Ricoeur's philosophy of translation see: Richard Kearney, Paul Ricoeur and the Hermeneutics of Translation. In: *Research in Phenomenology* 37, 2007, 147 – 159; Marianne Moyaert, *In Response to the Religious Other. Ricoeur and the Fragility of Interreligious Encounters.* Lanham/Boulder/New York/London: Lexington Books, 2014, 143 – 149.

② Friedrich Hölderlin, *Sämtliche Werke*, VI, 1, 425.

③ Richard Kearney, Paul Ricoeur and the Hermeneutics of Translation. In: *Research in Phenomenology* 37, 2007, 150f.

④ Paul Ricoeur, Reflections on a New Ethos for Europe. In: Richard Kearney (ed.), *Paul Ricoeur: The Hermeneutics of Action.* London: Sage Publications, 1996, 4.

the complex dialectic of expropriating oneself and appropriating the other also implies acknowledging that the translator and the interpreter always have to serve two masters, that they are bound by conflicting loyalties, so that they are inevitably somewhere between faithfulness and betrayal. ①

First of all, the need for translation is a direct consequence of the fact that while language is one, there is a multiplicity of languages. In a similar vein, the need for interpretation results from the fact that, although the capacity to understand is one, humans approach the world from different (cultural and religious) perspectives. Plurality is part of the human condition, and it exists in various shapes and in different ways of interaction: one can distinguish between political, ethnic, cultural, religious, economic shapes of plurality, as well as between a dialogical, indifferent and hostile interaction. The need for translation and interpretation corresponds with a basic capacity: although all of us speak a specific mother tongue and approach the world primarily from our own perspective, we are able to learn other languages and make ourselves acquainted with other cultural and religious perspectives. So, we want to translate and understand the other, because it enables us to enlarge our linguistic and intellectual horizon, and because, on a more fundamental level, we realize that our perspectives are limited, so that we need the input of the other to get a better view of ourselves and the world. We only discover ourselves through the other, and in order to realize this, we need translation and interpretation.

When translating and interpreting, we try to salvage meaning. Therefore, these practices are a work of *remembering*: they refer to the past of an immediate access to an original language, as well as to a world prior to the multiplicity of interpretations. In other words, translation and interpretation are driven by the attempt to retrieve a pure, completely transparent language or

---

① Paul Ricoeur, *Reflections on The Just*. Chicago: The University of Chicago Press, 2007, 26.

an absolute understanding of the world, a so-called God's eye perspective. This explains why we feel a kind of resistance when we permit foreign languages and perspectives access to the symbolic world created by our native language and original understanding. We spontaneously experience what is strange to us as a threat to the ideal of self-sufficiency, and hence we presume that our native language is untranslatable and that our own understanding of the world resists interpretation by others. From this perspective, every translation and interpretation cannot be but a bad or biased one, by definition as it were.

But nevertheless, there *is* translation and interpretation: people have always translated and interpreted, since it is a "remedy for plurality in a world of dispersion and confusion."① Consequently, engaging in translation and understanding is not only a work of *remembering*, but also of *mourning* over the loss of the claim to self-sufficiency of our native language and of our own interpretative perspective, over the temptation of omnipotence. In particular, mourning is a consequence of having to give up the illusion of a perfect translation, which would provide a perfect replica of the original, as well as that of a complete understanding, based on a perfect homology between our concepts and the world. Translation and interpretation are always *after Babel*, meaning that they are forever compelled to acknowledge the limits of my language and the multiplicity of languages, as well as the finitude of my own perspective and the diversity of perspectives. ②

So, we have to acknowledge that translation and interpretation are a work of remembering, that is, of salvaging the original meaning of linguistic and/or cultural and religious expressions in another context, as well as a work of mourning, that is, of accepting the loss of this original meaning. That is why translation and interpretation are situated somewhere between faithfulness and betrayal. In the case of translation, every language has a dif-

---

① Ricoeur, *Reflections on The Just*, 28.
② Ricoeur, *On Translation*, 3 – 5, 8.

ferent way of carving things up phonetically on the basis of phonological systems, conceptually on the basis of lexical systems, and syntactically on the basis of different grammars. Consequently, there is no agreement at each of these levels, let alone at all of them, about what would characterize a perfect language that could legitimately claim universality. Moreover, no one can tell how these specific languages, with all their linguistic peculiarities, are or even can be derived from the presumably perfect language. Hence, there is no universal language that underlies all the specific languages, serving as an absolute criterion of a good translation. This means that every language is prone to mistranslation. [①]In a similar vein, within the same linguistic community, each word is marked by polysemy, has more than one meaning. In order to find the 'right' meaning, we have to take into account the meaning that a word takes on in a sentence, and in the wider context of a discourse, both patent and hidden, intellectual and emotional. A sentence introduces a further degree of polysemy, related to the world as the referent of the sentence. This explains why we are never finished explaining how we interpret things, with words and sentences, to others who do not see these things from the same perspective as we do. A final level of polysemy occurs on the level of the narrative, referring to the fact that it is always possible to say the same thing in a different way.

These insights into the fundamental character of linguistic and interpretative plurality lead to the conclusion that we have to accept the loss of the perfect, universal language, and hence of the original meaning, as well as the loss of a complete understanding. A good translation can only aim at a presumed equivalence with the text from which it is translated, but can never claim to a demonstrable identity of meaning, just like a fair understanding can only aim at an equivalence of saying the same thing in another way but can never claim to be identical with the original saying. This equivalence with-

---

① Ricoeur, *On Translation*, 15 – 8.

out identity calls for multiple translations and retranslations that can be compared with each other, as the examples of the Bible, the writings of Lao Zi, Confucius etc. show. In a similar vein, equivalence without identity calls for multiple attempts to say the same thing differently, for interpretations from multiple perspectives. This explains why, in a situation of lacking an absolute criterion of a perfect translation or understanding, there is a desire to translate and to explain, which goes beyond constraint and utility. It enables us to prevent the bitter fate of enclosing ourselves in a monologue. This situation of equivalence without identity comes down to a call for linguistic and interpretative hospitality, "where the pleasure of dwelling in the other's language is balanced by the pleasure of receiving the foreign word at home, in one's own welcoming house. "①

The question then is how we can communicate with the other while respecting her linguistic and cultural integrity, in other words, while keeping at bay the lure of interpretative omnipotence, and of interpreting the other by our own standards. ② Phrasing this question in this way sheds some light on the discussion between Rorty and Habermas. Rorty, for his part, thinks that the diversity of languages and cultural and religious perspectives presents an incommensurable heterogeneity, implying that translation and interpretation are theoretically impossible, while Habermas thinks that translation and intercultural interaction rest on a common basis, which requires us to discover the unity of reason in the grammatical role of truth, rationality and justification that are common to all languages. The solution Ricoeur suggests, is to acknowledge that, since translation and interpretation are a work of mediation between one linguistic idiom and another, between one cultural or religious perspective and another, they are inevitably caught up in a double bind.

---

① Ricoeur, *On Translation*, 10; see also 26 – 9.

② Richard Kearney, Introduction: Ricoeur's philosophy of translation. In: Ricoeur, *On Translation*, xvif.

Translation and interpretation are bound by the vow of faithfulness to the text to be translated or to the phenomenon to be interpreted, but they are also under the suspicion of betraying these, since, by translating and interpreting, they have already given up the illusion of an immediate access to the original language and complete understanding. Translation and interpretation constantly have to serve two masters: the host language and the guest language, the phenomenon that is being interpreted and the interpretation. If the conviction of betrayal gets the upper hand, this leads to a resistance against every translation and understanding, because they are experienced as a threat of the original identity. This attitude is reflected Rorty's linguistic and cultural ethnocentrism, leading to a view on translation and interpretation as an assimilation of the other. If the conviction of faithfulness prevails, as is the case in Habermas's view that the unity of reason underlies the diversity of its voices, this leads to an unsubstantiated trust in the formal universality of truth, rationality and justification. This explains why his attempt to concretize this idea eventually fails, especially in the case where there are substantial linguistic, cultural, and religious differences. Furthermore, there simply is no third text or third party that could demonstrate the identity of meaning and of understanding, so that it could serve as the objective standard to distinguish qualitatively between various translations and interpretations. [1]

4. Conclusion

The above alternatives show, first of all, that translation and interpretation are risky practices, always in danger of assimilating the untranslatable into our own world, and of misunderstanding the other. There is no original language or a perfect translation, nor a complete and unbiased understanding of what is foreign to us that could serve as an objective criterion for our prac-

---

[1] Ricoeur, *Reflections on The Just*, 26; Idem, *On Translation*, 22.

tice of translating and interpreting. Moreover, we realize that there is always something untranslatable, something that eludes our understanding and that is thus incommunicable. Hence, "we can only aim at a supposed equivalence, not founded on a demonstrable identity of meaning. "[1] This aim at a supposed equivalence is concretized by the fact that the practices of translation and understanding consist in comparing our translations and interpretations with others. The result is that "we can translate [and interpret] differently, without hope of filling the gap between equivalence and adequacy. "[2] This answer offers us a way to live with the double bind of faithfulness and betrayal, but also points to the pleasures of linguistic hospitability. First of all, an imperfect translation and interpretation is preferable to no translation at all. Only through linguistic hospitality, we become sensitive to the strangeness of our own language, ideas, and practices. What is more, translation and interpretation enable us to understand ourselves, since this is only possible through the other, her language and culture. By staying in the space, in which we feel at home, we certainly will not feel lost in translation, but such an attitude inevitably leads to self-sufficiency and self-enclosure. Second, translation and interpretation are not only an appropriation through expropriation of an original other (a text, idea, person, culture or religion), but also a legitimate work in its own right. By transferring the original to other linguistic, cultural, and religious universes these practices give it a continued existence in a different context. Finally, translation brings forth a creative encounter between two worlds and makes meaning move. It develops new semantic resonances, makes unexpected allusions, and points to surprising new possibilities. Thus, translation and interpretation expand the horizon of meaning of the translated text and the interpreted object. [3] In sum, the idea of linguistic hospitality

---

① Ricoeur, *On Translation*, 33.

② Ibid. , 10.

③ Moyaert, *In Response to the Religious Other*, 149.

helps us to understand how to find our way in the labyrinth of translational, intercultural, and interreligious meanings, in other words, in a world 'after Babel'.

Universal Rationality across Cultures

Zhang Lihai[*]

Abstract: this paper follows the late Wittgenstein's approach to language and applies it to the discussion of rationality and incommensurability. It argues that there are universal standards of rationality which make the communication across cultures possible. Furthermore, it examines the concept of incommensurability, and maintains that incommensurability doesn't mean incomparability and untranslatability. Cultural diversity is just the results of various uses of universal rationality in different environments. Therefore, it is the evidence for the universal rationality instead of culture-bounded rationality.

Key words: Rationality Universal Rationality incommensurability communication across cultures

In this paper, I will follow the late Wittgensteinian approach to language to examine the problems of rationality and incommensurability. I will argue that there are universal standards of rationality which make the communication across cultures possible. I will further discuss the concept of incommensurability in the arguments of cultural relativism. I believe that incommensurability

---

* Zhang Lihai, Associate Professor, School of Philosophy, Wuhan University.

doesn't mean incomparability or untranslatability. Cultural diversity is just the results of various uses of universal rationality in different environments. Therefore, it is the evidence for the universal rationality instead of culture-bounded rationality.

I . The application of Wittgenstein's philosophical method

In *Philosophical Investigations*, Wittgenstein stated his method and purpose of philosophy as following: "And we may not advance any kind of theory. There must not be anything hypothetical in our considerations. We must do away with all explanation, and description alone must take its place. And this description gets its light—that is to say its purpose—from the philosophical problems. —They are solved, rather, by looking into the workings of our language, and that in such a way as to make us recognize those workings: in despite of an urge to misunderstand them. ——Philosophy is a battle against the bewitchment of our intelligence by means of language. "①

In this passage, Wittgenstein takes description as the method of philosophy, that is almost opposite to his early proposal about philosophy and philosophical method. He believes that philosophical problems can be solved by looking into the operations of human language. I think we can also use the method of description to deal with the problem of rationality. What is rationality? Whether rationality is culture-bounded or not? In order to answer these questions, we must examine the uses of the term ' rationality' in practical social communication. When we do this, we will find that rationality is not a single capacity. As Searle argued, it embodies in faculties and modes of consciousness (including faculties of language, perception, determination, etc.) which are biological functions of human being, and exist in all human actions and societies. They are traits of human species. Just like other func-

① Wittgenstein, Ludwig. 1986: § 109.

tions of human being, they are natural and universal. So, in some sense, to depict our faculty and use of language is to depict one of our faculties and modes of rationality.

Ⅱ. The meanings of rationality in ordinary language

In ordinary language, the term 'rationality' has many different uses and meanings. Are there some core or basic meanings in all the uses of the term? Let me examine it. In ordinary circumstances, when we say an action or a belief is rational, we mean that it is based on reason rather than emotion. But if an action or a belief is based on reason, it is not necessary to be rational. Because when a person reasons, he is likely to make a wrong reasoning or choice. In this case, although his action or belief is based on reason, but on a wrong reasoning, it is only an unreasonable action or belief.

From this examination, we can conclude that if an action or a belief is rational, it must be based on reason and conform to the rules of reasoning.

Even when an action or a belief is based on reason and conforms to the rules of reasoning, it may still be possible that it is unreasonable. Why? Because its presuppositions may be untrue or inconsistent with our intuitions or direct sense data, from which we make a claim or decision to take an action. Or maybe because the action based on the belief is self-harming. Therefore, we must add consistence with intuitions or direct sense data and being self-beneficial as the conditions of being rational.

So, what does it mean when we say an action or a belief irrational? It means that a belief or an action is based on reason or a reasonable choice, that it conforms to reality and rules of reason, and is beneficial to the agent. Obviously, a rational action stems from rational beliefs. Ultimately, rational actions and beliefs come from the operation of human rational faculties.

In ordinary language, the term "rationality" can also refer to human's intellectual faculties. According to Searle, rationality is not a separate faculty distinct from human's intellectual faculties such as of language, thought, perception, and intentionality. ① When we say a belief or an action is rational, we mean it is a result of people's normal or correct processes of language, thought, perception and intentionality. It is a result of people's normal use of their intellectual faculties which are universal traits of human being. In different social and natural environments, people use these faculties differently to deal with problems arising from their environment, which produce various social and cultural results, including social values, culture-bounded standards of rationality, political systems, etc. So, we can conclude that cultural diversity is not the evidence for cultural relativity of rationality or impossibility of cross-cultural understanding and translation. It is just the results of various applying of intellectual capacities of human being in different environments, therefore it is the evidence for the universal rationality.

A rational action is self-beneficial instead of self-harming. Rationality in this use falls into the concept of the practical rationality. For any action, if it is self-harming, it must be irrational. But whether rationality means maximization of self-interest as some social scientists and philosophers argued? In real social situation, it is very difficult or almost impossible for people to make sure which action is most beneficial to him. And to pursue the goal of maximizing the self-interests without considering other people's interests may be not allowed by social values, or draw fierce resistance from other people that may make the action fail to achieve its goal. But that is not to say, in many cases, to pursue the goal of maximizing the self interests is irrational especially in Eastern societies in which people usually stress a mean course or middle course. It is only to say, a rational action is an action that pursuing possible maximizaton of self-interests, but at the same time the rational agent must consider relevant people's interests and local social values. Only the rational

---

① Searle, John R. 2001: 22 – 23.

action with consideration of other people's interests and social values can be the most self-beneficial.

Above are examinations of the term 'rationality' used in ordinary language and social situation. We have seen that in both senses of the theoretical and the practical rationality, the faculties and standards of rationality are universal in human nature.

III. The relativist challenge to the universal rationality and the possible responses

I have argued that there are some basic rational traits in human nature. I will illustrate that these basic rational traits make it possible to understand concepts in different cultural systems. I will make a response to the relativist challenge by conclusions from the examination of human ordinary practice of communication.

Cultural relativists hold that different cultures employ radically different conceptual schemes which define what exists in the world, how things are organized, and how things influence others. [1] In other words, different cultures embody different conceptual systems; possess different standards of belief assessment and different systems of beliefs. For them, there is no universal rationality. Only the culture-bounded rationality exists.

Relativist challenge to the universal rationality indicates that there are some confusions occurring in relativists' thinking and using of language, especially in their philosophical thinking, and that we need some strategies to eliminate these puzzles. [2]

To some extent these relativist claims are true of real cultures. But from these claims we cannot make further inference that different cultures are not

---

[1] Little, Daniel. 1991: 203.
[2] Witt. 1986: § 119.

comparable and commensurable mutually. Cultural relativism claims too much, based on the confusion among the concepts of incommensurability, incomparability and incomprehensibility, accordingly, among the concepts of commensurability, comparability and comprehensibility.

The basic ideas beneath conceptual relativist claims are: (1) Two conceptual schemes are incommensurable if it is impossible to establish the definitional equivalence between concepts in the two schemes. (2) And further, if two cultures are incommensurable, we cannot compare them meaningfully and people in the two cultures cannot understand and communicate with each other.

Obviously, the basic ideas of cultural relativism are not true of existing cultures and human communication. It should narrow its claims in order to correspond to the practical communication across human cultures.

In reality, we can learn and understand different conceptual schemes, just like we can learn and understand different languages in the world. We cannot infer that because there are so many different languages in the world, people who speaking different languages must have different language faculties and that they can not understand mutually. Similarly, diversity of cultural rules does not demonstrate that rationality is culture-bounded, although some local cultural rules of rationality are culture-bounded which is different from but understood based on universal rationality. We can evaluate various cultural rules and values on the ground of universal standards of rationality such as veridicality, consistency, efficacy, welfare, etc. , which are found in all cultures in the world. So, although non-Western cultures embody different conceptual schemes, in terms of which non-Western people analyze and categorize everyday world, Western people can translate and understand these conceptual schemes.

Usually, incommensurability means that it is impossible to establish the definitional equivalence between concepts in two different schemes. [1]Some

---

[1] Little, Daniel, 1991: 205.

philosophers take the concept of incommensurability as equal to the impossibility of understanding and translating between two cultures. It is at this point that cultural relativists make a wrong inference based on confusions of concepts. If we look at the uses of these terms in ordinary communication carefully, we'll find that incommensurability doesn't mean impossibility of understanding or translating. Two cultures can be incommensurable, but people in the two cultures actually can understand each other and translate their concepts mutually based on the universal faculties and modes of cognition. The fatal error of conceptual relativists is that they wrongly infer from cultural diversity to incommensurability of cultures, and then from incommensurability of cultures to impossibility of understanding or translating between cultures, just because they fail to distinguish the three concepts. Once we recognize the difference among the three concepts, the puzzles caused by cultural relativist challenge disappear.

However, how can we understand alien cultural rules? Wittgenstein is right in answer to this question. He believes that through suitable training, people can understand rules and correctly follow rules. [1] People can also recognize whether other people correctly understand and follow rules. But how is it possible that suitable training lead to understanding of rules? "The common behavior of mankind is the system of reference by means of which we interpret an unknown language. "[2] These common modes and capabilities of behavior exist in all human's biological mechanism. They are parts of universal rationality of human.

Through training we can also grasp different languages, conceptual schemes and ways of thinking. For example, the processes of Chinese people learning the Western cultures, languages and sciences, are through the method of training. In the processes, usually teachers show the students the

---

[1] Witt. 1986: § 74; 223.

[2] Ibid. 1986: § 206.

rules and routines of language operations or scientific studies, and then the students exercise following the rules of language operations or scientific studies. Finally, people from different cultures can discuss and communicate about some common topics with common rules and routines. When turning to learn non-Western cultures and languages, the processes of training and understanding are similar.

Therefore, the relativist challenge to the universal rationality is untenable. People can understand the conceptual schemes which are different from theirs. It is just because all human possess the common cognitive faculties and modes that people in different cultures can understand each other.

IV. Some further arguments against cultural relativism

In his essay "On the Very Idea of Conceptual Scheme" (1974), Donald Davidson developed a concise argument against conceptual relativism. He points out that if various conceptual schemes are incommensurable, all communications between cultures would be impossible. But this impossibility doesn't exist. [1]

We can make further inference from Davidson's argument that there must be some common faculties in all humans and some basic concepts in all cultures because of the fact that communications between cultures do exist. Without these common faculties and basic concepts, communications between cultures would be impossible. The fact that all human beings have common faculties of cognition and biological natures enable us to understand other people's behavior in alien cultures.

One may refute Davidson's argument by saying that although communications between cultures occur ever, but people in different cultures don't really

---

[1] Davidson, Donald. 1974. "On the Very Idea of a Conceptual Scheme. " in *Analytic Philosophy*: *Beginnings to the Present*. 2001.

understand each other, the terms that they believe are equivalent and used in communications belong to different cultural systems and actually refer to different cultural and social objects.

This refutation overlooks the following facts that in various cultures there is a common natural world, and that there are some basic concepts that refer to real physical objects and properties in the world, such as mountain, river, people, tiger, etc. Because of these facts, people in different cultures can define and interpret their culturally unique concepts by the common basic concepts. Obviously, in this process, the common basic concepts and the universal faculties of recognition play the key role.

Further, even if we can suppose a situation, in which no shared beliefs and concepts exist in some alien cultures at the very beginning, people can still form some common principles, concepts and beliefs in the process of interaction and finally reach an mutual understanding and agreement, owing to the common biological faculties of human and the common natural world in different cultural systems.

The fact that people have different beliefs about the world is quite ordinary, even a same person may hold different ideas about the same world at different periods in his lifetime. But that does not lead to the impossibility of understanding and communication between people who have different beliefs about the world or in different cultures. Underneath the different cultural and metaphysical concepts, we can still find shared basic concepts and rational modes of formation of concepts.

V. A Refutation to Peter Winch's radical cultural relativism

In "The Idea of a Social Science" (1990), Peter Winch puts forward his radical cultural relativism. He argues that belief-forming processes are social practices in various societies. There are no universal standards for criticizing or justifying belief-forming processes. There is no an objective world, no such thing as 'truth.' [1]

Peter Winch's radical relativism of rationality does not correspond to the reality of human cultural and scientific development. People's beliefs and concepts about the world are different, that does not mean that the world in different cultures is not the same one. This is the second critical confusion in the relativist arguments. All nations have the same objective world. Cultural differences are just in their beliefs and conceptual systems about the same objective world. If different cultures have different worlds, the translation between cultures would be impossible. It is with the same objective world and common cognitive faculties that people can understand the different beliefs and conceptual systems in different cultures.

Different cultures have some distinctive standards of rationality, which are embodied in cultural rules, cultural belief-forming processes and modes of behaviors, and quite different, sometimes even opposite across cultures. This is the main evidence for Winch's cultural relativist arguments. His claim shows that cultural relativists have seen and understood the differences across cultures in some sense. Or how can they make claim about the diversity of cultures? They can make claim and understand the diversity of cultures, because beneath cultural differences, there exist universal modes of rational operation which are universal traits of human species and common across cultures. These universal traits enable people to understand and evaluate the differences between their unique cultural standards of rationality.

If Winchian inference is true that there is no sense to say one belief system is superior to another, the different belief systems in magic, myths, religions and modern science would be equally true or good. There would be no reason to say that modern science is superior to ancient magic or myth. Obviously, this inference is against our intuition. If ancient magic, myth and religion are equally true and good with modern science, human knowledge would

---

① Winch, Peter. 1990. *The Idea of a Social Science*. London: Routledge.

stop at the level of ancient myth and religion, there would be no need and motive to develop modern science as new form of knowledge about the world. Human interests (such as surviving, welfare and liberation) and the common basic rationality drive the development of human knowledge from ancient myth to modern science, because modern science is more valid and efficient in explaining the way the world really is and guiding human practice to success.

VI. Conclusion

It is the shared basic concepts and universal faculties of rationality that make interpretation between cultures possible. They are the shared foundation of all various cultures in the world. The diversity of cultures is just the result of the employment of human rational faculties and basic concepts in various social and natural environments.

The basic ideas that support the argument for the possibility of communication across cultures are that there are universal standards of rationality in all human cultures and that there is one objective world in all systems of concepts and beliefs. The universal standards of rationality are those principles and modes of cognition and action which produce true beliefs validly and reliably, and make correct choices for certain purposes, which are parts of human biological mechanism. They are universal and cross-cultural. Just for this reason, in one hand, beliefs should be evaluated by the criteria in the social context; in another hand, beliefs and the criteria of evaluation in local cultures should be examined with the universal standards of rationality.

BIBLIOGRAPHY

Davidson, Donald. 1974. "On the Very Idea of a Conceptual Scheme." in *Analytic Philosophy*: *Beginnings to the Present*. 2001. by Jordan J. Lindberg. California: Mayfield Publishing Company.

Searle, John R. 2001. *Rationality in Action.* Massachusetts: The MIT Press.

Little, Daniel. 1991. *Varieties of Social Explanation.* Colorado: West-view Press, Inc.

Winch, Peter. 1990. *The Idea of a Social Science.* London: Routledge.

Wittgenstein, Ludwig. 1986. *Philosophical Investigation.* Oxford: Basil Blackwell Ltd.

东学西渐的
哲学史考察

欧洲三位哲学家论孔子的思想
及其方法论的反思

吴根友[*]

摘　要： 魁奈与 17、18 世纪欧洲的大多数思想家一样，对于孔子与儒家思想基本上持肯定的态度，肯定了孔子与儒家的道德哲学对于中国人的正面价值，也肯定中国人在国内商业中的诚信态度。19 世纪以黑格尔为代表，开始猛烈地批评孔子与儒家思想，因此也极力地贬低中国思想的价值。20 世纪以后，雅斯贝尔斯以世界哲学的眼光重新评价孔子及其思想的价值，称其与苏格拉底、佛陀、耶稣一样，均是思想范式的创造者。雅氏还比较全面地分析了孔子思想的特征及其对人类文化的积极意义。不同历史时期欧洲不同的思想家对于孔子及其思想价值的评价差异很大，其主要原因是他们把孔子及其代表的中国思想看作是欧洲文明的参照系，他们希望借文化上的"他者"来校正自己文明的问题。因此，对于欧洲等思想家有关中国文化评价的观点，既要高度重视，但又不能简单地直接引用。由此我们也可以进一步地自我提醒，对于一切外国学者有关中国思想与文化的评价，都应当保持一种审慎的态度。

---

* 吴根友，武汉大学哲学学院教授。本文为教育部哲学社会科学研究重大课题攻关项目：《中国传统道德文化的现代阐释和实践路径研究》（项目编号：14JZD040）与湖北省重点项目《中国传统道德文化的现代阐释和实践路径研究》的中期成果。

关键词：魁奈　黑格尔　雅斯贝尔斯　孔子　儒家思想

在比较哲学的视野里重新考察先秦儒家思想，这是一个极有潜力的学术论域。自中国晚明以降，先秦儒家思想就已经开始进入了欧洲人的思想视野。尽管如此，对于欧洲的思想家而言，是否能够准确认识先秦儒家思想，到今天为止仍然是一个悬而未决的议题。作为欧美文化"他者"的先秦儒家思想，总是在各种各样的现实诉求中被研究、被解读，直到今天仍然如此。当代一些美国的学者注意到要向先秦的儒家思想学习一些什么东西，① 也有人要积极地阐释儒家思想的世界性意义，② 但在近四百余年的历史过程中，先秦儒家思想的价值其实是一个不断被发现，又不断遭遇贬低、误解的过程。比较文化视野里关于先秦儒家思想具有丰富的研究视角，如对先秦儒家的智慧观的研究，还有就儒家的"仁爱"思想与基督教的上帝之爱的比较专题性研究等，已有多种成果。③ 而当代英语世界里关于孔子的专门研究成果，要首推芬格莱特的《孔子：即凡而圣》④ 一书了。该书批评了西方学界对孔子思想的忽视，他说："西方思想家大都对于孔子视域中如此重要的人性的维度视而不见。"⑤ 此外，对先秦儒家、孔子进行系统研究的，还有郝大维、安乐哲二人。当然，美籍华人学者，特别是当代新儒家成中英、杜维明等人的研究成果更为丰富。本文择要回顾、述评 18 世纪以降欧洲三位思想家对于孔子思想价值的认识与评价，进而对当代世界性的比较哲学思想研究的方法进行一些理论上的反思。

---

① ［美］考普曼：《自然性重探：西方哲学家为什么应该学习孔子》，载姜新艳主编《英语世界中的中国哲学》，中国人民大学出版社 2009 年版。

② ［美］南乐山：《作为世界性哲学的儒家》，载姜新艳主编《英语世界中的中国哲学》，中国人民大学出版社 2009 年版。

③ 姚新中：《早期儒家与古以色列智慧传统比较》，陈默译，中国社会科学出版社 2013 年版。

④ ［美］赫伯特·芬格莱特：《孔子：即凡而圣》，彭国翔、张华译，江苏人民出版社 2002 年版。

⑤ ［美］赫伯特·芬格莱特：《孔子：即凡而圣·序》，彭国翔、张华译，第 2 页。

一 魁奈与黑格尔论孔子

自 17 世纪以降，欧洲部分思想家通过耶稣会传教士翻译的《论语》及其他儒家思想文献，初步了解到孔子的思想。其中有不少思想家将孔子比作西方的苏格拉底，当然也有人不同意这种类比。简洁地说，从维科、拉莫特·勒瓦耶、费内隆、李明，到伏尔泰、狄德罗，欧洲的启蒙思想家对于孔子的思想都有不同程度的涉及与论述。① 在 17、18 两个世纪内，欧洲启蒙思想家对于孔子及其思想的论述，大多是从正面的角度展开的。只有孟德斯鸠、康德对于儒家以及由儒家而涉及的孔子的一些思想，是持批评态度的，而这种批评多半是因为儒家与专制政治有内在的联系。19 世纪以后，以黑格尔为代表的德国思想家对于孔子及儒家思想，采取了激烈的批评态度。其中主要原因是欧洲已经从思想上完成对中世纪异化了的基督教的批判任务，而致力于建设一个新的资产阶级现代文明。孔子及其所代表的儒家哲学中的自然理性精神已经成为过时的东西。而现代中国，自"五四"新文化运动以来展开的对孔子与儒家的批判，也是与中国的现代文化追求的历史任务密切相关的。

1. 弗朗斯瓦·魁奈（1694—1774）论孔子

作为法国重农学派的经济学家，魁奈对孔子是保持高度尊敬之情的，他认可中国人对孔子的看法，将孔子看作是"所有学者中最伟大的人物，是他们国家从其光辉的古代所留传下来的各种法律、道德和宗教的最伟大的革新者"②。而魁奈本人则尊敬地称赞孔子道："这位著名哲学家坚贞不渝，忍受着各种非难和压制，而这些非难和压制有时在哲人们的著述似乎旨在重新建立他们自己国家的秩序时，也会遭到。"③

---

① 许苏民：《中西哲学比较研究史》上卷，南京大学出版社 2015 年版，第 104—127、194—200、214—225、262—265 页。

② ［法］魁奈：《中华帝国的专制制度》，谈敏译，商务印书馆 1992 年版，第 37—38 页。

③ 同上书，第 38 页。

魁奈对于孔子的称赞与对其人生努力的肯定，与后来黑格尔对于孔子的蔑视与批评，是截然相反的。他称赞孔子道：

> 这位贤明大师具有崇高声望，曾被推出任鲁国大夫。他以明智的立法，使全国面貌为之一新。他革除积弊，重新确立商业信誉。他教育青年人尊重老年人，敬奉父母，即使在父母死后，仍旧敬奉如常；他劝导女子要端庄淑贤，保持贞操；他要求在人民中间树立起公正、坦诚和一切文明的风尚。①

上述魁奈对于孔子的赞扬虽然并不是十分准确，但大体上较准确地刻画了孔子的精神形象。尤其是肯定了孔子对于女性道德行为的规范性要求，这一点与后来将孔子看成是蔑视女性的思想者的观点不同。

对于当时欧洲比较流行的一种歪曲的观念，即中国人在商业活动中不讲诚信、喜欢欺骗这一看法，魁奈提出了反对意见。他认为，对于中国这样的一个文明国家，这是不可能的。他认为，散布这些传闻的人，可能是把中国在广州口岸与欧洲人进行交易的活动与整个帝国内部的贸易活动混淆起来了。他认为，由于中国政府"对外国外贸易没有什么兴趣，它容忍那里的欺诈行为是因为它难以惩治那些远离本国达 3000 里格，一旦卖掉他们的商品便消遁而去的外国商人"②。由这一推测出发，魁奈甚至认为，这使中国人在与欧洲的贸易争夺中显得"比欧洲人更加精明"，是"运用竞争技巧更加沉着得多"③ 的表现。不过，这种猜测是没有根据的，也并不正确。

然而，上述魁奈对于中国国内一般性贸易与商业伦理的猜测既合乎情理，也大体上是正确的，他说：

> 不能想象在一个国家内，居民之间可以靠相互弄虚作假来进行

---

① ［法］魁奈：《中华帝国的专制制度》，谈敏译，商务印书馆 1992 年版，第 38 页。
② 同上书，第 70 页。
③ 同上。

贸易。相互欺诈的双方有何利可图呢？这只会引起令人棘手和非常麻烦的纷乱，从而使日常的商业活动变得十分困难，几乎不可能进行。甚至更不能想象这种诈欺现象是发生在像中国这样的一个文明国度中，在那里贸易方面的良好信誉和诚实、正直一直是令人瞩目的；这是孔子伦理学的主要论题之一，而在这个帝国内，伦理就是法律。①

魁奈对于当时中国社会商业伦理的诚信行为的基本肯定，并将其与对孔子的肯定与赞扬联系在一起，表明他对孔子的思想及其教化的成效是持肯定与赞赏态度的。这种肯定与赞赏当然有夸张之处，但比起同时代的一些欧洲思想家，如孟德斯鸠对于中国社会普遍道德状况的激烈批评，可能更接近中国社会的真实，但这并不是说孟德斯鸠不应该批评当时中国社会的专制政治制度。

2. 黑格尔论孔子

欧洲的近现代历史进入黑格尔的时代，在生产技术、制度革新方面已经远远地超越了中国。欧洲开始了以自己为中心的新的历史时期。黑格尔对中国哲学的蔑视与批评，对孔子的肆意诋毁，与欧洲的自我中心主义的时代精神，特别是与日耳曼民族意识的觉醒密切相关。黑格尔知道中国哲学，特别是孔子的哲学在莱布尼兹时代曾经在欧洲轰动一时的历史事件，但他自以为发现了人类"绝对精神"的真理之后，便以十分傲慢的态度与口吻说道，孔子的哲学里没有什么高深的东西，《论语》里面所讲的"是一种常识道德，这种常识道德我们在哪里都找得到，在哪一个民族里都找得到，可能还要好些，这是毫无出色之点的东西。孔子只是一个实际的世间智者，在他那里思辨的哲学是一点也没有的——只有一些善良的、老练的、道德的教训，从里面我们不能获得什么特殊的东西"②。他甚至认为，古罗马西塞罗的道德教训的著作，比

① ［法］魁奈：《中华帝国的专制制度》，谈敏译，商务印书馆1992年版，第70页。
② ［德］黑格尔：《哲学史讲演录》第1册，贺麟、王太庆译，商务印书馆1995年版，第119页。

孔子所有著作的内容更丰富、更好。这些有关《论语》与孔子思想的评价，在今天看来是极其浅薄的、傲慢的，但他之所以敢于公开地蔑视古老的中国圣人，是因为他认为自己已经找到了人类的"绝对精神"这种哲学真理。

不仅如此，黑格尔还以他自己所信奉的"自由"精神来贬低孔子思想的价值与中国道德的精神价值。他认为，所谓的中国哲学、孔子的哲学，也无非就是指"这种道德"：

> 这种道德包含有臣对君的义务，子对父、父对子的义务以及兄弟姊妹间的义务。这里有很多优良的东西，但当中国人如此重视的义务得到实践时，这种义务的实践只是形式的，不是自由的内心的情感，不是主观的自由。所以学者们也受皇帝的命令支配。凡是要想当士大夫、作国家官吏的人，必须研究孔子的哲学而且须经过各样的考试。这样，孔子的哲学就是国家哲学，构成中国人教育、文化和实践活动的基础。①

上述黑格尔对孔子哲学思想的评价，与魁奈的评价完全相反。孔子思想本身的性质没变，变化的是欧洲的社会，以及思想家要求一种新的秩序与关于秩序的基础，因此，作为文化"他者"的孔子，就沦为黑格尔等人思想与需求的反面材料，因而受到了以黑格尔为代表的19世纪其他欧洲思想家的批评。这种批评，有一些合理的因素，但主要方面是错误的。因此，当代的中国学者不能简单地用黑格尔的观点与结论来对待孔子的思想。

二 雅斯贝尔斯论孔子

经过两次世界大战的欧洲，使得欧洲的思想家们不得不重新反省现

---

① ［德］黑格尔：《哲学史讲演录》第1册，贺麟、王太庆译，商务印书馆1995年版，第125页。

代性以及鼓吹现代性的思想所带来的负面影响，他们开始把眼光再一次
地投向了东方，投向了中国。与雅斯贝尔斯同时的德国另一位大哲学家
海德格尔，主要把眼光投向了老子与庄子，而雅斯贝尔斯则以更加广阔
的"世界哲学"的眼光投向了全人类，在中国，他同时关注了孔子与
老子两位哲人。

　　雅氏对于孔子思想的评价，自然也带着欧洲文化的烙印，但在整体
倾向上表现出对孔子思想的贴切理解。雅氏努力深入孔子的思想深处去
理解孔子思想的动机与时代问题意识，进而试图为我们今天的人类提供
一些有价值的思想参照。因此，雅氏对于孔子思想的研究与评价，主要
表现为一种学术上的对话与理解。这一点与黑格尔的傲慢与批判的态度
截然不同。雅氏对孔子与柏拉图、耶稣、佛陀等思想范式的创造者的相
同之处的揭示，以及就孔子与犹太先知之间不同特点的分析，孔子作为
思想改革形象的论证，已有学者在著作中作了基本的总结。① 此处依照
雅氏自己的思路，简述他对孔子思想的整体看法，并在此基础上给予扼
要的评价。

　　在雅氏的"世界哲学"的视野里，孔子与苏格拉底、佛陀、耶稣
一道，成为"思想范式的创造者"，他认为，孔子的根本思想是"借对
古代的复兴以实现对人类的救济"。这即是说，孔子是一个托古改革式
的思想人物。简而言之，雅氏是从如下五个方面来概述孔子思想体系
的，其一是对于古代的认知，其二是其道德、伦理规范，其三是孔子所
关注的根本知识，其四是孔子的极限意识，最后，雅氏对孔子的人格形
象及其特征作了简明的勾画，并对孔子思想在后来时代里的影响及相关
评价，也作了择要性的概述。相对于黑格尔而言，雅氏对于孔子思想的
认识及评价更加深入，也更加富有启发性。下面我们就着重从五个方面
介绍雅氏对于孔子的论述与评价。

　　1. 孔子的根本思想

　　在比较哲学的视野里，雅氏考察了孔子对于古代思想借用的方式。

---

① 参见许苏民《中西哲学比较研究史》下卷，南京大学出版社 2015 年版，第 473—477
页。

他说：

> 通过将流传下来的文献转变成有意识的根本思想，实际上是产生了一种与古老的文化融而为一的新哲学。自己的思想并不通过其自身而展现：犹太的先知们宣告了上帝的启示，孔子则宣告了古代之声。对于古代的自我尊崇，阻止了傲慢自大，可以从渺小的自我之中提出很高的要求。古代传统使得那些依然生活在本源之中的所有的人，获得更多的机会、信仰以及信众。那种源自纯粹理性的空无的独自思考，乃是徒劳无益的。①

在雅氏看来，孔子与犹太教先知虽然有不同之处，但也有类似之处，即希望通过将自己融入历史之中，来表达一种真理。比如孔子本人对于学习的态度、对于孝的态度的诸种说法，其实表达的是这样一种思想倾向："我们存在的本质乃处于历史之中。孔子勾画出了一幅应当能够使得这唯一的真理发挥更好效果的历史画卷。但他并不重视诸如车、犁、船的伟大发明者伏羲、神农、黄帝。对于他来讲，真正的历史始于社会和政府、礼仪和秩序的奠基者。"② 因此，孔子只重视 尧、舜、禹这些人物，因为这些人"从内心感知着上天那永恒的原始典范"③。

尽管孔子非常重视历史，但他所倡导的绝对不是简单地照搬古代。雅氏认为孔子对于古代社会的态度有两点：一是批判性，这表现在能区分"在古代何时为善何时为恶"，能够"选择值得纪念的典范或作为警戒的例子"；④ 二是他并不追求与古代的外表的同一，因此，孔子"倡导的是对永恒真理的温习，而不是对过去的模仿"⑤，进而希望这"永恒的思想"能够在他所处的黑暗时代里重放光彩。正因为如此，孔子

---

① ［德］卡尔·雅斯贝尔斯：《大哲学家》（修订版）上卷，李雪涛等译，社会科学文献出版社 2010 年版，第 128 页。
② 《大哲学家》，第 129 页。
③ 同上。
④ 同上。
⑤ 同上。

对于"权威"的处理方式就值得我们学习:"他认为权威并非仅仅是通过行使暴力的垄断而获得的权力。真正的新生事物在同传统相重合时是如何从永恒存在的本质中产生的,在历史上这是首次借助于一个伟大的哲学而使人们意识到一种保守的生存方式,这一生存方式是通过开放的自由思想而运动着的。"① 应当说,雅氏对于孔子如何向历史学习的思想做出了精彩的阐发,修正了人们一贯认为孔子是文化保守者的观念。

2. 孔子的道德、伦理思想

雅氏从六个方面阐述了孔子的道德、伦理思想。第一,对于孔子的礼论,雅氏有不同于 20 世纪以来中国学者的看法,他认为,在孔子的思想中,"礼并没有绝对的特性"②。因为,作为一种单纯形式的礼,如果缺乏展示仁的价值,其本身是没有价值的;而且,在孔子的思想中,并没有区分"礼、伦理以及法",因此,"他更能清晰地看到他们的共同根源";并且,孔子也没有区分美与善,这样,反而使人更清楚地了解到:"美中没有善便不再是美了,而善中没有美,也不再是什么善了。"③ 第二,对于孔子的乐论,雅氏没有多少特别的论述,不过他从"个人生命秩序"的角度来考察孔子"放郑声"的主张,还是颇有启发意义。第三,雅氏特别提出了孔子重视"自然与陶冶"的问题,尽管他并没有提出足够的文献证据。他说:"孔子对一切自然而然的东西都要表示赞同。他给万物以应有的秩序、程度、地位,而不是否定他们。"④ 孔子虽然主张克制自己,但不主张做苦行僧,他希望通过陶冶本性让人变善,认定强施暴力只能带来灾祸。第四,雅氏考察了孔子的"与人交往"的思想,并将"与人交往"看作是"孔子生活的要素"⑤。在此细节部分,雅氏对于孔子的妇女观提出了含蓄的批评,他说:"孔子对于妇女的冷漠态度,着实令人惊讶。在夫妇关系的方面,他沉默

---

① [德]卡尔·雅斯贝尔斯:《大哲学家》(修订版)上卷,李雪涛等译,社会科学文献出版社 2010 年版,第 129—130 页。
② 同上书,第 133 页。
③ 同上书,第 134 页。
④ 同上。
⑤ 同上书,第 135 页。

了，提到女人，他用轻蔑的口气予以评价。在他听说一对相恋的人双双自尽的消息后，则表现出了轻蔑的态度。他还爱讲，没有什么比女人更难办的了。孔子所处的氛围，显然是以男性为中心的。"①

第五个方面，雅氏也考察了孔子的政治观，并认为孔子的政治观与柏拉图的哲学王观念很相似。雅氏将孔子的政治观概括为两个基本原则，一是"有能力的必须在他相应有位置上"，二是"公共的政治环境必须使得革新行为成为可能"②。应当说，雅氏所说的第一个原则应该是正确的；第二原则，在孔子的思想中能否找到证据，还有可以进一步讨论的空间。

第六个方面，雅氏引用了大量的文献，仔细地考察了孔子的君子人格，并对孔子的"君子人格"的精神内涵作了非常有意思的阐述。应该说，这是雅氏对孔子道德、伦理思想阐述得比较精彩的地方。雅氏说："在孔子看来一切的善、真、美都蕴涵在君子这一理想人格之中了。在这一理想之中融进了高贵的人格思想，以及他们所处的高高在上的社会阶层，融进了高贵的出身与天性，并且也融进了绅士的举止以及贤者的心境。"③ 不过，既然雅氏如此肯定孔子的君子人格理想，那么如何来处理孔子对仁者、圣人的人格理想评价，就会引发出很多学术的讨论。

3. 孔子的根本知识

在雅氏的思想框架里，孔子对根本知识的认识包括在四个方面：

> 首先是人的本性；其次是社会秩序的必要性；再其次是我们思维的基本方式，真理的根源与分支问题，根源的无制约性以及表象的相对性问题；最后用是统摄万物并且同万物都有关联的一以贯之的大"一"。④

---

① ［德］卡尔·雅斯贝尔斯：《大哲学家》（修订版）上卷，李雪涛等译，社会科学文献出版社2010年版，第136页。
② 同上书，第138页。
③ 同上书，第139页。
④ 同上书，第141页。

　　第一，就人性的问题，雅氏正确地看到，孔子对人的本性认识是建立在"仁"观念基础之上的，"人的本性乃是仁。仁包括人性以及伦理道德"①。这一人性问题主要是从两个方面展开的。首先，人应当成为人，让人与禽兽区别开来，而使人与禽兽区别开来的根本特征，就是让人成为具有"仁的品德的人"。雅氏正确地看到，在孔子的"根本知识"中，"仁乃是统摄一切的，它不是诸道德中之一员，而是一切道德之灵魂"②。正是由"仁"出发，"所有的有用性、规则性、正当性、才能成为真理"③。但是，"仁"又不是一个僵硬的规则，恰恰相反，正是从"仁"出发而"产生了没有任何目的约束的无制约者：'有道德者把困难作为前提，之后便可以获得酬劳'"④。

　　雅氏在此将"仁"理解为一种极其根本而又没有任何具体的功利性的"无制约者"，这是一个极富启发性的认识；但他所引用的"仁者先难而后获，可谓仁矣"这个具体的例证，并不是十分恰当，只能看作是比较哲学视域下的一种特定的理解。

　　雅氏特别看中"中庸"的概念对于理解"仁"的帮助，这是不可定义的"仁"通过语言而表达出来的一种相对明确的意思。他说：

　　　　依照仁而行事并非遵循某一明确法则，而是赋予所有特定法则以价值，同时剥夺它们的绝对性，以此行事而已。尽管仁是不可定义的，但它的特征还是在孔子的言语中描述了出来：孔子在被他称作适度和中庸的概念之中看到了仁。⑤

　　其次，对于"人是什么"的问题，孔子恰恰给出了多元性的回答，

---

　　① ［德］卡尔·雅斯贝尔斯：《大哲学家》（修订版）上卷，李雪涛等译，社会科学文献出版社 2010 年版，第 141 页。
　　② 同上书，第 142 页。
　　③ 同上。
　　④ 同上。
　　⑤ 同上。

人在本质属性方面，如仁这一点是相近的，但在"习惯"上，是因人而异的。而就人的类型来看，人可被分为不同的层次：最高的是圣人，其次是通过学习而获得知识的君子，再次是在学习方面感到有困难但不气馁的人，最差的一类是既难以学习，又不去学习的人。

第二，就秩序而言，孔子的根本知识中有三种基本秩序：第一重要的秩序与原则是"恕道"原则："己所不欲，勿施于人"；第二个重要原则是通过典范的权威来建立秩序，成为表率与典范；第三个重要原则是不要使用暴力的方式直接地干预事物，而是要在事物的开端处施加影响，以使之朝向正确的方向发展。① 不过，对于第三条原则，雅氏并未引证出相应的原文，而是作了一种引申性的解释。

第三，就思维方式与"根源的无制约性"问题，雅氏作了如下的阐述："根源的无制约性进入现象的相对性之中。因此这一切取决于根源性之中的诚实的真面目，并涉及现象之自由度。"② 这就使得孔子的思想具有极强的灵活性，这种灵活性不是一种基于利益计算的方便性，而是表现为恰当性，因为"真理与现实不可能存在于一种或一种最终确定下来的独断的陈述之中。因此，固定化是被拒绝了的"③。雅氏对孔子思维方式的理解与解释，与我们今天所理解的中国化的马克思主义的活的灵魂——"具体问题具体分析"的态度与工作方法，有高度的相似性。灵活性，具体问题具体对待的处事方法，可能真是中国人的真精神。

第四，贯穿万物的"一"。雅氏认为，要清楚地理解孔子所说的"一"，是很困难的。这个"一"既可以是"恕道"，也可以说是"天命"，是"礼"，甚至还可以是"类似于老子无为的观念"。④ 的确，我们很难说清楚孔子思想中的"一"。孔子不是我们今天意义上的哲学家，一定要建立一个统一的思想体系。他的一生处于变化发展之中，其

---

① ［德］卡尔·雅斯贝尔斯：《大哲学家》（修订版）上卷，李雪涛等译，社会科学文献出版社 2010 年版，第 146 页。

② 同上书，第 144 页。

③ 同上。

④ 同上。

思想的前后期可能各有侧重。因此，对于孔子思想中的"一"，我们似乎要注意到他的思想在前后期的不同，而不能把他看作是一个固化的人物。这是我们理解其思想一贯性时所要注意的问题。

4. 孔子的"极限意识"

雅氏从西方哲学的立场出发，探讨了孔子对于终极实在的态度。通过认真地研究，他发现，孔子在这方面没有作过多的思考。雅氏认为，孔子对于"临界"这一话题总是小心翼翼的，孔子对于不可知事物虽然"并没怀有冷淡的无所谓的态度"，但却有"一种非常令人震惊的态度"，即"他不愿将令自己内心触动的经验转化为虚伪的知识，不愿真实的意义丧失于所说之中。我们不得不承认，在孔子那里从来没有过对无限的事物以及不可知事物的冲动，可以感觉得到，这两个问题足以让伟大的形而上学家耗尽毕生的精力"。① 但通过"孔子对礼俗虔诚的执行之中，以及在窘迫情景下所回答的问题之中"，还是为人生指明了方向，还是"可以感觉到他对人生终极状况的关怀的"。②

雅氏对于孔子"极限意识"的分析，有助于我们理解孔子思想的边界及其在形上问题思考方面的边界之所在，从而有助于深受经学影响的中国人从孔子思想内在的角度去思考其思想的局限性，这与从政治、阶级的立场去分析、批判孔子思想局限性的外在批评做法是极不相同的。

5. 孔子的人格形象

在相对占有充分的思想资料的前提下，雅氏对于孔子的认识要比他的前贤黑格尔等人的认识深刻得多、全面得多，也客观得多。其中对有些材料的解释虽然与汉语世界里长期居于主流地位的解释有很大的不同，但也颇有启发性。下面几段话是雅氏对孔子的整体评价，也可以说是对孔子人格形象的刻画，它有助于我们从文化的"他者"角度来理解孔子。原文稍长，但颇有启发意义，故笔者在此分段摘录下来，以供

---

① ［德］卡尔·雅斯贝尔斯：《大哲学家》（修订版）上卷，李雪涛等译，社会科学文献出版社 2010 年版，第 149 页。

② 同上。

学人们参考。

其一，

孔子没有只为他自己考虑，他个人是否应当逃避这世间。他也没有设计任何形式的经济技术制度、立法以及形式上的国家制度，孔子所热烈努力以达成的目标并非是可以直接渴望得到的，而只能间接来促成，这是一切其他之物都依附于它的根本：亦即伦理政治善中的整体精神，以及作为整体一部分的每一个个体人的内在的状态。①

其二，

孔子没有宗教的原始体验，不知道启示，不相信他生命的转世，他也不是一位神秘主义者。不过他也不是一位理性主义者，在他的思想中，引导他的是人间社会的统摄理念，只有在这样的社会中，人才能成为人。孔子热爱世间的美、秩序、真诚以及幸福，而这一切并不会因为失败或死亡而变得没有意义。②

其三，

孔子把他的思想限制在现世的可能性之中，是因为他客观冷静的性格所致。他慎重保守，并不是因为恐惧，而是出于他对责任的意识。他尽可能地避开可疑与危险的事情。他渴望获得经验，故而到处倾听，对于古代知识的学习是从不知足的……他保持节制，并时刻修身以待，真正能打动他的并不是对力的冲动，而是真正的自

---

① ［德］卡尔·雅斯贝尔斯：《大哲学家》（修订版）上卷，李雪涛等译，社会科学文献出版社 2010 年版，第 154 页。
② 同上。

主意志。①

其四，

　　孔子的性格乐天知命、开放、自然。他拒绝对他个人的任何神化。他生活在市井之中，作为一个人也有他的弱点。②

其五，从孔子与老子的比较中，亦能显示出他的某些突出特点：

　　与老子不同，他参与世俗的事务，并受一种天命的思想所驱动，即认为应当去改善人类的状况。他创立了一所学校，以培养未来的政治家，并编辑发行古代的典籍。③

与这些实际的行为相比，雅氏认为，更重要的是：

　　在中国，孔子使理性在其全范围与可能性之中首次闪烁出看得见的耀眼光芒，并且这些表现在一位来自百姓的男子汉身上。④

通过老子与孔子的异同比较，雅氏还进一步得出了一个极富有启发性的结论，即孔子、老子的思想"实际上立足于同一基础之上。两者间的统一性在中国的伟大人物身上则一再得到体现，这并不是通过系统地统摄这两种思想于一体的哲学而予以反映，而是存在于中国人那乐于思考而又富于自我启发的生命智慧之中"⑤。

　　在《历史的起源与目标》一书中，雅氏对于"轴心期"里的中国

---

　　① ［德］卡尔·雅斯贝尔斯：《大哲学家》（修订版）上卷，李雪涛等译，社会科学文献出版社 2010 年版，第 154—155 页。

　　② 同上书，第 155 页。

　　③ 同上。

　　④ 同上。

　　⑤ 同上书，第 158 页。

诸子百家思想有另一种评价的视角，这与其在《大哲学家》一书中着重从"世界哲学"的学术角度评价孔子及其他诸子思想的视野有所不同。他认为，"轴心期"的特征可以从社会现象与精神运动两个层面来理解。从社会现象的层面来看，主要有三个特点。其一，在古代中国、印度和西方三个互不知晓的地区，众多哲学流派出现了。在古中国有孔子、老子、墨子、庄子、列子和诸子百家；在古印度出现了《奥义书》与佛陀；从伊朗到以利亚，先知纷纷出现；而古希腊贤哲如云，有荷马、哲学家巴门尼德、赫拉克利特和柏拉图，还有许多悲剧作者，以及修昔底斯和阿基米德等。其二，这些哲学流派分别展开了精神传播运动。孔子、墨子和其他哲学家，游历中原，到处赢得信众，建立了学派；希腊诡辩家和哲学家到处漫游；而佛陀则在各地云游中度过一生。"在孔子受挫于魏国和柏拉图在锡拉丘兹的失败之间，在培养未来国士的孔子学塾和服务于同一目的柏拉图学园之间，可以找出社会学的类似现象。"① 其三，三个地区内有大量的小国和城邦，有国家对国家、城邦对城邦的斗争。古代中国由于周天子软弱无力，大诸侯通过征服其他小国而扩张领土。"在希腊和近东，一些小城邦，在某种程度上，甚至包括波斯所征服的城邦，都享有独立地位。在印度，有许多邦国和城市。"②

在这段文字里，雅氏将孔子的教育活动与古希腊哲人柏拉图的学术与政治活动相提并论，这一横向比较研究所得出的结论是耐人寻味的。孔子与古希腊哲人的相似性问题再一次被提示出来。

三　方法论的反思

上述三位欧洲思想家对于孔子的论述，对于我们如何思考传统在当

---

① ［德］卡尔·雅斯贝尔斯：《历史的起源与目标》，魏楚雄、俞新天译，华夏出版社1989年版，第12页。

② 同上书，第11页。

代的价值，具有方法论的启示意义。就魁奈而言，他在占有极少资料的
情况下，对于孔子与中国传统的道德与商业伦理的认识与评价，虽然很
难说是十分准确而全面的，但没有过分地从自己的哲学立场出发来对中
国文化做出"判教"式的评判，而是给予了相当的尊重。特别是他能
够从商业伦理的一般原则出发，推论中国社会的整体道德状况不可能是
像有些传教士发回的材料所说的那样，具有普遍的欺诈、不诚实等，这
一点颇能体现一个经济学家的基本学术良知。作为现代西方哲学史上的
著名代表人物黑格尔，其哲学思想的深刻性与巨大的启发力是无可怀疑
的，但他的哲学中所具有的现代性的傲慢与强烈的欧洲中心主义的倾
向，也是十分鲜明与突出的。从现代性对于传统专制政治批评的角度
看，他对于孔子及其所代表的儒家道德思想的批评有合理之处，即看到
了基于个人自由基础之上的现代道德与专制政治所需要的奴性的道德之
间的尖锐矛盾；但他由此而对孔子的哲学思想、道德观念，乃至于对中
国传统社会道德思想进行全盘否定的做法，则是十分错误的，而且是非
常粗暴的。

　　相比较而言，雅斯贝尔斯对于孔子及中国传统思想的认识更为全
面、态度更为亲和、评价更为合理，且颇有启发意义。首先，雅氏最大
限度地超越了欧洲中心主义的观念，从更具有哲学普遍性的高度，将孔
子看作是一种思想范式的创立者。其次，他能较为深入地理解孔子思想
的内容，并从欧洲哲学家的视角对孔子思想的内容进行分类梳理，尽管
其分类未必恰当，其具体结论未必允当，但作为一种不同的分类、解读
本身，为我们重视理解孔子及其道德观念提供了新的视角，因而具有思
想上的启发意义。最后，他能在更加广阔的世界哲学的视野里考察孔子
的思想局限及其价值，这为我们今天在全球化的时代里重新诠释中国传
统道德与文化的当代价值及其世界性的意义，提供了有益的思想启迪。

　　实际上，如何在跨文化的视域里恰当地理解先秦儒家，理解孔子，
发掘其思想的当代意义，这是一个开放的问题。在世界文化相互交融的
时代里，我们似乎只能在理解与解释的历史过程中来尝试着给出新的理
解与解释。当代中国哲学家张祥龙运用"生存—现象学"的方法来解
读《论语》与孔子思想的做法，或许对我们有一种启示意义。他要求

学人"让思想透入生存脉络和时机化视域,在诗与思的某种交织中开出哲理新境",同时"又能穷本究源",这样,就"不会以现成框架切割之,以形而上概念塑造之,以科学、逻辑硬化之,而是容吾夫子回到深刻意义上的原文,也就是回到原本的人生起伏、时潮语境、诗书礼乐、家国之忧、好学之乐中;让《论语》回到上下文,其根得土,其叶得舒,其微言大义得以滋生攀缘,开花结果,从容展现于当今的哲学话语世界"①。张氏的这一要求,用中国传统的学术语言来概述之,即是要以"知人论世"的态度与方法来理解孔子,而不是仅仅按照作者自己的时代要求来任意肢解古代经典文本。研究古代哲人的思想,尤其是在跨文化的语境里研究思想领域里的"他者",更应该持有这种"知人论世"的精神。这种精神若用乾嘉学者的话语来说,即是"实事求是"。若用现代中国人的话语来说,即要以追求思想史的真相为基本要求,将"求真"的学术价值精神放在首位。比较哲学的研究并不是一种"判教",而应当首先是一种思想异同真相的分析。因此,芬格莱特的观点是值得我们重视的,他说:"将孔子翻译成西方的语言,典型地反映了通过将孔子西方化从而使之可以理解这样一种努力。通过使用那些对于西方耳熟能详的概念,那些翻译试图帮助西方的读者。但如此一来,孔子思想中最为独特的东西却就此丢掉了。"② 通过对西方学界理解孔子的历史经验的反省与批判,芬氏采取了另一种方式,即以努力贴近孔子原意的方式来解读孔子,他说:"我希望重新检视孔子的《论语》,以其自己的用语来探讨它。我希望发现孔子本人认为是重要的东西,而不是我认为重要的东西。我希望发现孔子所要提出的问题以及他认为是合适的那种答案,而不是我所要提出的问题以及我认为的合适的答案。"③ 芬氏的这一意图在实际的研究中是否能实现,是另一回事,④

---

① 张祥龙:《孔子的现象学阐释九讲》,华东师范大学出版社 2009 年版,第 3 页。

② [美]赫伯特·芬格莱特著:《孔子:即凡而圣》,彭国翔、张华译,江苏人民出版社 2002 年版,第 2 页。

③ 同上。

④ 尽管芬氏在主观上努力接近孔子,但安乐哲对于芬氏有关孔子思想的解读是不认同的。(参见安乐哲《自我的圆成:中西互镜下的古典儒学与道家》,彭国翔编译,河北人民出版社 2006 年版,第 11—18 页。)

但他能以尊重文本，尊重孔子的态度来对异域文化中的"他者"进行研究，这种态度与思路是值得肯定的，而且与张祥龙的想法在原则上是相通的。因此，当代中国人文学研究，应当在更加广阔的比较哲学与比较文化的视野里研究自己民族的传统文化与道德思想，同时一方面要吸取近现代以来西方学者合理的学术与思想成果，另一方面也要批评黑格尔式的文化"判教"方法。这样，我们既可以避免对传统文化的盲目推崇，也可以更加全面地看清中国传统文化的内在价值与现代意义，进而增强民族的文化自信心。

"像中国人那样思考"

——论杜威对西方哲学的批评及其中西哲学比较研究

许苏民 *

摘 要: 杜威通过揭示康德如何从"启蒙运动的儿子"走向"与启蒙运动决裂",以及法国哲学与英美经验论哲学的不足,奠定了其心仪中国哲学的思想基础。他评说了中西道德哲学的不同流派,在哲学和文化的一些基本问题上,他的观点多有与马克思、恩格斯相通之处。他看到了五四新文化运动的"中国味儿"或"中国特点",提出了"两个适应"的理论,即:使古老的中国观念"适应现代的情况",使西方思想的精华"适应中国的情况"。他从老子和孔子的哲学中发现了为世界上其他民族所不及的精神品格,强烈谴责西方列强向中国转移其社会危机,以中国的人生哲学为"救世之灵药"。他说中国哲学更多地把大自然"当作娱心悦目的事物看"。他所提出的"像中国人那样思考"的主张,是后来诺斯罗普关于中国哲学审美特征之研究、公正的世界秩序之建立应引进中国价值观的先声。

关键词: 杜威 德国古典哲学 老子哲学 孔子哲学 中西哲学比较研究

---

* 许苏民,教授,南京大学中国思想家研究中心。

这篇文章的正标题来自杜威于 1922 年 1 月发表于 *Asia* 第 22 卷上的 *As the Chinese Think* 一文，该文是杜威在结束其两年多的访华行程后取得的最重要的理论成果。该题目本身就包含着对中国人的思想和追求给予设身处地的理解、对中国哲学的现代意义无比珍视的双重意蕴。在访华前，他于 1915 年在北卡罗来纳大学作了《德国的哲学与政治》的系列讲演，着重分析了康德哲学的学理失误，并涉及对法国哲学和英美哲学的批评。1919 年来华后，他既看到了新文化运动的蓬勃开展，也看到了主张维护旧道德和恢复帝制的人还和义和团运动的人数一样多，他既支持新文化人引进德、赛二先生和变革儒家伦理的诉求，也把对西方文化的反思带到了中国。他敏锐地看到了新文化运动的"中国味儿"或"中国特点"，提出了"两个适应"——使古老的中国观念"适应现代的情况"，使西方思想的精华"适应中国的情况"——的主张。与中国学者的交流加深了他对中国哲学的认识，由此他才在回国后向西方人发出了"像中国人那样思考"的呼唤。回顾杜威的这一思想历程，重温其在研究中西哲学的过程中所提出的真知灼见，对于今天的中国和世界皆不无裨益。

一 关于中西人性论与政治哲学和道德哲学的关系
——论西方哲学的弊病，兼论中西"灭人欲"之学皆为乡愿之学

1. 论康德如何从"启蒙运动的儿子"走向"与启蒙运动决裂"，以及法国哲学与英美经验论哲学的不足

杜威是以研究康德哲学而于 1884 年获得博士学位的。那时，"回到康德去"是西方哲学界的流行思潮，但他在 1915 年的《德国的哲学与政治》的讲演中却开始全面反思康德哲学，他公正地指出，康德是"启蒙运动的儿子"，但却走向了"与启蒙运动决裂"。在他论证这一观点的千言万语中，有一句话最为关键，就是："（康德）与启蒙运动决

裂最显著的表现，就是他否认了人性的本善。"他紧接着说，正好相反，在康德那里，"人的本性是恶的——这是原罪教义在他的哲学中的体现。他并不是说激情、爱好、感觉本身就是恶，而是说它们夺取了责任的主权，而责任是人类行动的驱动力。于是，道德就是一场无休无止的战斗，它要把人的一切自然欲望转化为完全受理性的法则和目的支配的意愿。""即便人类遵循其友好的和社交的本能，由此而找到道德规范和组织有序的社会基础，但这样的本能也还是受到康德的谴责。"①人性论常常被哲人们当作道德哲学和政治哲学的逻辑起点，特别是近代以来，对人性的不同理解，往往会导致根本对立的道德哲学和政治哲学体系。

这里有必要回顾一下马克思、恩格斯关于 18 世纪启蒙运动之特点的论述。马克思、恩格斯在大量引证法国启蒙者的论述后说：

> 并不需要多大的聪明就可以看出，关于人性本善和人们智力平等，关于经验、习惯、教育的万能，关于外部环境对人的影响……的唯物主义学说，同共产主义和社会主义之间有着必然的联系。既然人是从感性世界和感性世界中的经验中汲取自己的一切知识、感觉等等，那就必须这样安排周围的世界，使人在其中能认识和领会真正合乎人性的东西，使他能认识到自己是人。……既然人的性格是由环境造成的，那就必须使环境成为合乎人性的环境。②

马克思和恩格斯都认为承认"人性本善"是法国启蒙学说的一个首要的和根本的特点，这一论断是合乎实际的。法国启蒙者的"人性本善"学说，是在中国哲学影响下形成的，尽管也带有向基督教《圣经》的原始教义回归的意味。但马克思和恩格斯以及杜威所一致肯定的法国启蒙学说的这一根本特点在康德那里却消失了。

---

① ［美］杜威：《德国的哲学与政治》，载《杜威全集·中期著作》第 8 卷，何克勇译，欧阳谦校，华东师范大学出版社 2012 年版，第 129 页。

② ［德］马克思、恩格斯：《神圣家族》，载《马克思恩格斯全集》第 2 卷，人民出版社 1956 年版，第 166—167 页。

　　路德、加尔文把具有善恶两重性的原罪说改造为性恶论，并不合乎《圣经》原义。读过《圣经》的人都知道，亚当、夏娃在没有偷吃禁果以前，只有上帝赋予的纯善无恶的第一天性，故可以说是"人之初，性本善"；而犯下偷吃禁果的原罪以后，也并不意味着人性就完全变恶了。"原罪"作为人的第二天性，其中有两重意蕴：其一，是以人类的祖先曾经违背过上帝的意志来说明人在外物的诱惑下很容易犯错误；其二，是说人在吃了禁果以后，从此就具有了分辨善恶的智慧，也就是上帝所说的"那人已经变得和我们相似了"。这两重意蕴无论怎么说，都与性恶论不沾边。还是利玛窦说得对："吾以性为能行善恶，固不可谓性自本有恶矣"，恶是由于"接物之际，误感而拂于理"所造成的。①

　　康德也曾摇摆于性善性恶之间，但他的所谓"理性"却驱使他拒绝了法国启蒙者的性善论，而像路德、加尔文一样把原罪说解释为人性天生为恶的学说。他不仅认为人会因本性的脆弱和不纯正的动机而在无意中犯罪，而且认为更有一种作为一切现实的恶的总根源、作为一种具有普遍性的族类倾向的"根本恶"，驱使着人一边在蓄意犯罪，一边又伪善而自欺地标榜自己在道德上何等纯洁。这说明人从"根本"上就是败坏的，不是一般地坏，而是坏透了。这一说法有没有片面的真理性呢？当然是有的。"相研史"视角下的人类史可以作为康德关于人性恶的先验论证的经验事实依据。以动机纯洁来蓄意犯罪的情形在历史上也屡见不鲜，但这并不意味着可以说人从"根本"上就是败坏的，更不意味着可以把性恶论作为道德哲学的基础。如果这么做，并将其在学理上彻底贯彻下去，那就不仅与启蒙运动所追求的合乎人性的社会这一"善"的理想大相径庭，而且也就没有所谓道德哲学可言了。

　　正如以往的哲学史上从不曾有过彻底而纯粹的性善论或性恶论一样，康德的性恶论也不例外。他要通过改造人性来改造世界，这种由恶变善的改造若是在人性中没有丝毫依据，那么其一切关于道德的高言宏论就不能立足了。于是，在康德那里，人就有了天生的善良意志，可以

---

　　① ［意］利玛窦：《天主实义》，载朱维铮主编《利玛窦中文著译集》，复旦大学出版社2001年版，第76页。

认识到绝对命令的普遍性和合理性；意志的软弱使人不能自觉地服从绝对命令，于是人们就通过皈依上帝来赋予绝对命令以神圣感。按照康德的说法，人生活在感性和理性、现象和本体的二重世界之中，感性世界由自然规律所支配，所以没有自由；而只有在理性世界中，人才有按照绝对命令行动的"自由"。这种"理性的自由人"的特点是：他不在乎个人的幸福，也没有任何同情心和获得道德美名的愿望，更不考虑行为的后果，他唯一知道的，就是服从命令、忠实履行其义务和责任。如果不考虑到康德作为"启蒙运动的儿子"曾经讲过"人是目的而不是工具"等言论，仅就其在人性论上"与启蒙运动决裂"而发表的这些言论，我们就只能看到一个加尔文式的狂热的宗教徒，或一个自以为保持着"思想自由"，但在行动上却无条件服从命令的普鲁士士兵。

虽然杜威批评了康德的先验论及其用德国的责任原则去反对法国的权利原则，但这并不代表他认为法国哲学和英美经验论哲学就是完美无缺的。他说康德的"绝对命令使人想到出操的军士"，而英国人的明智的利己主义则"至少使人在脑海里呈现出商人讨价还价的图画"。他赞同边沁对法国哲学的批评，说权利就像责任一样，仍然是先天的原则，来自假设的人性或者人的本质。英国人发现法国人讲的那些权利是可以讨论和权衡的，也多少允许妥协和调整，这是其在道德方面的独特贡献。他认为：

> 伦理的讨价还价要人们放弃一些想要的东西，才能得到另一些东西，这虽然不是最崇高的一种道德，但从社会的角度来看，至少是负责任的。……这种道德要求思考，要求讨论；但却是（康德式的）来自上级权威的声音所不能容忍的，这是一个不可饶恕的罪状。①

特别令杜威警觉的是，康德把科学方法和科学结论排除于社会生活

---

① ［美］杜威：《德国的哲学与政治》，载《杜威全集·中期著作》第8卷，何克勇译，欧阳谦校，华东师范大学出版社2012年版，第128页。

之外的观点也渗入了英美学界和政界:"我们也接过了这种倾向;……当我们面对所有需要社会决定来解决问题的时候,都没有采用科学的方法而使得交流变得更加理智。"①

杜威又说:

> (英美人) 讨价还价、互通有无、皆大欢喜的道德规范,在某个遥远的未来可能会寿终正寝,但迄今为止,这些道德规范在生活中发挥了巨大的作用。德国伦理学打着纯洁的道德唯心主义的旗号,大肆嘲笑注重实际动机的理论,……但是,如果一个咄咄逼人的商业国家完全从服从天职的动机出发来进行商务和战争,人们就会被唤醒,就会感到不安,就会怀疑这是一种被压抑了的"心理综合征"。当尼采说"人类并不渴望快乐;只有英国人才这样"的时候,我们对这个彬彬有礼的批判置之一笑。如果一个人宣称把不在乎幸福当作对行动的一种检验,那么,他履行原则的方式便是不幸的了,因为这种方式会造成他人的不幸。②

马克思从德国哲学中发现了"被压抑的利己主义",而杜威则发现了"被压抑了的心理综合征",真可谓所见略同了。

杜威对康德哲学之弊病的揭示及其对法国哲学和英美经验论哲学之不足的评说,表明了他的最基本的价值立场。明确了这一点,就可以理解他在中国发表的演讲和他在美国发表的一系列关于中国的论文中所阐述的观点了。

2. 对一个常见的错误说法的廓清,兼论中国和西方都有大致相同的几种人性论学说

杜威把他对康德哲学的反思带到了中国,他的《社会哲学与政治哲学》的讲演就是从人性论讲起的。他说:

---

① [美] 杜威:《德国的哲学与政治》,载《杜威全集·中期著作》第8卷,何克勇译,欧阳谦校,华东师范大学出版社2012年版,第352页。

② 同上书,第128—129页。

前几天看见一部学者著的书，说西洋的政治制度根据于人性本恶的学说，所以提出许多牵制政府的方法；中国古代的政治制度，根据于人性本善的学说，所以只以为君主自能仁民爱物，用不着议会等等制度去限制他。这话很可研究，但是太偏一点。西方政治制度的根据，其实并不是说人性本来恶的，不过说人类有了大权，若没有限制，一定有滥用大权的趋势，就是好人也会变成坏人。并不是以为人性本来坏的，不过防备他、制限他不做坏事罢了。①

应该承认，杜威的这一对权力制衡理论的哲学基础的解释是正确的、合理的。首先，这一观点合乎西方政治哲学史和制度史的实际。譬如在英国，恰恰是认为"人对人像狼一样"而力主性恶论的霍布斯，提出了绝对君权的学说；而与此相反，认为原始状态的人彼此之间充满善意而主张人性本善的洛克，则提出了权力制衡的学说和与此相应的制度设计，从而为现代英美政治制度的建立奠定了理论基础。其次，这一观点从人类政治实践的经验事实出发，把人尤其是被选出来担任公职的人看作好人，而不是一开始就把人看作是本性邪恶，且注定要作恶的动物，不仅在事实判断上合乎实际（因为坏人是不大可能被选出来担任公职的），而且在价值判断上也体现了以忠厚之心待人（把人往好的方面想）的君子之道；同样是从人类政治实践的经验事实出发，杜威强调权力对人有腐蚀作用，认识到要防止好人变坏人就必须着眼于限制权力的制度建设，这不仅体现了人们维护自身权利不受非法侵害的愿望，更体现了对于被选出来担任公职的人的爱护。

与康德的人性论不同，儒家哲学的主流传统是性善论，以孟子为代表，所以杜威认为，孟子的政治哲学"强调了儒家教义中的比较倾向于民主的方面"②。且儒学特别强调统治者应该具有道德上的合法性，"皇天无亲，惟德是辅"，只有"内圣"，才能"外王"，"行一不义、

① ［美］杜威：《社会哲学与政治哲学》，载《杜威五大讲演》，胡适译，安徽教育出版社 2005 年版，第 53 页。

② John Dewey, *As the Chinese Think*, John Dewey The middle works Volume 13, Carbondale：Southern Illinois University Press, 1983, p. 225.

杀一不辜，得天下而不为"，这无疑也是其优于德国古典哲学之处。但这种政治哲学显然也有不够完备的地方，对此，杜威作了委婉的批评。他说：

> 我们理想中可以想象一个开明专制的国家，里面有好的君主、好的官吏，政治、法律都很修明，只有人民没有政治权，这也未尝不可能。但从人类经验上看来，这种理想，大概是梦想了。好的皇帝、好的官吏，也许可以有的，但只是暂时的。我们从前讲过，人们一朝有了大权在手，无论如何好人，总有自甘堕落、滥用大权的趋势。这是人类的一个大毛病。故无论如何，非有政治权保障不可。①

在这里，杜威重申了权力制衡的依据不是人性论上的性善性恶，而是权力对人的腐蚀作用；而制约权力的最重要的手段，就是对公民的政治权利的保障，特别是法律应赋予公民以选举和罢黜政府官员的权利。从政治哲学的学理上来说，应该肯定杜威的批评是具有合理性的。杜威的上述观点，开了20世纪自由主义与儒学之对话的先河。

　　杜威认为，在人性论上，中国和西方都有大致相同的几种学说。在中国古代，有人说人性本善，但后来被外欲习俗浸渍熏染，就变坏了；有人说人性本恶，全仗礼教来节制纠正；还有人说人性是不善不恶，好像水，决诸东方则东流，决诸西方则西流；主性善的又驳他说，人性趋善，好像水之就下。在西方，对于人性的观念也有两种。一是主善派，他们说人性本来是善，但后来受了物质的影响，就变坏了。卢梭也曾说过这种话，其理由是：要是天性彻底地为恶，那么任凭有如何良善的环境，人性也不会受影响；必定先有可善的因，才有感化迁善的果。二是性恶派，他们讲性是恶的，因为性要是善，那就不容教育训练了，而正因为要教育训练，所以性不是善。杜威认为，平心来论，两说各有毛

---

　　① ［美］杜威：《社会哲学与政治哲学》，载《杜威五大讲演》，胡适译，安徽教育出版社2005年版，第65页。

病。其实，人的本能本无所谓善恶，把他造成善行或凶德，都无不可。① 杜威认为，要培养具有良好道德品质的人，就必须有良善的环境，有良好的教育训练。同理，为了使被选出来担任公职的好人不变坏，就必须有好的制度环境。在宅心仁厚的哲人看来，制度所限制的乃是权力对人的腐蚀作用，从而使人更好地行使权力，而绝对不是把人当贼防。

3. 论中西"灭人欲"之学皆根源于性恶论，且皆为"乡愿之学"

杜威在中国讲哲学，不能不面对程朱理学的影响。当时中国学界已注意到程朱理学与康德哲学的相通之处，毛泽东在 1917—1918 年读新康德主义者泡尔生的《伦理学原理》时就写道："吾国宋儒之说与康德同。"②正因为在中国也与西方一样存在一种影响很大的"灭人欲"的学说，所以杜威探讨了"欲望应否寂灭"的问题，企图在关于"人欲"的两种对立的见解中寻求一种折中的解决方式。

一种见解是：人类的苦恼，大半由于多欲，要是将种种欲望寂灭干净，自然是天真泰然，百体从命了。杜威认为这种见解"立说未免过激"③，而其立论的基础正是性恶论：

> 他们既信他恶，所以用狮子搏兔的法子，将种种本能欲念、冲动意志都寂灭得干干净净，使道德完全成消极的，不是积极的。……他们所谓道德，大概都尚束缚本能，贬损意志，节制喜怒哀乐之情，不准他们妄发。诸位要知道，现在世界最可痛恨的是什么，就是这种非积极而为消极的道义德行。所以今日所谓良民，就是庸行庸言的乡愿（Mediocre Person），不是那有创造能力、积极精神、轰轰烈烈去改造世界的人物，这不是很可痛恨的事吗？依

---

① ［美］杜威：《伦理讲演纪略》，载《杜威五大讲演》，胡适译，安徽教育出版社 2005 年版，第 272—274 页。

② 毛泽东：《〈伦理学原理〉批注》，载《毛泽东早期文稿》，湖南出版社 1990 年版，第 196 页。

③ ［美］杜威：《伦理讲演纪略》，载《杜威五大讲演》，胡适译，安徽教育出版社 2005 年版，第 303 页。

我看来，要是不利用本能，而以束缚为德行正规，顶好也不过养成一种柔怯的德性（Wishy-washy Character）。Kipling 有一首诗，叙一个人死了要想登天堂，他是个庸言庸行无功无过的人，但是他没有积极地去做什么好事。所以天帝不准他登天堂，还打他下地狱去受审。……这首诗不但骂尽天下乡愿，也将主性恶的流弊和盘托出。①

在中国，程朱理学表面上讲性善论，骨子里却是性恶论，故主张"灭人欲"。章太炎先生认为这是"乡愿之学"，初学者往往对此论断茫然不得其解，读了杜威以上论述，也许可以真切地领会太炎先生的深意。

另一种见解恰恰相反："英国某诗人又说，欲望是不可少的，因为欲望能鼓动我们努力去改进环境。人无欲望，便蠢如鹿豕。因为有欲望，才能不满意于现状，才能发扬踔厉去从事改造事业。所以奢望为进化发展和改革之本源。有人问某德国社会改造家说，什么是改良社会最大的阻力？他说，就是难使社会不满意于现状。因为不满意，才有改良的欲望，才能努力去行。"对于这种见解，杜威审慎地指出："说句平心话，这也是片面之词。"他指出不知足的人也有许多毛病：愤郁多忧，难与为欢，或吹毛求疵，得陇望蜀，和世人多龃龉；浮躁易怒，责人重而责己轻，或自私自利，不顾公益。所以，在杜威看来，"有欲无欲，各有利弊。无欲望，便不能奋发去行；有欲望而常不知足，又必妄于非分，徒劳无功。"

在这两者之间，应如何善以处之呢？杜威认为：一方面，欲望和不知足心，万不可寂灭，因为不知足的目的，是要唤起努力，改进环境；另一方面，又不可操之过急，乃至贻祸无穷，这就要"善用不知足心"②。至于如何做到"善用"，显然就不能不从中国哲学中吸取合理的思想因素了。（见本文第三节）

---

① ［美］杜威：《伦理讲演纪略》，载《杜威五大讲演》，胡适译，安徽教育出版社 2005 年版，第 273—274 页。

② 同上书，第 304 页。

二 "实行道德之方法不同而原理相通"

——东西方伦理思想之比较，兼论新文化运动的中国特点

1. 论东西伦理思想的差异

在《伦理学演讲》中，杜威对东西方思想作了比较。他在比较中所说的"东方伦理"实际上指的只是儒家伦理，而他所说的"西方伦理"，则主要是指古代雅典和近代英美等国的伦理思想。在作此比较之前，他先有一个声明："我并非要度长较短，尊彼抑此。道德本应环境而起，某种道德对于某种环境为善，对于他种环境又不然，所以东西（方）道德，实无长短之可言。我所讨论，是智理上的比较，是东西思想的对照。"① 其关于东西伦理学之比较的总论点，可以一句话来概括，即："实行道德之方法不同而原理相通。"可谓善于异中见同矣！他认为东西伦理思想的差异主要有以下三个方面。

第一，"东方思想更切实更健全，西方思想更抽象更属智理的"②。杜威所说的"健全"，是指与"抽象"相对的"具体"或确实性。他说东方的五伦，都是确定的、切实的、天然的人生关系。西方思想却不同，作为其主要观念的正义与慈爱都是抽象观念，是由理智推究出来的，并没有实指哪种伦常事物。东方切实的道德观念的好处是有确定的标准，其弊病是因确定生执拗，不能通权达变以适应时势。西方理智的抽象的道德观念的好处是能权能变，如正义与慈爱，应用到各种伦理关系中都可以，虽有含糊的毛病，但却是平等的、普遍的、活的，能权能变以适应环境。对于杜威的这一观点，史华兹（Benjamin I. Schwartz）提出了不同看法，他认为中国古代也有"仁"和"义"这些与具体的

---

① ［美］杜威：《伦理讲演纪略》，载《杜威五大讲演》，胡适译，安徽教育出版社2005年版，第300页。

② 同上。

例示相分离的理智的抽象的道德观念。① 指出这一点当然非常重要，但杜威说中国伦理思想更切实，大体上还是可以成立的。

第二，"西方伦理根据个性，东方伦理根据家庭"②。这一差别与第一点差别有着密切的关系：正因为西方人不承认有确定不变的伦理关系，所以他们只知道有我、有个人，所以没有尊卑的分别，产生出正义和慈爱这种普遍适用于一切人的道德观念；而东方经书所说的五伦，有三个属家庭（即父子、夫妇、昆弟），其余君臣是父子的变相，朋友是昆弟的变相，所以说东方的道德观念，简直可说是全然以家庭为根据。经书说孝是德之本，而孝的范围也最大：不信不诚，败坏家声，可算不孝；建德立功，扬名显亲，就可算孝。因此，西方的道德说到底是个性的道德，东方的道德说到底是家庭的道德。这是一个为中西学者所普遍认同的观点。

第三，"西方伦理尊重个人利权，东方伦理蔑视个人利权"③。杜威说，西方一二百年来，个人权利最受尊崇。所以，个人有行动自由的权利，他人不得干涉；有保存财产的权利，他人不得强取；有养护身体的权利，他人不得毒打；有保全荣誉的权利，他人不得败坏。凡干涉他人自由、强取他人财产、破坏他人荣誉的，都是不道德的。后来这种权利观念渐渐被推入政治领域。从道德方面说，个人不能侵犯他人权利，所以从政治方面说，政府就应当保护人民的权利。这就是"个人主义的真表现"。父有权利，子也有权利，君臣同有此种权利。"君不尊重民权和民不尊重君权，一样的不道德。"④ 认为东方伦理蔑视个人在西方是一个比较流行的观点，但英国学者休斯（E·R·Hughes）却对此提出了异议，他认为"中国公元前五世纪以降，形形色色的思想者探索

---

① ［美］本杰明·史华兹：《古代中国的思想世界》，程钢译，刘东校，江苏人民出版社2004年版，第11页。
② ［美］杜威：《伦理讲演纪略》，载《杜威五大讲演》，胡适译，安徽教育出版社2005年版，第301页。
③ 同上。
④ 同上。

人类个性的本质以及对社会的价值，带来了了不起的发现"①。

杜威认为，东西方伦理学虽然具有以上几个方面的差异，但从伦理学的基本学理方面来看，却也具有相通之处，这就是他所说的"原理相通"。他认为"公益的尊崇"（Regard for Common Good）乃是东西方伦理思想的共同特征：

> 世界种种道德或规律（Moral Codes），或文或野，或东或西，或古或今，都有一相同而不变的地方，就是尊崇公益。实行道德之方法，条理万端，各各不同，但目的总在谋最大多数的最大幸福。孔夫子说："己所不欲，勿施于人。"耶稣说："视敌如友。"立说各异，而原理不过为人类谋公共幸福。②

这一论述，从抽象的学理上看应该说是正确的。

2. 评"引进西方经济，保留旧道德"

杜威批评了一些中国学者关于"引进西方经济，保留旧道德"的主张，他在批评这一主张时所阐发的哲学学理，竟然与恩格斯和列宁的观点达到了高度一致。对于生活在中国的各个对外口岸和中心城市的西方资本家及其文化侍从执着坚持的只给中国人经济和商业的实用技术而不给他们新观念的主张，杜威像鲁迅一样一针见血地指出，这些人之所以如此，是"因为各种新观念的引入会搅乱他们赞扬和借以获利的那些东西"③。

杜威看到，一方面，新文化运动正在中国蓬勃开展；但另一方面，"认为现存的种种罪恶是由共和引起的，并且欢迎君主统治回归的人比甚至旧时的共和人士人数更多——人数之众，正如20年前认为赶走外

---

① E·R·Hughes, *Introduction*, *The Individual in East and West*, *Oxford*：Oxford University Press, 1937, p. 3.

② ［美］杜威：《伦理讲演纪略》，载《杜威五大讲演》，胡适译，安徽教育出版社2005年版，第271页。

③ ［美］杜威：《老中国与新中国》，载《杜威全集·中期著作》第13卷，赵协真译，莫伟民校，华东师范大学出版社2012年版，第95页。

国人将会治愈一切罪恶，并尝试用义和团这种万灵药的人那样多"①。
这些人认为，只要引进西方的经济，而保留中国的旧道德，那么一切就
都会好的。对此，杜威坦率地表明了自己的看法，他指出：

> 这种观点是感伤的理想主义最具乌托邦色彩的想法。经济与财
> 政改革，除非伴随着新的文化理念、伦理，以及家庭生活（这些
> 构成如今所谓学生运动的这场运动的真实意义）的成长，否则就
> 如同隔靴搔痒。它会弥补一些罪恶，又创造出另一些罪恶。从其本
> 身来看，它是一个有价值的实际措施。但是，如果把它用作一根棍
> 子来打击男女老少对新信念、新观点、新的思想方法、新的社会科
> 学与自然科学——一句话，对一个新的年轻的中国的渴望，那么，
> 这真是荒唐透顶的事情。②

杜威认为，真正从根基上削弱作为古老中国之基础的家庭体系的，
不是归国学生的教导，也不是一小群人为了选择他们的伴侣而要求打破
家长权威、由此通过改变妇女的传统地位来变革中国的渴望。"这些事
情最多只是征候，不是原因。真正的原因，恰恰是工业革命产生的现代
方法。……铁路与工厂系统正在从根基上削弱家庭体系。即使每一个学
生都发誓永远保持沉默，这些东西也将继续发挥作用。"③ 这一观点与
列宁的观点惊人的一致。列宁在与俄国的民粹派论战时指出："欧洲思
想情感方式，对于顺利使用机器来说，是和蒸汽、煤炭和技术同样必
需的。"④

受康德哲学的影响，在中国，也有人说尊重个人权利好像有点自私
自利，道德应当根据义务，不应当根据权利；东方道德就是尊重一己对

---

① ［美］杜威：《老中国与新中国》，载《杜威全集·中期著作》第 13 卷，赵协真译，
莫伟民校，华东师范大学出版社 2012 年版，第 92 页。

② 同上书，第 91—92 页。

③ 同上书，第 93 页。

④ 列宁：《我们拒绝什么遗产?》，载《列宁选集》第 1 卷，人民出版社 1992 年版，第
136—137 页。

人应尽的义务，所以没有自私自利的毛病。杜威不同意这一看法，他说尊重权利并非蔑视义务，况且义务权利，本非二事。所谓义务，不过是尊重他人的权利罢了。假使我们拿个人做中心，认为我们的权利为神圣不可侵犯，那么，推己及人，自当会尽义务，自然会尊重他人的权利。所以你的权利，就是我的义务；我的义务，就是你的权利。政治上对个人权利之尊重，就是民治主义的基础。所以，中国的新文化运动致力于改变严尊卑上下之分、缺乏平等的权利观念的儒家伦理是正确的。①

杜威还进一步论述了现代社会中权利平等与社会正义的内在关系，阐明了"正义即权利"的哲学学理："利权和直道，有密切的关系，你尊重我的利权，我尊重你的利权，就是直道。所以可说直道等于利权（Justice ＝ Rights）。"② 在这里，是否尊重个人权利，被看作是衡量人的行为是否合乎道德、社会有没有公正和正义的准则。这一论述与恩格斯的观点相一致，恩格斯在《反杜林论》哲学编中说：

> 一切人，作为人来说，都有某些共同点，在这些共同点所涉及的范围内，他们是平等的。这样的观点自然是非常古老的。但是现代的平等要求与此完全不同；这种平等要求更应当是从人的这种共同特性中，从人就他们是人而言的这种平等引申出这样的要求：一切人，或至少是一个国家的一切公民，或一个社会的一切成员，都应该有平等的政治地位和社会地位。③

3. 论五四爱国运动和新文化运动的"中国味儿"或"中国特点"

杜威敏锐地看到，五四爱国运动和新文化运动具有明显的"中国味儿"或"中国特点"，其中有两个积极的主导特征："一是对文化方面的改革作为其他改革的前提的需求；二是领导权回归那些在态度方面

---

① ［美］杜威：《伦理讲演纪略》，载《杜威五大讲演》，胡适译，安徽教育出版社 2005 年版，第 301—302 页。

② 同上书，第 302 页。

③ 恩格斯：《反杜林论》，载《马克思恩格斯选集》第 3 卷，人民出版社 1995 年版，第 444 页。

特别倾向于中国的人的一种趋势，以此来针对那些引进与照搬外国方法的人。"然而，这两个特点看上去似乎是矛盾的："中国人领导权的回归如何与对中国习俗和思想习惯的攻击相一致呢？它如何与这样一种意识相符，即意识到西方优势的真正来源不在外部技术，而在思想与道德问题呢？"① 杜威认为，历史从来就不是逻辑的，许多在逻辑上矛盾的运动在实践上却是有效的。而其之所以在实践上有效，就在于其具有"中国味儿"或"中国特点"。

首先，无论是学生的爱国运动，还是主张新文化的白话文运动，都在中国历史上有过先例：

> 五四运动是由中国学生们直接发动的，不仅没有归国留学生的鼓动，而且与他们的建议是相反的。它是自发的和本土性的。语言改革的运动……从本质上说，它是一场由中国人为了特定于中国的目的而进行的运动，并且在中国历史上有过先例。②

杜威的这一论断，可能是与胡适交流的结果。胡适就认为，白话文是中国历史上就有的，新文化运动是中国的文艺复兴；胡适还在1921年5月4日的《晨报》上发表了《黄梨洲论学生运动》一文，其中讲到了东汉的太学生运动、宋朝陈东和欧阳澈领导的学生爱国运动等。

其次，新文化运动以思想和道德为救国之根本途径，"在某种意义上说，是向中国思维模式的回归，是一种古老的中国观念的恢复，以及对该观念的力量并未穷尽和终结于儒家的确信。"因为：

> 思想与道德因素的优越性超过所有其他因素的观念，本身就是一个中国本土的观念。它与认为能够通过引进枪炮和工厂以及技术管理的改良来获得拯救的观念相比，中国味儿浓得多；……某些新

---

① ［美］杜威：《中国的新文化》，载《杜威全集·中期著作》第13卷，赵协真译，莫伟民校，华东师范大学出版社2012年版，第101页。

② 同上书，第98—99页。

的领导者也许会断言说，他们通过抨击儒家思想——就像他们经常做的那样——比那些固守儒家思想的人更忠实于儒家。因为他们会说，孔夫子那里真正的观念、有活力的观念，是对理念、知识的首要性的信念，以及对传播这些理念的教育之影响力的信念。①

20世纪80年代流行的"五四学者是最传统的反传统者"的观点，其实是杜威早就讲过的话。

还有，杜威看到，在中国的道德改革浪潮中：

> 人们组建起成千上万的社团来医治各种各样的罪恶，这是反缠足社团、反鸦片运动、反赌博协会、重塑旧的教育体系以及诸如此类事物的时代。虽然基督教的影响是这些改革发起的一个重要原因，但它们中的绝大多数是以一种儒家复兴的形式进行的。②

杜威主张"中国味儿"或"中国特点"应该在实践中加以发展，他提出了"两个适应"的理论：一方面，中国文化要现代化，要"适应现代的情况"；另一方面，西方思想之精华要中国化，要"适应中国的情况"。他指出：

> 如今僵化为儒教的这些观念（指孔教在道德上和思想上的标准——引注）无法适应现代的情况。……而儒家教育已经成为贵族式的，是为了少数人的。因此需要一种新文化，西方思想中的精华在这种文化中应自由地得到吸纳——但是要适应中国的情况，作为手段被用来建立一种重新焕发青春的中国文化。③

---

① ［美］杜威：《中国的新文化》，载《杜威全集·中期著作》第13卷，赵协真译，莫伟民校，华东师范大学出版社2012年版，第101页。
② 同上书，第97页。
③ 同上书，第101页。

三 "取东西洋文明兼而有之"
——论中国哲学为救世之灵药与
中西哲学的互补和调节

对于中西哲学的差异，杜威主张以历史的眼光去看。他说：

> 希腊最初的哲学，与现在的哲学不同。他们所研究的都是自然现象，并非关于人生问题。拿现在的名词说起来，他们都是想做科学家的，不是想做哲学家的。……雅典的哲学家，才稍稍有进一步的研究，然而还是大概关于自然现象。他们都以为人是自然界的一部分。就是苏格拉底（Socrates）的人生哲学，也是逃不掉自然现象。于此就能看出东西哲学的异同。东方中国的哲学，是偏于人生日用的问题。西方的哲学，是偏于自然现象的问题，……后来由自然转到人生的研究，……所以生出人生的哲学，社会的哲学。①

这里"偏于"一词用得极佳，远比那些动辄说"西方有什么，中国没有什么"的学者们高明。

他在论述中西哲学对于自然的不同态度时，表现出了一种很深邃的哲学眼光。他说：

> 我们要把世界一切现象，比较一下，去下一个总括的断语，这是很难的一件事。但有几句话说来，有几分真实，而且可供大家研究的，就是以科学征服自然，是西洋文明的特长；目天然界现象为神秘，而且拿来当作娱心悦目的事物看，这是东方人最显著的

---

① ［美］杜威：《哲学史》，载袁刚学编《杜威在华讲演集》，北京大学出版社 2004 年版，第 277 页。

态度。①

这一论述实在非常精彩，因为它道出了中国哲学的审美特征，说明了西方哲学更多地是以科学的眼光去看待自然的，而中国哲学则更多地诉诸审美。这一论述，是后来诺斯罗普关于中国哲学审美特征之研究的先声。

但问题在于，世界已经进入了一个东西方文化密切交流的时代，中国与西方如何增进相互理解，如何善于吸取对方的优点，也就成了迫切需要探讨的问题。杜威最重视"生活的哲学"，或"人生哲学"。他认为"不同民族有着深深渗透于他们各种习惯之中的不同哲学"，要增进相互理解，真正做到取人之长，补己之短，就"必须从努力真诚地了解对方的生活哲学开始"②。正是在这些问题上，杜威又发表了许多至今仍有重要意义的真知灼见。

1. 论东西方两种不同的精神性尺度及其融合

杜威发现，在日本有一种流行的观点，即东方文明是精神性的，而西方文明是物质性的。中国人从日本那里接受了这一观点，而许多来自西洋的人则会把这个观点完全颠倒过来。杜威认为，之所以会形成这种误解，关键在于：在东方与西方，关于精神的和理想的东西的真正意义用的是不同的标准或尺度。东方人衡量精神性的尺度使他们没有看到，"在乍一看来似乎是西方生活的物质性方面的东西中，存在着某些理想的或精神的要素、经常受到忽视的一些要素"③。

杜威说，东方人衡量精神性的尺度是"通过沉思与冥想来宁静地修养心灵"，在东方人的观念中，"最宽泛意义上的审美要素，包括一种对普遍之物的形而上的冥想与沉思，这是首要的"④。与此不同，西

---

① ［美］杜威：《造就发动的性质的教育》，载袁刚学编《杜威在华讲演集》，北京大学出版社2004年版，第373页。

② ［美］杜威：《像中国人那样思考》，载《杜威全集·中期著作》第13卷，刘华初等译，马荣校、刘放桐审定，华东师范大学出版社2012年版，第191页。

③ ［美］杜威：《国家之间相互理解中的一些因素》，载《杜威全集·中期著作》第13卷，赵协真译，莫伟民校，华东师范大学出版社2012年版，第231页。

④ 同上书，第232页。

方人看起来似乎是忙碌的、主动的，并且把活动看得比任何其他事情更重要。他们看来似乎不赞赏闲适，以及沉思的修养、思辨、对自然之美安宁而平静地鉴赏、文学与艺术。虽然他们也创造出了精美的艺术与卓越的文学，但这些东西在西方似乎是文明的附带产物，而不是最重要的东西，并且没有进入生活的主流。对大众来说，获得空闲似乎只是为另一种活动提供一个机会，而不是通过沉思与冥想来宁静地修养心灵。在西方，保持忙碌显然首先意味着被称为商业的事情，买进卖出，制作用以售卖的东西，追逐金钱。如此看来，说西方文明是物质性的，又有什么不对呢？

杜威又说，东方人衡量精神性的尺度，西方哲学家也可以接受，但西方的大众却接受不了。西方大众衡量文明的精神性的尺度是"公益精神和投入"。他说："对我来说，……高雅的修养与闲适的享受，减少直接的活动——商业的、政治的、竞技的社交集会，是重要的。"但在西方的大众看来，这种因素就是相当次要的了。

他们认为，伦理因素比审美因素更加重要。服务于他人，对社会进步、人类福利的热情，甚至连那些在自己的人生中未曾以此为业的人都把这看作是理想的。为了服务于他人的福利而牺牲个人的享受，甚至是闲适的高雅享受，被视为精神的东西中重要的成分。或多或少有意识地把这些尺度铭记在心，使许多西方人……认为他们自己的文明更具精神性。因为他们（在中国）没有找到像他们在家乡找到的那样多的公益精神和投入。①

那么，如何评价这两种互相矛盾的精神价值呢？杜威认为：

服务的理想是活动的理想，是保持忙碌的理想。从闲适及其修养的观点来看，它会相应地显得像是沾染了物质主义，虽然是一种

①　［美］杜威：《国家之间相互理解中的一些因素》，载《杜威全集·中期著作》第13卷，赵协真译，莫伟民校，华东师范大学出版社2012年版，第231—232页。

高品质的物质主义。另一方面，从服务的伦理理想观点来看，审美
鉴赏与沉思显得像是沾染了物质主义，虽然是一种高级得不同寻常
的物质主义，因为它们看上去似乎带上了自私的色彩。

这一批评与中国晚明学者对宋明理学的批评如出一辙。至于如何在这两
种理想之间作出选择，杜威认为：

> 最合理的结论应该是：一个真正的理想会把来自两边的因素都
> 包括在内；到目前为止，每一种观点都是片面的，并且有些东西能
> 从对方那里学到。①

他认为，把各种理想的因素包含在看似物质性的西方文明内部，似
乎是"东方最需要从西方学习的东西"。他提醒中国人，"借鉴科学与
工业的专门技术应用，尤其如果后者与科学精神和社会服务相分离的
话，甚至可能是有害的，而在西方家园中，它们确确实实是联系在一起
的"②。回顾百年来的中国历史，杜威的这段话的意义很值得我们深沉
思索。

2. 论如何使中国人发挥其原创力，从而成为世界上最伟大的民族

杜威引用了一位美国教师的话，说如果中国人获得了盎格鲁—撒克
逊人的原创力，他们将会是世界上最伟大的民族。但问题是，在中国有
没有使人充分发挥原创力的环境？即使是盎格鲁—撒克逊人，如果在受
到周围人持续不断地监督的状况下生活几个世纪以后，他们是否还能够
发展或者保持住那股原创力？他说中国人的思考习惯是：在想要做什么
事情之前，先考虑"面子"问题。也许在他们看来，考虑一件新事情
的时候，踌躇三思对于创造来说更加重要。③

---

① ［美］杜威：《国家之间相互理解中的一些因素》，载《杜威全集·中期著作》第13
卷，赵协真译，莫伟民校，华东师范大学出版社2012年版，第232页。
② 同上书，第236页。
③ ［美］杜威：《是什么阻碍了中国》，载《杜威全集·中期著作》第12卷，刘华初等
译，马荣校，刘放桐审定，华东师范大学出版社2012年版，第43页。

　　杜威发现，在中国人的生活中，为他人考虑，体谅他人，与对他人缺乏同情心和主动帮助并不完全矛盾，因为谁也不想自找麻烦。他举例说，不仅在大街上人们对被撞伤的人都只当没看见，甚至看见自己的恩人受到伤害也不肯伸出援手。"这并不是说中国人的习惯性礼貌是不真诚的。……（因为）那些助人的人可能会惹祸上身，可能会被指责为同谋。在中国，事不关己，高高挂起；不要惹火烧身，祸从口出，这是生活的法则。"① 连主动帮助别人都怕惹祸上身的人，哪里还敢冒着风险去创新呢？因此，要使中国人成为世界上最伟大的民族，就必须改造不利于人发挥其原创力的社会环境。这一结论固然是对的，但他不知道，"事不关己，高高挂起"等生活法则是中国人用了多少血和泪才换来的教训；他的观察也有片面性，杜威在中国期间，鲁迅在北京《晨报》上发表的《一件小事》，就热烈讴歌了一位北京的人力车夫救助他人、勇于担当的高贵品质。

　　杜威思考的问题，孙中山先生早就在思考了，他是从中国哲学知行观的视角来思考的。1919 年 5 月 18 日，他们二人在上海会晤，孙中山以即将发表的"知难行易"学说质证之。据杜威回忆：

　　　　在与前总统孙逸仙一起愉快度过的一个晚上，他提出了与日本的快速发展相比中国的变化显得缓慢的理论。就像中国古谚所说，"知易行难"。孙先生这样解释，中国人人把这个谚语记到了心里。中国人不行动，是因为他们害怕犯错；他们想在事先得到保证，不会有任何失败或者严重的麻烦才行动。

杜威认为，孙中山所反对的"知易行难"说，正是对群居生活造成的"面子"心理阻碍创造性发挥的印证：

　　　　改革与试验遭到挫折，不是因为缺乏智慧，而是因为智慧对于

_____

　　① ［美］杜威：《是什么阻碍了中国》，载《杜威全集·中期著作》第 12 卷，刘华初等译，马荣校，刘放桐审定，华东师范大学出版社 2012 年版，第 46 页。

可能导致的错误的过度敏感、过度关心会引来麻烦。"远离麻烦"
变成了（行动中的）指导原则。①

杜威为中山先生的这一学说当起了义务宣传员。在《伦理讲演纪略》中，他说：

> 实行就是求知。知识要经过实践的陶炼才能正确。中国大政治家孙逸仙先生说，"知之非艰，行之维艰"两句话，贻祸中国不浅，就是使人怕事偷懒，养成泄沓昏沉之风，这话实在很对。我们虽然不能逆料成败，却不能不冒险去行，多行一次，就多一番经验，多一番经验，就增一度智识。②

在《教育哲学》的演讲中，他又说：

> 我闻中国古代有"知之非艰，行之维艰"的话。试验的方法，却与之相反。这是只有行然后可以知，没有动作便没有真的知识。有了动作，然后可以发现新的光明，有条理的事实，以及从前未发挥的知识。故曰：没有行，决不能有真的知。③

所有这些论述，既表示了对孙中山创造性地发展中国哲学知行观的高度认同，同时也提供了中西哲学会通的一个典型范例。

3. 论老子和孔子的哲学对中国民族性的影响及其现代意义

杜威对中国人讲西方的积极进取创造，对西方人却讲要"像中国人那样思考"，这大概就是李卓吾评说孔子时所说的"随机处方，因病

---

① ［美］杜威：《是什么阻碍了中国》，载《杜威全集·中期著作》第 12 卷，刘华初等译，马荣校，刘放桐审定，华东师范大学出版社 2012 年版，第 47 页。

② ［美］杜威：《伦理讲演纪略》，载《杜威五大演讲》，胡适译，安徽教育出版社 1999 年版，第 299 页。

③ ［美］杜威：《教育哲学》，载《杜威五大演讲》，胡适译，安徽教育出版社 1999 年版，第 133 页。

发药"吧。从老子哲学中，他发现了作为中国人生观之根底的崇尚自然，以及世界上其他民族都不及的对于自然无为的执着；从孔子哲学中，他发现了崇尚和平的理性，以及世界上其他民族都不及的把道德看得比什么都重要的精神品格。他强调："中国人的人生哲学，对于人类文化有一个非常有价值的贡献，而且含有一种为急促的、燥烈的、过于忙碌而焦虑的西方人所无限需要的素质。"① 他建议西方人要"像中国人那样思考"，正是第二次世界大战后诺斯罗普提出的"世界秩序中的'善'的标准之确立必须引进中国价值观"② 之主张的先声。

他说老子哲学是中国人生观的根底，认为从根本上来说，老子哲学对中国人的影响超过了儒家，人们往往是以老子的态度去接受儒家学说的。老子的教训最扼要的一句话，是自然超过人为，由此得出的结论便是"无为"主义。他特别欣赏老子的"听其自然"的人生观，对其"无为"思想作了中肯的评论。他说：

> 所谓"无为"，不完全是没有行动，它是道德行为的一种规律，是教人积极的忍耐，坚毅，静待自然工作的一种教训。……一味的夸高争胜，临了反要把自己缚在人为的网中。这一种见解，自然不是中国人所特有的，但是从这见解所得的结论，却没有像中国人那样的坚执的了。因为有了这种见解作根底，所以才有中国人"听其自然"、知足、宽容、和平、幽默、乐天的人生观。③

他说老子的学说之所以能有这样大的影响，是因为它与中国人的性情和生活习惯相合的缘故。

---

① John Dewey, *As the Chinese Think*, *John Dewey The middle works Volume 13*, Carbondale：Southern Illinois University Press, 1983, p. 223. 以下引用的译文，凡由该书译出者，皆为《东方杂志》19 卷 3 号（1922 年 2 月 10 日）所载之译文及华东师范大学出版社中译本《杜威全集·中期著作》第 13 卷之译文的综合。

② F. S. C. Northrop, *The Meeting of East and West：An Inquiry Concerning World Understanding*, New York：The Macmillan Company, 1946, p. 496.

③ John Dewey, *As the Chinese Think*, *John Dewey The middle works Volume 13*, Carbondale：Southern Illinois University Press, 1983, p. 222.

他认为老子哲学有助于西方人正确处理人与自然的关系。他说一个美国农学家写了一本书，叫《四千年的农夫》（*Farmers of Forty Centuries*），这一书名便足以引起我们无穷的反省。世界上其他民族从前也是农民，他们的耕种方法导致了地力枯竭和农业的衰落。但中国人还是照旧耕种着，他们的土壤至今还是多产的。

> 这是人类的一种莫与伦比的成就。借此可以说明中国人的保守主义（conservatism），可以说明他们尊重自然和蔑弃一切用人力奋斗并求速成的那种态度。他们的心灵和自然程序的契合，就像他们的肉体和农业劳作的契合一样。他们是保守的，因为从几千年来他们保守着自然的富源，坚忍而又顽强的看护着保存着。①

他说尽管中国人的风水学说和堪舆实践带有神秘色彩，但其中却包含着一个合理的信念，即："土地的开发必须顾及过去现在未来的全人类的利益。"②

他主张西方人应学习中国人"知足、宽容、和平、幽默、乐天的人生观"，以此来补充和调节西方人那种永远也不知满足的人生观，防止欲望过度膨胀所带来的社会弊病。他批评西方列强在第一次世界大战后"把他们自己的麻烦和不安向中国'投射'"的损人利己行为，建议他们学习中国的人生态度："如果采取中国人的恬静和耐心，只采取裁减军备、废止特权等必要措施，然后静待时间来调整目前的困难局面，那才是一服救世的灵药哩。"③

他扬老而并不抑孔，认为二者似相反、实相成。与道家崇尚自然无为相反，儒家强调的是艺术、文化和道德努力的重要性。但其实际效果在许多方面和道家学说是相似的：通过反复劝导，把先人的经典作为智慧的源泉来尊重，为保守主义提供了思想上的理由；通过把道德的和思

---

① John Dewey, *As the Chinese Think*, *John Dewey The middle works Volume 13*, Carbondale: Southern Illinois University Press, 1983, pp. 222 – 223.

② Ibid. , p. 224.

③ Ibid. , p. 227.

想的力量看作优先于其他力量而加以颂扬，教人耐心地漠视最后一定会被理性挫败的军事与政治力量的展示。他认为，从中国人对孔子的特别尊重，以及孔子对中国民族性的持久的影响力中，可以看到中国人生活的一个显著特点，即："中国人更倾向于依靠和平的理性而不是靠打架的力量来解决争端。"① ——这对于在第一次世界大战的硝烟中生活了好几年的西方人来说，是一阵凉爽和畅的清风。

他平静地问道："有哪一个别的民族如此持久地相信，孔夫子的影响最终是一切社会力量中最有力的吗？有哪些其他国家的英雄们是道德教师，而不是超自然事物的揭示者、僧侣、将军、政治家？"② 这一发问令人想起了伏尔泰记载的 18 世纪初英国人的一次集会上关于"谁是这个世界上最伟大的人"的争论，对这个问题的回答是："牛顿，只有牛顿，才是这个世界上真正伟大的人。"③ 这反映了 18 世纪英国人崇尚科学的时代精神。从 18 世纪初到 20 世纪初，历史的车轮又转过了两个世纪。杜威的发问表明，在科学昌明的时代，世界需要新的时代精神，需要像中国人那样崇尚道德。而这一意味深长的发问，正印证了狄德罗在 18 世纪作出的"有朝一日善意与道德的科学将跃居一切科学之首位"④ 的伟大预言。在这一意义上，似乎又可以说，在老子与孔子之间，杜威更重视的还是孔子。这或许是蔡元培把杜威与孔子并论，杜威亦由此获得了"西方的孔子"之雅号的原因吧。

杜威在赞扬中国哲学的同时也承认，无论是老子还是孔子的哲学都有消极面，因为"优点与缺点，长处与短处，总是互相伴随"的。他比较了中西定命论，指出：

> 西方的定命论是这样的：既然要发生的事情一定会发生，那么

---

① John Dewey, *As the Chinese Think*, *John Dewey The middle works Volume 13*, Carbondale: Southern Illinois University Press, 1983, pp. 224 - 225.

② ［美］杜威：《像中国人那样思考》，载《杜威全集·中期著作》第 12 卷，刘华初等译，马荣校，刘放桐审定，华东师范大学出版社 2012 年版，第 196 页。

③ ［法］伏尔泰：《哲学通信》，高达观等译，上海人民出版社 1981 年版，第 44 页。

④ Denis Diderot, *Lettres à Mademoiselle Volland*, *XLI. Le 30 septembre 1760*, *Oeuvres complètes de Diderot*, *Tome Dix-huitième*, Paris, 1876, p. 479.

我们还是要走自己的路。……但是东方人的定命论却更多地注目于现在而不是未来。为什么要去做呢？为什么要去尝试呢？为什么要花费精力去改变现状呢？"无为"容易变为消极的服从，保守容易变为习故安常，变为恐惧及不喜变换。①

他在1924年回答康乃尔大学中国学生关于"中国积弱的主要原因何在"的问题时，只说了一句话："中国文化过度了（China is over civi-lized）。"② 文化过度，自然也就文弱，缺少了生命的激情和探索创新的勇气，这其实主要也是针对儒家而言的。但他强调：

> 我的意思，以为完全生活，须取东西洋文明兼而有之方可。所以在西方人应当把东方人的恬淡安详的态度，收取些去；在东方人却应当把西方人的创造精神、科学精神吸收些来；这才能达到兼而有之的目的。③

作为一位有远见的和负责任的大哲学家，他憧憬着东西方文明相互交融、世界各民族和平相处、共同繁荣和发展的美好前景。

---

① John Dewey, *As the Chinese Think*, *John Dewey The middle works Volume 13*, Carbondale: Southern Illinois University Press, 1983, p. 224.
② 萧公权：《问学谏往录》，学林出版社1997年版，第75页。
③ ［美］杜威：《造就发动的性质的教育》，载袁刚等编《杜威在华演集》，北京大学出版社2004年版，第373页。

访谈与对话

关于"理想人格"的对话

吴根友　刘素民[*]

吴根友教授（以下简称"吴"）：刘老师，非常高兴。您是武大毕业的学生，现在在中国社会科学院任职，在基督教方面有长期的深入研究。我们今天就基督教文化和儒家文化中对理想人格的不同论述作一个比较。在世界化的过程中，对儒家文化圈和基督教文化圈中"人应该成为什么样的人？"这个问题，我们其实可以作一个更深入的讨论。

刘素民研究员（以下简称"刘"）：非常荣幸，感谢吴教授吴院长的精心策划！

一　儒家人格理论与基督教人格理论

吴：在儒家思想中，从孔子开始，特别提倡人要成为君子，然后在君子之上呢，可能更高的境界是要成为仁者，仁者爱人嘛，最高的境界当然是圣人，这是孔子提出的理想人格。孟子特别提到要成为大丈夫，这很重要。当然，他也提倡"圣"，认为"圣"是人伦最高的境界。荀子也提倡君子，继承孔子"君子儒""小人儒"之分的思想，特别批评"贱儒"。在荀子的思想中，不仅讲"圣"，还讲"圣王"。"圣人"要

---

* 吴根友，教授，武汉大学哲学学院；刘素民，研究员，中国社会科学院哲学研究所。

"尽伦"，"圣王"要"尽制"，"制"就是在制度中把最好的东西体现出来，所以，"圣王"是荀子思想中最高的理想。除此之外，在《易传》传统里面也讲"大人"，这个"大人"在德行、知识这两个方面都达到了一个完美的境界，所以在《易传》里，专门有一个说法，"大人者，与天地合其德"，就是大人的德性跟天地的德性是一致的。所以，他既不违背天地的规则，又能够根据天地的精妙规则来实现人的理想。关于这种理想，后期儒家如宋明儒学把整个前期儒家的这一思想作了一个非常好的概括，构成了一个图示。比如说，一般人，就是庶人，要向君子学习；那君子要向谁学习呢？君子要向贤人学习；贤人向谁学习呢？要向圣人学习。圣人是不是最高？不是，圣人要向天学习。所以宋代的哲学家周敦颐，就有一个梯度式的说法，叫"圣希天，贤希圣，士希贤"，"希"就是希求，希望的意思。宋儒对整个前期儒家的理想人格作了一个梯度推进的论述。所以我想了解，在基督教的文化传统中，对"要成为一个什么样的理想的人"有没有一整套类似的说法？比如说，从普通人到教士，到信奉上帝者，再到能够被上帝拯救进入天国。我想求教于您。

刘：谢谢吴教授。刚才听您讲儒家理想人格的建构过程当中，从孔子到宋儒整个这样一种设定或者说诠释，我们可以从中发现丰富的内涵。从您刚才这个介绍来看，我觉得儒家理想人格的建构讲求"内圣"，同时也讲求"外王"，但理想人格最终指向"天"，恰恰这一点让我觉得儒家的理想人格跟基督教的理想人格是有可比性的。为什么？因为一旦儒家理想人格最终指向"天"，那么它的这个超越性就出现了，它不仅仅是世俗层面的一维了，而是有超越的维度的。《论语》中孔子谈"天"之处比比皆是，且多有"天道"之意。如，"四时行焉，百物生焉，天何言哉"（《阳货》），"子在川上，曰：'逝者如斯夫，不舍昼夜'"（《子罕》），说的是自然法则；"获罪于天，无所祷也"（《八佾》），君子"畏天命""小人不知天命而不畏"（《季氏》），说的是惩恶扬善的天；然而，孔子谈得更多的是与个人命运息息相关的有意志、有人格的天，如"天生德于予，桓魋其如予何？"（《述而》），"天之未丧斯文也，匡人其如予何？"（《子罕》），"五十而知天命"（《为政》），

"不怨天，不尤人，下学而上达，知我者其天乎!"（《宪问》），"颜回死，子曰：'噫! 天丧予! 天丧予!'"（《先进》），"予所否者，天厌之，天厌之"（《雍也》），如此等等。无论是孔子的"自然之天"（不等于自然界）还是"义理之天"（不是抽象的原则），两者基本上是一致的，即以上观下或由下达上——以上观下，则万物一体，人事亦不例外，也服从自然法则；由下达上，则人与天相通，天也有道德属性，正所谓"天与人离形异质，而所继者惟道也"（ 王夫之《尚书引义》）。虽然天与人是两个相互独立的领域，但"天道"与"人道"却不是表示两个独立实体的范畴，而是一种你中有我、我中有你的关系范畴。以天道观人，人有天性；由人道达天，天也有人性。因此，我们可以在此找到针对儒家理想人格与基督宗教对话的可能。

我们知道，基督宗教是一神教。先说这个"人格"，"人格"这个概念，在英语当中就是"personality"，"personality"如果从词源上来说，应该是希腊语当中的"persona"，"persona"这个词的原意就是舞台上演出所戴的面具，它在词源上是这样一个意思，这个面具就类似于京剧中的"脸谱"。所以从这个意义上我们就可以引申，"persona"的"角色"的意义来源于最初的"脸谱"的意义。"personality"就是由这个词而来的。在基督教文化中有一个很重要的前提或者说设定，就是说，人是有罪的，人从受造那一刻，就是罪孽深重的。我们看《圣经》的时候，无论是《旧约》还是《新约》，都可以看到它记载了很多的小故事，都是在讲人的罪孽深重。有一些故事，比如说亚伯拉罕，他曾经拉皮条；还有雅各，他爱上了他的妻妹，就是他老婆的妹妹；还有大卫王曾经欺凌下属之妻以及彼得三次不认上主；还有耶稣在克西玛丽园祷告的时候，就是为即将到来的死亡感到极度悲哀的时候，门徒们却都犯困睡着了。这些记载中的人物都是很关键的，都是后来了不起的圣徒，对吧? 但是呢，他们也确确实实犯了这样的错误，这样的罪。也就是说，《圣经》中所记载的这些事情，它所涉及的人物都是后来成为圣徒的人物，但是在当初他们的罪过跟普通人没什么区别，比如说，懦弱啊、好色啊、肉体战胜不了自己的意志啊等等。这都说明在基督教文化当中所强调的一个设定，就是人是有罪的，是吧? 因为人是有罪的，那就需要对人进行救赎。于是基督教就利用希伯来信仰和希腊哲学，尝试建构一种叫"道成肉身"的神人之间的一种关联，这样就把既是神又是人的上帝作为人生的最终追求目标。那么对人来说，人的理想人格的追求，就以"神人合一"为最终目的，就是这样一个指向。所以，基督教理想人格的最终指向就是"神人合一"。"神人合一"在基督教中有一个词叫"vision"，它是以这样一个目标来设定人格的。我刚才说"personality"有一个希腊文的词源"persona"，那么，在基督教的神学当中呢，我们也可以见到另外一个跟它相关的词，也就是说，当我们谈到基督教理想人格建立的时候，我们不能不说，"personality"这个词的神学来源就是"person"。"person"这个词在基督教神学中有一个很特殊的含义，叫"位格"，它指的是上帝三位一体的神格。基督教在强调人是罪孽深重的同时，也有一个前提，就是人是受造的，人在受造的那一刻其实是具有一点点的神性的。"person""位格"的特性当中的一些东西，在上帝创造人的时候就赋予了人一部分。但是人的"personality"跟上帝的"person"相比在量上是不一样的。因为，对神来说、对上帝来说，"person""位格"是一个"perfection"，是一个"完满"。但是人的"personality"——也就是人的"人格"，在分有"上帝"这个"perfection"的意义上存在，所以人的"personality"是不完满的。那么，在这个意义上，人才有可能去追求最终的理想人格目标"神人合一"。基督宗教哲学中与儒家"天道"最接近的概念大概是"自然法"（natural law）。这里的"自然"不是指一个独立的实在即所谓的自然界，而是指万物的本性，首先是人的本性即"human nature"；自然法也不是后来所谓的统摄自然界的自然规律（law of nature），而首先并主要指道德律，是在人心中起作用的神圣命令。这与中国儒家的天道和人道合一的传统极为相似，为我们比较中西思想传统提供了一个新的切入点。

吴：好，非常好。圣人要跟天达到"合一"，那么在基督教神学里也有一个"人神合一"，但是这两个"合一"之间是不是有一些细微的差别？譬如说，"圣希天"，圣人希望能够跟天合一，但是他不是希望成为跟天一样那么有能量、能够造化万物，他可能在价值层面上能够更有涵盖性和包容性，比如说，他超越一种很狭隘的是非判断，对各种各样的价值采取一种包容的态度，对吧？圣人在人格上能够跟天合一指的是这样一个意思。另一方面，圣人与天合一还有另一个意思，那就是人在整个精神境界上保持着一种刚健不已的状态，所谓"天行健，君子以自强不息"。所以，"圣希天"里头包含着一种刚健不已，没有消极啊、被动啊、死亡啊等这样一些东西在里面。所以我觉得，儒家"圣希天"的内涵里有很多很多的主动性和胸怀上的包容性。用我们今天非常通俗的话来讲，就是圣人能够达到天的高度。他既是一个有情怀的人，对这个世界保持着一种高度的关爱，像慈母、慈父对孩子那样；另一方面有胸怀，对各种价值都采取一种包容，不是讲此是彼非、此非彼是。所以我觉得，在整个中国的儒家文化传统里，"圣希天"这样一个"天"的境界，可以说接近于一个完美的状态。那么，我觉得在基督教的"人神合一"里头，据我对基督教的粗浅的理解，人总是被拯救的、受上帝启示的。当人如果被上帝拯救、回到伊甸园的状态的时候，我不知道在这样一个位格上人跟神之间的关系是怎样的？尽管在整个基督教中也讲，人是按照上帝的形象塑造的，但是它能不能像中国人讲的，达到像"圣人"这么高的境界？我提这样一个问题。

二　狂狷、中道与救赎

吴：其实我接下来还有第二个问题，等会你可以再思考。就是我觉得儒家的文化中除了这个圣人啊、君子啊，还有一些很有意思的、跟圣人君子之间稍微有偏离的人格，但这也是很不错的，比如说"狂"和"狷"这两种人格，是吧？狂狷人格，其实除了有些疵瑕之外，它还是得到肯定的。比如说孔子就有限度地肯定过"狂者"。所谓"狂者"，即这个人老是讲"古之人、古之人"，意思是说，我虽然做不到某些事，但古代有那么一个理想的人是我们要模仿的。按照口语讲，就是这个人老是喜欢讲大话，但其实他是有所进取的人。"狷者"呢，他这种人，心胸可能狭隘一点，但是他持守一个原则：绝对不后退。就像我们今天讲的底线伦理一样，他有一个底线，超越这个底线，他宁愿死，都不会去做。这种人虽然没有达到君子的"中道""中行""不偏不倚"的状态，但也是非常值得肯定的。不知道在基督教文化传统里，有没有类似"狂"和"狷"这种中间的类型，这个也希望您能给我们讲一讲。

刘：嗯嗯，我先顺着吴教授说这个"中道"。在基督教伦理学当中特别强调中道。中道不是机械论意义上的，它是一个三思之后的非常审慎的斟酌，所寻求的是一个黄金点。所以，中道毋宁说是人之行为选择过程中的一个最高的目标。亚里士多德也强调中道，而正是因为承袭了亚里士多德的哲学传统，中世纪基督宗教的伦理学特别强调中道。

现在回到吴教授刚才的话，在基督教里面，人究竟怎么样去达到人的理想人格，有没有主动性？从基督宗教创造观的角度说，作为受造物，人是罪孽深重的，那么，我要想建立跟上帝的神人关系的话，我究竟有没有主动性呢？是否我就是完全被动地等着被救赎、等着弥赛亚的到来才是正确选择呢？从基督宗教的角度讲，是有主动性在此的。为什么？基督教讲人是受造物，上帝按照自己的形象造人，人是上帝的肖像，即"image of God"，基督教特别强调这个"image of God"。那么，有了这样一层关系之后呢，人和神在本体论上就形成了一种关联性。这种关联性就是通过从希腊哲学借鉴来的一种方法来建构的。这种方法是什么？刚开始我在讲的时候，我说基督教利用了希伯来信仰和希腊哲学方法来建构它的理论体系。那么，这种方法就是从希腊哲学、特别是从柏拉图那里借鉴来的一种方法，这个方法叫"participation"，意思是"分有"。人与神之间是通过"participation"这样一种关系建构起来的。也就是说，人在受造的那一刻，分有了上帝的神性，分有了上帝的理性和善性，这样一来，人与神就在本体论意义上建构了一种关联。从这种关联性出发，既然人是上帝的肖像，既然存在着这样一种本体论的关联，那么，在基督宗教的语境中，人的整个的人生就没办法离开对上帝神性这一完满性的追求。因此，从人的内在动力上来说，个体人生的内在动力是永远指向神的，最终目的是与神合一的，这个最终目标就是"Vision"，即得到永福。除此之外，基督宗教在建构它的理论体系的时候，在伦理学上设定了几种德性，首先我们知道的就是信、望、爱，它们在基督教哲学里面叫"三主德"。作为受造物来说，为了建构神人关系，人必须去爱上帝，并且在"爱上帝"的前提下"爱邻人"，在这个过程中逐渐去放大、增强作为罪人原本有的善性和神性，这是人的主动。除了"三主德"还有"四枢德"，就是基督教强调的审慎、正义、节制和刚毅。我们想一下，这四种德性其实就可以帮助人主动地去追求理想人格，来建构自己和神之间的理想的关系。与审慎、正义、节制、刚毅相反的这些错误，就像您说的那个"狂"啊、"狷"啊，在一定程度上，它是有益的东西，但是超过了那个程度，它也是有害的，也就是说，与审慎、正义、节制、刚毅相反的也会产生一些负面的作用。所以，我觉得基督教在这些方面是可以和儒家产生类比和对话的。

吴：您刚才讲到两点，非常有意思。就是"image of God"，是吧？（刘：对，对）像上帝，是吧？（刘：对）在汉语里头，其实在儒家里，包括在道家里也有类似的说法，人跟天地间的相似就是"肖（qiào）貌天地"。

刘：肖（xiào）天地。

吴：对，在发音上有"xiào 貌"、有"qiào 貌"，这在古音中都是可以的，以"x"声母和"q"声母发声的字在古音上其实是相通的。"不肖子孙"就是说不像天地生下来的。那么，儒家或者中国传统文化中的儒道两家，在讲作为一个个体的人，或者作为一个被天地制造出来的人跟他的本体有相像这一点上，可以说与基督教有非常类似的地方。但是，你刚才讲的有一点非常有意思的就是，在"四枢德"那里，跟神圣相反就是骄傲。我印象中，基督教非常批评人的这种骄傲。

刘：是的，基督宗教将骄傲、自大狂妄视为大忌。

吴：嗯，自大狂妄。我曾经请来过一位美国的耶尔李教授，他是斯坦福大学的，他专门来给我们讲过基督教传统里对骄傲的批评。在中国文化里的"狂狷"，它的负面情况恰恰都是"傲"，"狂傲""狷傲"，就是狂、狷在一定程度上是可以接受的，但超过那个度就是"傲"，就不行了。所以我觉得在这一点上也非常有意思，就是基督教也反对"傲"，儒家和道家也反对走向极致的那种"傲"，这种"傲"也是有问题的。所以，可以说在"谦虚""内省"的层面上，它们都有可以对话的地方。

三　达到理想人格的方法

吴：那么还有一点，我觉得，在儒家人格上面，有"希天"这样的内在动力。在方法论上，儒家特别强调两点，一个是向外学习，像孔子或荀子主张学习"文"，是吧？所以讲君子"学不可以已"，这是荀子的，孔子也是讲"学而时习之"。所以在孔子这个传统里，人要成为君子，学习是一个非常重要的手段。而且，只要你不是天生的圣人，你只有通过学习才能由普通人进为君子，由君子再进为贤人，这是学习非常重要的地方。那么，另一条路数，像孟子所开创的心学的路数，它更多地强调一种向内的追求，就是追求本原。一个是向内追求，一个是向外追求。向内追求就是要追求你的四端、本心，就是"求"放佚的良心，把丧失的良心找回来。这种"求"，称之为得之在我。这种"求"的结果是，通过我自己不断地追求，完全靠我个人的努力是能够有效果的。另一种"求"是追求外在的功名利禄，这种"求"，你得还是不得不是完全由你自己决定的。所以孟子讲，我们君子应该怎么求，我们只能求那个通过我自己的努力，能够达到理想结果的，也就是说，只能求我内在人性的这个"善"，至于外在的权势、名誉、地位，这不是求就能够得到的。所以，他把人生的整个的追求就放在内心，在这点上就非常有意思。我觉得在成就理想人格的过程中，一方面是学习经典、经文或者说文献，一方面是求人性，求内在的本体之善、"四端"之心。那么，在这个问题上，基督教要告诉我们的，除了受牧师的教化之外，作为一个普通人，我不是牧师，但我也相信基督教，那我怎么样能够变得更好？有没有一些方法？

刘：是的。我觉得刚才您提到的孟子的主张非常好。孟子以"不忍人之心"论"本心"，确立性善论。孟子看重心的道德本性"恻隐之心，人皆有之"，然后由本心论本性，由不忍人之心得出"四端"说，所以人才有"仁义礼智"四德。即将善这种本性看作生而有之的先验的。在孟子看来，人之有是四端也，犹其有四体也。（《公孙丑》上）四端是人之本性的自然呈现，是人与动物的不同之处。所以孟子认为没有四端，则不能成为人。孟子讲求"尽心""知性""知天"，他认为，人只要尽自己的道德本心去行事，就可以知晓自己的本性是善的，在内心上不会抗争，由此知本性与本心。而了解自己的本心是善的就知天了。孟子确认人的善来自于天，从而将人的价值源头客观存在化。无论孟子还是基督宗教，在这一点上是有共识的，即强调外在的、物质的、肉体的东西是次要的，人生最重要的还是在于人性的善的追求。

吴：如何追求这种善？

刘：在关于善的追求这个问题上，我觉得基督宗教有丰富的理论主张。首先，基督宗教有信仰主义的一方面，因此，一部分神学家强调纯粹的精神性而贬斥肉体，就像奥古斯丁曾经说到"肉体是禁锢灵魂的臭皮囊"；然而，另一个方面，基督宗教神学家的理论中也有理性主义的思考成分，比如说，中世纪的经院哲学家托马斯·阿奎纳提出"神恩成全自然"。自然意义上的东西，当然包含人的肉体、人的物质追求。在基督宗教看来，人作为受造物，其最终目的是借助于"神恩"获得救赎，而"神恩"也是为了成全这个自然意义上的价值的。也就是说，尽管肉体的快乐不是最终的快乐和最终的幸福，但是，人是一个由灵魂与肉体组合而成的复合实体，人的最终幸福即得到神恩的拯救并非只是灵魂的得救，而是整个人的得救，因此，人不必总是因为牵挂"旅途之终"而忘记当下的努力。也就是说，人可以借助于现实人生去追求最终的灵魂的快乐和精神的幸福。阿奎那把"Grace"作为最终目的，而这个"Grace"就是我刚才所说的"Vision"，就是"神人合一"意义上的最终目的。那么，在这样的追求当中，他将灵魂的幸福作为人生的最高目标，与孟子讲的精神层面的追求一样，提倡通过这个"meditation"或者"contemplation"最终达到"Vision"这样一个状态。可见，中西方这些大哲学家的想法在此有一致之处，也有明显不同，这个不同就在于，基督宗教虽然也发展了知物的物理学、知人的伦理学和知天的形而上学，然而，终究是将人得救的希望即人的最高幸福交给了超越的上帝。相较而言，孟子则讲求"尽心""知性""知天"，显然路径不一。刚才吴教授对我很有启发。儒家在进行理想人格建构的时候，它在真真切切地倡导"内圣"的同时主张慢慢地、外在地去影响社会，就是所谓的"外王"。但同时它又提倡一种超越性，就这种超越性而言，我记得好像是孔子说，对尧舜也不能称王。

吴：不能称圣。

刘：对，称圣。

吴：他的意思就是说，如果对天下所有人都有所拯救，就是尧舜在这一点上也是有缺点的，不是完美的。

刘：是啊。这样就说明一个问题，就是说理想人格的建构其实是一个不断追求的过程，用一个词来表达，这个过程是一个"生成"的过程，一个"becoming"的过程。基督教的理想人格建构跟儒家的理想人格建构尽管路径不一，却都是包含着一个不断生成的过程，是永无止境的。就此而言，两者也是可以对话和比较的。

吴：好。除了自觉地学习之外，儒家认为在成就理想人格的过程中间，老师的作用是很重要的。这一点可以说在荀子和孔子那里都有，尤其是在荀子那里，他特别强调师是重要的，如果没有师的正确引导，你的学习就很容易走上弯路、邪路和歧路。荀子的这一思想，应该说在唐代韩愈的《师说》里得到了一个全面地理论的总结和提升。他讲"师"有三种。传道是一种，"道之所存，师之所存"，这是最高境界的"师"。授业、解惑各是一种，"授业"仅仅是把知识传授给你，"解惑"可能不一定直接给你上课，但像郭沫若讲，有时候一字之师啊，这都属于"师"的范围。所以，如果按照韩愈的讲法，"师"其实有三种类型。最高的"师"，跟"道"结合在一起，这还是儒家的，就是"道"之师；第二个就是"业师"，业师就是在学业上、知识上的老师，像我们今天的硕导、博导一样，给你培养成硕士、博士，拿到文凭；然后就是"解惑"，比如说你在任何一个地方，哪怕你是在坐火车、在路上，跟别人相处的时候，你有一个疑问，你问了别人给你解答，他也是你的"师"，所以，今天有"一字之师"这样的说法。那么，在基督教传统中的牧师里面有没有类似这样的划分？或者有？或者没有？

刘：嗯，谢谢吴教授。这个问题非常好。同学们现在是在大学读书和研究，大家都知道大学是目前我们获得知识最理想的地方，因为这里有系统的学科设置和科学有效的讲授与学习方法；大家也一定清楚，现代中国大学的学科设置与讲学方式在很大程度上借鉴了西方大学的建制。可是，同学们是否了解，西方最早的大学是天主教的教会建立起来并完善的，特别是以经院哲学学术发展的地点即教会学校和修道院为基础建立起来。在中世纪，"大学"（*universitas*，university）原意为"统一体"，原指教师与学生的行业公会。教师按授课专业分成不同学院，一般分艺学院、神学院、法学院和医学院四部分。各大学的专科各有侧重，比如说巴黎大学、牛津大学是以神学院著名。大学的艺学院和神学院成为继希腊学园之后的哲学摇篮。在此，学生要学习"七艺"，而授课与争辩则是两个重要的教学环节。毫无疑问，这些方法与教学内容也被我们现在的大学所普遍采用。在中世纪修会建的大学里面，教师是有双重身份的，即教师和神职人员。所以，他承担着两种角色，一个是在大学的课堂里教书，另外一个是在修院里面去布道。而大学学科的设置也充分体现出一种整全人修养或者说建构理想人格的设计与实践。师生在课堂上讨论宇宙和人生的各种问题，亦即说，他们在知识论上特别注重"知物""知人"和"知天"的问题。在"知物""知人""知天"中，他们尝试从人的角度，以人为中心去理解天和物，建构"顶天立地"的大全理论体系，从而实现宗教信仰意义上人与上帝之间的关系。"七艺"的内容、授课与争辩的方法逐渐演变，并在后世各地的大学推广，最终成为我们今天学科设置和教学内容的重要组成部分。在这个意义上，儒家虽然没有像基督宗教这样建立一个系统的现代教育理论和技术，但是在方法上也是有可比较之处的，是吧？

吴：对。好，我们接着"师"这个问题讲。在宋以后，"师"已经变得在整个制度建构中有它的地位，叫天、地、君、亲、师，就是"君""亲"，然后"师"，"师"在整个国家的价值建构中有非常重要的位置。那么，在整个基督教的社会里，牧师在整个社会的结构中间是处于什么样的位置？

刘："牧师"（priest）是一种职业，是在一般基督新教的教会中专职负责带领及照顾其他基督徒的人。圣经原文的用字是牧羊人之意。治疗和支持是牧师的主要职责——牧师怀仰着对基督教信念的忠诚，治疗并保卫他的同伴们。因此，"牧师"之师不同于"天、地、君、亲、师"之"师"。在中世纪担任大学教职的许多人是天主教神学家，其中也有不少人是神父（Father）。神父即神甫，司祭、司铎的尊称，是一个教堂的负责人，介于主教与助祭之间，属于七级神品，是罗马天主教和东正教的宗教职位。牧师也好，神父也好，在基督宗教社会制度建构中都有一定的地位，所发挥的作用是沟通教徒与上帝的关系。不过，从特定的历史时期来看，特别是在中世纪，在基督宗教价值观占统治地位的时期，神学家曾经被赋予比较高的社会地位，特别是，一旦他们因为对神学教育、对社会教育做出了特殊贡献而取得各种封号之后，他们的地位就更是非同寻常。例如，神学家托马斯·阿奎那是巴黎大学的名师，1323 年，他被教皇册封为圣徒。教皇宣布"托马斯著作的每一章节都是正确的"。托马斯还被授予"天使博士"的称号，其学说被确立为天主教的正统学说。20 世纪末，英国广播公司举办了人类第二个千年最伟大思想家的网上评选活动，结果，托马斯·阿奎那力压霍金、康德、笛卡尔、麦克斯韦和尼采，以排名第五的身份跻身于"千年十大思想家"之列，足见其非同寻常的社会影响力。再例如，9 世纪爱尔兰神学家爱留根那是一个通晓古代语言与文化的宫廷教师，因为他的智慧而备受法国皇帝和社会名流的喜爱，因此一度被赋予极高的社会地位。中世纪时，整个社会赋予了神学家和神职人员非常崇高的地位，大到皇帝的老师，小到普通百姓去教堂，在遇到非常难以解决的问题的时候，去教堂请教神父。不过，随着宗教世俗化的加剧，基督宗教在世俗社会中发挥影响的程度逐渐减小，特别是，随着世俗教育的独立化与专业化的加深，神职人员所担任的"师"的角色逐渐被限定于神学院或有限的哲学专业，因此，神职人员的社会作用与其发挥作用的程度也相应地非比从前。然而，无牧师也好，神父也罢，其所承担的沟通人与上帝关系的核心角色无论如何都没有改变，因此，不管是从担任世俗教育的教师的角度，还是从个人信仰的角度看，他们的社会影响力和社会地位虽然有所减弱，可是，他们在西方整个社会的价值建构中曾经提出的理论已经和正在发挥着非常重要作用。

吴：我能不能这样理解，就是基督教社会中"师"的地位很高。中国人讲，天地是最高，然后国君是其次，然后就是亲人，"天、地、君、亲"，然后就是老师。在这个人格的塑造中间，老师是最末端，但也让你从一个无知者到有知者。那么在基督教传统中是不是这样，比如说我们人跟神有一个内在的关系。但是，以我对西方文化的理解，神职人员其实在一定程度上比皇帝还高，因为皇帝登基时毕竟还要教皇去加冕。这能不能叫上帝、神、国君到亲人，或者其他？有没有在类似的社会结构上来安排神职人员的这种特殊地位？

刘：这个理论上是没有的，但是社会实践上确实曾经有过这么做的，特别是中世纪。君权神授，世俗皇帝要登基的话就必须借助于上帝的权威来赋予他合法性、合理性。因此，神职人员的价值在于赋予世俗权力跟天沟通的神圣性，这是最根本的。所以在某种程度上，他是至高无上的代表，然而，他只是代表，因为上帝才是最高权威，而无论谁，都不可以僭越上帝的威严。

吴：所以在这点上，其实他的位置比中国的老师的位置还要高。

刘：从神职人员对皇帝"君权神授"发挥影响力的角度看，你说的有道理。然而，中世纪时，作为教师的神学家一般不具有发挥如此影响力的角色担当，因此，其对当权者的影响力有时候是只能是间接的。而如果同样是作为宫廷教师（皇帝的教师），我想，中国的老师与西方具有神职身份的老师受当权者尊敬的程度也许是大同小异的。

吴：好，我接下来要问的就是上面没讲的，就是儒家的君子人格是正面的，但是与君子人格稍微偏离一点的，有"狂者"有"狷者"，那么在基督教的理想人格中间，相对于比较好的牧师而言，有没有类似"狂"和"狷"的概念，来表明这种人也还是可取的，但是只不过有所偏失而已。

刘：就是跟这个"狂"和"狷"相同的说法？

吴：类似的。"君子"是最好的，是不偏不倚的，但是"狂"和"狷"也是君子类型，不过是有瑕瑕的，"狂者"代表说大话的，"狷者"代表持守原则的。这样的理想人格的概念，我们在基督教中能不能找到类似的两者？但又不是犯罪的。

刘：刚才我说道，基督教有信、望、爱"三主德"，"三主德"太抽象太宏观太大了，为了辅助这个大的目标的实现，基督宗教还提出审慎、正义、节制、刚毅，特别是，强调中道原则，强调"狂"而进取，而一旦进取之途被堵塞，就要学会"狷"而自守。一张一弛乃文武之道，狂狷是中庸之道的两极，也是基督宗教思想在继承亚里士多德思想时的进一步发挥。

四　理想人格形成的动因

吴：类似的。好，我们进入第三个问题。对基督教文化和儒家文化中理想人格形成的动因，我们也可以做一个对比。儒家讲为什么要成为君子，这基于人之为人的本质这样一个设定。比如说，我们讲你之所以是人，而不是禽兽，你应该做到什么。所以在先秦的儒家特别讲，如果一个人不孝顺父母，那是不能成为人的。儒家文化有一个非常重要的区分，它在人跟禽兽之间划了一道界限，人不能成为禽兽。但是如何来规定人呢？儒家在讨论人向理想人格迈进，由比较低的人的品位向更高的品位迈进的时候，要寻找其内在动力。所以把仁者爱人看作是人之为人的本质，就是我们对同类要爱，如果你不爱，你就不配作为人。那你的父母当然是人，而且他们是养育你的，你对他们不仅是一般地爱，还要孝，对你的兄弟要敬，所以从人的本质上讲，它使我们朝着一个理想人格奋斗，不是有一个外在的东西压迫着你，而是内在的本质召唤你成为理想的人格。在动力上，孔子开创的儒学是这样讲的。

刘：其实就是人性决定的。

吴：哎，人性内在决定的。孟子讲得更清楚，所谓恻隐、羞恶、辞让、是非，这四端是所有人都有的，这叫普遍本质，没有做到这些就不配称为人。所以孟子把这些视为人性固有的，而且是分为四个层面上讲的。所以在这点上，儒家成为君子、成为圣贤的理想，不是别人要求的。你要成为人的时候，内在的本质召唤着你。按照海德格尔的现象学说法，它是由内在的本质召唤出来的，不是出于外在制度的压迫或者神的要求。所以这样一个人之为人的召唤，使你朝着君子、贤人、圣人这样的目标去奋斗。那么，基督教讲人是被上帝创造出来的，是"creature"、被创造物，只有上帝是创造的。所以，在这样一个理想人格的塑造过程中，基督教传统可能强调拯救，或者强调启示，没有上帝的光的启示，你就不会开悟，没有上帝的拯救，你永远都是罪人。那么，在这一点上看，每个人的存在好像是被动性的。在儒家思想中，每个人理想人格形成的动力在于内因的召唤。那么在基督教中，人去信、望、爱的内在动力是怎么展现出来的？

刘：您讲的这些对我有很大的启发。刚才您提到孟子，他似乎是在强调人性意义上的一种内在召唤。实际上，基督宗教在建立理想人格的时候，强调人是有内在动力的，这个动力于人是有最终目标的。孟子强调内圣外王是发自内心的、发自人性的，是一种本质的要求。在基督教的哲学建构当中有一个非常关键的词叫"natural law"，我们都知道这个词，但是很多同学会认为它是一个近代产生的西方概念。其实不是这样的，在基督教理论当中对"natural law"有系统的论述。那么，近代的"natural right""human right"也是从这儿生发出来的。现在回到人性问题上，"natural"是从"nature"而来的，"nature"就是自然，自然的也就是人性的，所以，自然法也叫人性之法，自然法的规定就是人性之法的规定。自然法有丰富的内涵，总的来说它的诫命就是趋善避恶，趋善避恶其实是人的本能的、本性的要求。自然法有三个诫命：第一就是保全生命，这是一种本能的要求；第二就是繁衍后代，因此需要结婚生子；第三是所谓神学意义或形上意义的追求，即对真理的追求、与上帝合而为一的追求。由此，我们看到，它的内容实际上是上下贯通的，既有世俗层面的指向，也有最终指向神人合一的目标，从这个意义上来说，人作为受造物有一个与创造者相沟通的可能性，即人天生具有主动地去追求理想人格的天性。不仅如此，作为"image of God"，人在受造的那一刻，就被上帝赋予了这个"personality"，而这个"personality"跟上帝的"person"有一种本体论上的关联性，这就决定了人必须以上帝为最终目的，终身追求上帝的完满性（Perfection）。因此，人生的追求根本目标是具有人性意义的。这一点上跟孟子的说法在内涵上是比较接近的。从基督教的角度来讲，这里首先是一个目的因的带动，而后才生成了人的动力因。否则，它就是外在的，就不是人性意义上的，所以我觉得孟子那里也应该是一个目的因，而不是动力因。

吴：但中国哲学不是从动力因、目的因上说的。

刘：对，没有四因说。如果从四因说的角度说的话，我觉得目的因更恰当，因为它是人性，发自内心的。

吴：其实在儒家这里，它把一切来自于人性内部的追求看成是一个内在的动力。

刘：对，目的因的作用大概在于此。

吴：在儒家看来，如果是被制度所压迫、所驱使，则是外在的、不能成为内在动力的，所以动力在汉语里头具有自我发动的意思。

刘：自我发动。

吴：像阳明学，在讲良知的时候，它与朱子学的一个非常不一样的地方就是，它特别强调良知是内在的自我觉醒。

吴：自我发动，譬如说，西方道德哲学中特别讲到道德拖延症，我明明知道这是善事情，但我就是不去做，心里有一些内疚、亏欠，但我还是不去做，道德动因乏力。所以阳明他讲我们每个人之所以在现实生活中知行不合一，就是因为内在的动力启动系统出了问题、被遮蔽了，要么被物欲遮蔽了，要么被世俗的名利遮蔽了，所以阳明一再讲我们要彰显自己的良知。

刘：致良知。

吴：对，致良知。所以所有的学问都是致良知，致良知之后让你的生命有了"主脑"，"主脑"就像打仗指挥部，这个指挥部是很灵敏的。

刘：就是这个原则。

吴：指挥部是灵敏的，一切就像太阳光是照着的，所以其他一切物欲啊，其他一些妖魔鬼怪，自然而然就被驱逐了。所以阳明讲学问其实很简单，没有那么复杂，你把你的良知照亮了，时时处在这个醒着的状态、不睡觉的状态，你干什么事都是对的。

刘：其实这个跟启蒙说、跟基督教的光照论是相似的。

吴：但我是从人格的成长的角度讲，就是儒家有一个内外之别，内就是发于人性的，所以我把它理解为是一个动力，外就是我们要实现的一个社会目标。比如说当老师有很多硬的条件，要不是为了保持这个教职啊，其实我很懒得做的，这就是被压迫的；但是我要是觉得我有一种使命（刘：使命感），对，觉得当老师要传道啊什么的，那你就会发于内心地自我驱动去做。

刘：基督宗教的传教士的确是怀抱着使命感去传教和做事的。同学们看小说看电视看电影，都看到过那些苦行僧吧。苦行僧不光是佛教当中有，基督宗教当中也是很多的。有些隐修士苦修的程度不得了的。像托马斯·阿奎那，他家是贵族，他原本是富家子弟，可是他就要尝试一下托钵僧的滋味，以此修行，这其中就包含了一种使命感。还有一些历史上去其偏远贫困地区传教、帮教的传教士，如果不是使命感驱使而生成的意志力的坚守，面对穷山恶水和无知暴民，就会有犹豫和退缩。当年我在武大读书时，听说来自美国天主教大学的 Maclin 教授曾经自费吃住在这里给同学们举办讲座、给同学们上课。他是美国天主教大学的教授，同时又是一个天主教徒，无论如何，他的奉献精神当然离不开他作为教师所具有的传授知识的使命感；然而，除此之外，即使他在给我们上课时从未传教，而只是讲授哲学理论，可是，谁又能否认他的敬业与认真与他作为天主教徒而怀揣的使命感无关呢？使命感会产生一种内在的力量，这是一种强大的动力。

吴：对对。

刘：要达到一个理想的目的，我觉得可能阳明哲学跟基督宗教在向着理想人格迈进的时候，是具有可供比较的理论的。

吴：只不过我们是在不同的体系下说法不同。

刘：对。就是说，在基督教这边更愿意作为一个目的因去说，当然动力因也是有的，但动力因就是外在的动力。

吴：我们这里说的动力是内在人性的召唤（刘：良心，良知），所以这里存在一个内在诠释系统的差异。

五 "君子"与"小人"之称

吴： 在儒家文化传统中，作为一个普通人在道德上有君子和小人之别。普通人就是没有像基督教牧师那样有一个职位的人，基督教有没有类似于君子这样的人格，然后跟小人存在一个道德上的差异？比如说基督教有异教徒和教徒，那么异教徒是不是相当于我们这样一个小人，或者是怎么样的，在人格上的区分上有什么样的一些概念和观念可以沟通？

刘： 总的来讲，基督教理想人格的最高点就是神，"person"既是神格，又具有人格的意义。基督教里面又有另外一个说法，就是"incarnation"，道成肉身。正是通过道成肉身，神有了人形，祂在具有神性的同时，也具有了人性，这才给了人成为类比上帝存在的存在的一种可能性。在这个意义上，人是平等的。那么回到您刚才的问题，您的意思是？

吴： 我的意思是讲，比如说，生活中间，你尽管不是一个神职人员，我称你很有道德，这个人是一个君子……

刘： 就是有没有"小人"这个意思？

吴： 不是。是这样的，在基督教的理想人格塑造中，一个人不是牧师，也不是神职人员，但我觉得这个人在基督教信仰上已经达到一个很高的地位，我怎么来称谓他？这在汉语里很好说，在儒家传统中，可以说这个人很君子，是吧？那就是一个褒扬性的称法。但在基督教中，我不能称扬你是一个牧师，我也不能称你是一个异教徒。我们讲"这个人做事很差劲，这是一个小人"，在儒家里头，这样一个普遍性的人格有一个普遍性的二元对立，不是君子，可能就是小人，或者就是庶人、普通人，是吧？但是，我们至少有这样一些分别。那么在基督教中，如果我是你的教友，我的修为很好，但我不是神职人员，在我没有社会架构中的职位的时候，有没有对正面人格的一些称谓？

刘： 从圣经上的角度来说，所有的基督徒，无论年龄大小都是上帝的儿女。所以，他们在教会大家庭里自然就互为弟兄姊妹；神父称平信徒为教友。基督宗教有许多尊称，对修为好的智者和大德之人，天主教教宗有授予尊称的习惯，例如"天使博士""圣徒""全能博士"等等称号，将获得者树立为人生楷模教人学习。基督宗教没有"小人"的称呼，然而，历史上，对异教徒却有比"小人"之称更恶劣的称呼，那就是"恶魔""撒旦"。历史上，布鲁诺就被当成异教徒恶魔而处死。值得注意的是，《圣经·旧约》当中有对异教徒采取"以牙还牙"的针锋相对的态度的教义，而《圣经·新约》则一改过去，强调"他打你左脸，你把右脸给他"的宽容态度，目的是弘扬上帝拯救的大爱。中世纪基督宗教伦理学强调"恶是善的缺乏"，因此，它是反对二元论的。

吴：我们讲，在汉语世界，包括汉语佛教里面很有意思，它对人格是有阶位的，比如说有善男、善女……

刘：对，善男、善女。

吴：信男、信女。

刘：对，信男、信女。

吴：然后有菩萨道，再往上是佛。

刘：基督教也有。

吴：基督教有没有类似地描述这些人？

刘：天主教的教阶制度就是规定天主教神职人员的等级和教务管理的制度，是教会法中的一项重要制度。教会教阶一般分为教皇、大主教、主教、神甫等，统称为大职教，下面是修士、修女等上职教，在教务方面按照级别逐级对下行使管理权。教阶是天主教会按照等级制度组成的教职体系和教会管理体制。罗马帝国后期参照帝国的官阶体系而形成，后逐步扩展并定型于中世纪西欧封建社会。教阶制的主体由主教、神父和助祭三个品位组成。主教品位又分作教皇、枢机主教（红衣主教）、首主教（即首席主教，一国教会组织之首或首都所在地的主教）、大主教、主教和一般主教等级次。助祭之下还设有一些其他较低品位。教会管理体制则依照这一等级层次，逐级对下行使管理权。罗马教廷把整个西欧的基督教组织及神职人员，按着这一等级森严的教阶制度，统统纳入一个巨大而完整的组织体系之中。

吴： 它这个仅仅是代表着宗教组织里面的阶层，但它是跟人格连在一起的吗？因为在儒家，比如说，我是一个厅级官员，或者我是一个尚书，或者我是一个侍郎，或者我是一个知府，我有这样一些官位，但这不必然说我是一个君子啊。在基督教文化的理想人格里面，有没有一套职位之外的语词或称谓？

刘： 神职人员有被封圣或者被授予尊称，例如"全能博士""天使博士"等，就是职位之外的称谓，这种称谓既对是对拥有者出类拔萃智慧的肯定，也是对其理想人格的称颂与宣扬。不是每一个神职人员都可以封圣或者被授予尊称的，只有很少一部分被封圣，包括修女也是，很少一部分修女被封圣。但是历史上有一些人，比方说托马斯·阿奎那和奥古斯丁这样一些是被封圣的，但是跟他们同时代那么多优秀的神学家和教师，得到尊称的并不多。

吴： 都是一般的。

刘： 教阶制是非常严格的。对于普通人来说，加入天主教之前要学道理，这种学道德即学习基督教理想人格的一些内容、一些理论，并在这个过程中慢慢地去实践与塑造自己的理想人格，当然是基督宗教的理想人格。只有达到一定程度后才允许学道理者受洗。

六 "人格"意涵与异质文化

吴： 另外一个问题就是关于"人格"这个词，"人格"这个词是对英文"personality"的翻译，邓晓芒老师其实是不同意汉语里有"人格"这个说法的，就是说汉语里没有"人格"，只有"品格""品性"等等。

刘： "人格"是一个多层次的概念，可以用"品格"解释，但是它比品格内涵更丰富。

吴： 对，是这样，我就是这样认为的。我们用现代汉语的"理想人格"来解释整个中国古代以儒家为主的文化里面人的不同的道德境界，就是君子、贤人、圣人，然后就是圣人与天合一的最高境界，我们把它称为"理想人格"。实际上在整个中国古代并没有"人格"这个词，更没有现代汉语"理想人格"这个词。我是用现代汉语的语言来讲人怎么样成为人，达到不同的道德境界。

刘：您很严谨。

吴：所以在这里我们是用现代汉语谈古代的道德境界，因为中华文化的传统特别是儒家，是以成为一个道德的人作为一个目标，跟整个基督教或者是世界上所有的一神教不太一样的地方是，一神教里面可能更强调人向神的皈依。

刘：有道理。

吴：在这样两个不同的文化传统里面，比如说，未来的"一带一路"，或者是未来的美国、欧洲的大批人到中国来，就像今天的中国人向欧美移民、定居一样，那么，这样一个异质的文化，到中华文化传统中来，这涉及一个怎么样做人的问题，他不能够按照儒家的方式做，只能按照一神教的方式做。就是说，我们如何在现代汉语的"人格"的意义上来理解这个问题，即不同的文化传统特别是一神教文化传统的人与儒家文化的人联系在一起时，如何能够和平共处的问题。比如说，我一骂你，哎呀，这是一个小人，他要是知道汉语小人的意思肯定很生气，我是一个上帝的选民呐，或者说我是一个信上帝的，你怎么能这样讲呢？但是外来的这些文化有时会把你称为异教徒，以一个异样的眼光对待你。比如说，在今天新疆的伊斯兰教的清真寺，它不怎么允许汉人进去。有一些很激烈的地方，你进去他会杀你，是吧，这当然是很极端的，不太多的。在这样一个多元的文化中，把它更简化一些，在一神教的文化传统和儒家的文化传统中，普通人在接触的时候怎么样以一种比较好的心态去对待对方？在这个问题上，我觉得探讨一下理想人格是非常有意思的。因为中国人对人在道德境界上是有分寸的、有分别的，这种分别如果在对方一神教系统中他不理解，那在语言上、在做法上，他肯定就要产生误解。所以，我觉得考虑儒家文化对以基督教为代表的一神教文化的对话，其实是为一个未来开放的世界打开一扇门，就是我们这些普通人之间怎么交往。这些可是活生生的人呐！

刘：我觉得您有一个很大的抱负在这其中。随着中国这个新的对外开放，特别是"一带一路"政策的实施和活动的展开，中国传统文化与伊斯兰教、基督宗教接触会越来越多。从基督教这个角度说，它始终面临着一个新的基督教本土化的问题，即如何让基督教文化跟中国现当代文化发生有效的碰撞，而不是产生摩擦和斗争。这应该是作为了解基督教文化和儒家文化的老师们或者一些学者去思考和尝试做出一探究的问题。说到这里，也许应当提一下汉斯·昆。

吴：对，全球伦理。

刘：汉斯·昆当年提出来一个宏大的理想，他要搞一套全球伦理提供给联合国通过。他虽然有点乌托邦的感觉，但也不是说不可以借鉴。当前，在儒家文化跟基督教文化相互碰撞的时候，我们可以发挥我们传统文化中特有的专长去发掘一些共有的价值，就像您今天设计的这样一个对话，借此，我们可以尝试挖掘出一些共性的东西，建构一些可能对话与比较的平台，也就是要寻找两种文化深层中所蕴含的一些共性或有关的东西。目的是减少彼此的矛盾，协调共同的未来。当然，这需要通过哲学层面的一种反思后而形成一定的理论成果，然后再推广开来。

吴：再举一个简单的例子，我们的"君子"和英文里面的"gentlemen"这两个词在含义上能不能真正地对等呢？

刘：也许是有交叉的。"gentlemen"的意思指的是"出身高贵的人""绅士""君子""有教养的人"。它可以指一定的外在的地位即出身，但在深层次上它更是一种高深的修为与涵养。儒家文化中的"君子"强调的就是涵养。所以在涵养、修养的意义上它俩是完全对等的。显然，"gentlemen"不仅仅指高贵的出身与显赫的地位，它更多的是强调内在的"君子"性格。一个出身并不高贵也无显赫社会地位的神父，当他在走向贫瘠之地的偏僻教堂中做善工的时候，他的物质条件是非常差的，但是，一旦他以爱岗敬业的态度锲而不舍地取得成就造福一方时，他又何尝不能被称为"gentlemen"或者"君子"呢？

七　人格平等与权威主义

吴：好，非常有意思，一下子讲了一个半小时。

刘：哦，真的。

吴：从九点开始的，九点多一点点开始的。

刘：谢谢吴老师。

吴：我的意思是讲，基督教文化——广义地讲是一神教文化，跟儒家文化还是有很大差异的。

刘：是的。不过，我在尝试去寻找对话的可能性。

吴：特别是在讲人要成为一个什么样的理想人的时候，我觉得儒家文化对基督教的一套信、望、爱的系统不太理解。

刘：不太理解吗？

吴：不太理解，但是按照现代性的平等观念来看，儒家可能有一些等级性、有一些阶位，比如说小人、君子、贤人，圣人，好像是一步一步往上走的，这在基督教一神教中好像不是那么明显。

刘：基督宗教理论上似乎是要尽量避免这种外在的区分，以体现作为"image of God"的个体人之间人格平等原则，亦即在"personality"这个意义上是平等的。

吴：我的意思是讲，儒家有一个非常鲜明的小人、君子、贤人、圣人的区分，这在道理上实际上也隐含着一定的权威主义的东西，因为贤人比君子要高明，圣人比贤人更高明，所以我们虽然有一个非常清晰可辨的区分让你在道德上不断地达到一个更高的境界，但要是从一神教的角度看，人都是上帝的子民，各个宗教组织都是兄弟，除了一个神之外，大家都是平等的，在世俗层面都是一个平等的人格，中华文化恰恰缺这个东西。

刘：实际上，基督宗教的确一方面尽量避免区分人格，但同时又特别强调神父、牧师对一般信徒的引领作用。这种引领不只是信仰上的指导，更多的是世俗伦理和理想人格塑造方面的影响，目的是一步步走向上帝。而其严格的教阶制度所体现的也是这样的一种模式，就此而言，基督宗教内部的等级性、阶位性也是非常明显的。

吴： 而儒家恰恰是在人的道德境界上也有一个高低的位阶，所以儒家礼制所构筑的不仅是社会制度层面的等级，就是在人格的成长上也有等级，这里有好处，有坏处。

刘： 是的。

吴： 好处就是让你的道德境界不断地向上打开。

刘： 开放的态度。

吴： 但坏处就是它有意无意地形成各种各样的道德权威，道德权威主义在基督教或者以基督教为代表的一神教里头，恐怕还是不太一样的。

刘： 有道理。基督教不但在最初最原始的意义上提倡人格平等，尽量地不去区分人格上的等级，而且在马丁·路德宗教改革之后，在外在做法上也是非常彻底的。宗教改革之前普通人是看不到圣经的，必须通过神父的讲解，只能聆听，但是看不到圣经文字，没有权力直接读圣经。马丁·路德他看不惯这个东西，他说我要直接跟上帝沟通，我要取消神父的所谓中保。我直接跟上帝沟通，亦即要彻底地去除所谓的不平等，无须神父作为一个所谓的桥梁（吴：中介），中介。这种思想直接影响了近代的所谓自由、平等思想，人的主体性由此凸显出来，各种等级制度和宗教禁锢逐渐去除。这其中需要一个漫长的过程。无论如何，儒家思想在中国影响久远，精英主义和等级制度的影响比较明显。

吴： 很深。所以我今天搞这个对话，其实也是与我自己最近研究的现代哲学家有关。我在开幕式①上讲到冯契先生，冯契先生做了很多工作，他在综合中国传统的儒家的理想人格加上马克思的一些思想再加上近现代的一些自由平等的思想之后，提出一个新的概念，叫"平民化的自由人格"。

刘： 有深意。

---

① 指的是 2016 年 11 月 19~20 日在武汉大学召开的 "'在比较中前进的中国哲学'高端论坛暨第二届比较哲学学术研讨会"。

吴：所以，"平民化的"也是中国近代的，也是现代西方启蒙的，"人格"这个词也是来自于西方的，但是他用现代汉语来表达的对理想人格的建构，其实是在适应社会主义的现代的市场化改革。

刘：中国化的。

吴：中国人，怎么样成为一个理想的人。就是不再有所谓的从君子到贤人到圣人这样一个等级，大家都是平民化的，都是自由的人格，在这一点上，在某种程度上，吸收了基督教一神教这样一些内容。

刘：似乎是这样的。您刚才提到孟子的理想人格最终是指向天的，无论我的理想人格建构经历一个什么样的过程，君子啊，大丈夫啊什么，最终一定要指向一个最高的、永恒的、永远生成着的过程，在这一点上与基督宗教理想人格建构有相通之处。您说到冯契，这让我想到台湾的谢扶雅。

吴：谢扶雅我还不太熟，没读过他的书。

刘：谢扶雅是既想当儒家、一个好的儒者，又想成为一个非常好的基督徒的人。他想从一个"noble Christian"到达一个"Christian nobleman"。他想这样做，这也就是像您说的，他其实是一个想把儒家文化跟基督教文化做一个很好的糅合，然后在自己身上体现出来的学人。我觉得有一批学人是这样做的。

吴：所以我觉得儒家跟基督教的对话最终还要达到一个现代性的人格。

刘：很有启发。

吴：冯契先生给我们开创了一条道路，"平民化的自由人格"，就是我们不再像古代的圣贤、君子那样，但还是要有一个理想的人格。

刘：是啊。

吴：又是自由的，又是平等的，没有贵族气的，没有奴颜婢膝的。

刘：赞成你的观点。

吴：但也没有盗寇之心。在中国古代社会、包括现代社会（**刘**：投机心理很强）中，下层社会其实有很多不健康心理（**刘**：的确如此）。一旦有钱就要称王称霸，这叫盗寇之心。然后是没钱，要么是人的依赖，我的主子啊，我的领导啊；要么是物的依赖，成为商品拜物教。冯契先生提出的"平民化的自由人格"恰恰是针对近现代资本主义社会所带来的商品拜物教和中国传统社会所带来的人身依附的，他要把这两个方面消解掉，所以提出一个"平民化的自由人格"。在这里，儒家讲理想人格，没错，是吧，但是怎么样把它变成一个现代性的，怎么样从基督宗教和其他的一神教里头汲取一些东西，这恰恰是这个对话的非常重要的动因。

刘：您讲得很有道理。我觉得其实现实也已经告诉我们，当下正是一个很好的机会，无论是就外在条件还是内在的动力来说，现在都是一个非常好的时机去进行这样的一种研究和对话。

吴：对，我觉得这样的话，中国文化其实也有能力来消化吸收一神教所带来的各种各样的人格上、文化上的一些内容。

刘：所以，从这个意义上说，中国哲学，就是大的、广义的中国哲学，它的研究范式也好、内容也好，将是非常有前景的。

吴：是啊，所以我觉得要多开展一些基督宗教和儒家文化的对话，或者在基督宗教和伊斯兰教之间，搞一个几个宗教在一起的对话。

刘：对对，比如说利玛窦所在的那个时代，他是很有抱负的，可是因为外在条件的不具备、整个国民文化素质和眼界的局限，那会儿很少有平民百姓能了解到，甚至平常知识分子对基督教也不感兴趣、没有了解，就没有推广的渠道，再有价值的理论和方法也都无以发挥效用。现在我们有这个条件了，是吧？国家鼓励文化对话，也鼓励宗教对话。这就为我们打开思路建构理想的对话与研究平台创造了一定的良好条件。

吴：最近最大的问题就是一神教带来的矛盾和冲突问题，因为它只相信一个上帝。

刘：对。

吴：忠于自己的上帝，认为自己的上帝是唯一的。这就搞不好。

刘：对，这就不允许其他的平起平坐。

吴：对，儒家文化恰恰有这样一个（刘：包容），所以我觉得今天的对话是一个开始。

刘：好，特别好，这是一个好时机、好时代。

吴：我们以后可以开展多种多样的对话。

刘：好的，开展多层面的对话。同时，也希望在座的同学们认识到，中国哲学研究，即广义的中国哲学研究，在方法论的建构和问题的选择上是非常广阔的、很有意思的。因此，只要踏实读书认真选取课题，你们的前途将是非常好的。

提问互动

吴：你们提两个问题，跟刘老师交流一下，我们马上结束对谈。

学生1：我想问一下，基督教怎么看待和处理意志软弱的问题？

刘：您说的是心理学上的意志软弱吗？

学生1：不是，我虽然知道这件事是善的，或是好的，但是没法实现，就是实现不了。

刘：实现不了？是你不愿意去实现还是有外在困难限制？

学生1：就是基督教怎么看待这个现象？怎么让这个现象消除？

刘：就是意志薄弱这个现象？

学生1：对。

刘：如果从这个基督教理想人格建构来说，意志薄弱那就是不够刚毅、不够勇敢。

学生1：儒家讲一些慎独，以文会友，以友辅仁，然后通过友道相互扶持，来克服这种现象，基督教有这方面的吗？

刘：有。您说克服这样一个障碍的话，它会从神学修养和基督教心理学两个角度给你提供帮助。神学修养即包含你讲的慎独方面的修养。当然你同时也可以向神父去求助，寻求心理安抚和改正的方法。此外，基督教心理学是一个非常专业的研究方向，具有一定的实践性。它会从理论上给你提供非常系统的辅导，同时辅以专业技术的帮助来克服这样的问题。当然，基督宗教的有些团体也会提供一些类似于训练营的活动，有可能帮助你改善。

学生2：我想问一下，在基督教里面，我们在比较中西哲学的时候有一个忽略的角度，就是基督教的上帝是全知全能的，但中国的"天"

好像不能用全知全能来说。"圣希天","圣"在汉代的时候可能有一个全知全能的含义,因为神学色彩比较重,但是发展到后来,基本上是在价值层面。我不知道基督教到底是怎么看待神是全知全能的?

刘:如果是在做中西比较的话,你完全可以抛开其他层面,在价值上去谈中国的"天"和西方的"上帝"。

学生2:但如果对神的这种感觉下不来,那人永远是被动的,因为人是有限的,人的理性不能窥测上帝,因为上帝是完全自由的嘛。

刘:你说错了,人不能够完全领悟上帝,但却是能够有限地认识上帝的,亦即说人对上帝的认识是无限趋近于上帝的完满性的。上帝是全智,它是一个完满的智慧。人在受造的那一刻分有了这一智慧,人的智慧是类比上帝的完满智慧的一个存在,也就是说,人的理性是上帝赋予的,所以在本体论上,人在受造的那一刻即被赋予了理性,从而具有认识能力,因此才可能去认识上帝的智慧。所以,人天生就具有认识能力认识上帝,只不过人没有完全的洞察能力,从而完全地了解上帝作为"perfection"意义上的全智。然而,无论何何,人的认识能力是在类比上帝完满性的智慧的存在当中存在的,这就意味着我的智慧是逐渐提升的。

学生2:逐渐提升的,那就是说,因为荒谬所以才相信。

刘:那是神学,那是信的意义上的,那不是智的意义上的,就是说理性跟这个信还是要分开的。

学生2:那我们现在谈的基督教,对西方社会来说,是信的成分大还是智的成分大呢?

刘:你如果去做哲学研究的话,那你是在理性的意义上去做的;你如果是您刚才说的因为荒谬所以我才相信,那可能是在神学意义上的。神学意义上就无须论证上帝所谓的全智全能全善性,你只信就好了。如果是哲学思考和哲学论证的话,你可以借助于本体论的东西,可以借助于知识论,尤其知识论非常重要,知识论讲求你的认识是如何产生发展和发挥作用的,知识如何可能。你可以这么思考,就是分别从不同的层次去思考。但是思维不能混在一起,你在论证它的形而上学意义的时候,要借助于知识论的方法去论证,这样可以达到伦理学的这个最终的目的，就是落实到伦理学，但是也可以放弃完全在形而上学、本体论的层面去论证。可是呢，在这个过程当中，你不能一会儿是哲学的，一会儿是神学的，这个不行。理性和信仰要分开的。

学生2：那像近代的好多哲学家不都是既在"信"又在"知"上谈上帝的吗？

刘：可以啊，我不是说你不能谈，而是说你在谈论一个问题的时候，你要在到达一定的清楚点的时候再回到另外一个思维层次上。

吴：神学跟哲学不能混在一起谈。

刘：你的前提如果是认识上帝，那显然是从哲学角度去谈的，就是我从理性的角度，借助我的理智去认识上帝。那你又说，正是因为荒谬所以我才相信，这个是纯粹神学层面的，混在一起就没办法得出任何结论了。而分开来谈就比较清楚了。西方近现代哲学家都离不开对宗教问题的讨论，这说明他对以往的神学思想是有认识的。你们如果做中西比较哲学研究，那基督宗教哲学这块儿是一个大的任务，一定不可以抛弃和逃避。年轻人很喜欢的海德格尔的思想，你们知道吗，海德格尔的《存在与时间》，他的基本的观点早在托马斯·阿奎那那边就谈得很清楚了，就给你们推荐一本书，《论存在者与本质》，就是 *On Being and Essence* 那本书，很薄很薄，它就是谈存在问题的。

吴：段老师翻译的。

刘：是的。可见，谈论存在和本质问题不可以逃避开基督宗教哲学的原创理论。基督教哲学持续了一千多年，你们知道这一千多年在西方整个历史上意味着什么？它是时间最长的哲学理论阶段。古希腊哲学影响很深远，可是它只有几百年的历史，加上古罗马时代，不过千年。而古罗马时代是没有什么创造的。

吴：没有哲学。

刘：斯多噶学派的伦理学算是比较有影响的。

吴：对。

刘：因为那个时代很荒谬嘛，古罗马、古希腊加在一起才不到一千年，但是中世纪基督教哲学持续了一千五六百年，这个影响力大家可想而知。所以不能忽视，做中西比较哲学，就像吴教授他这么多年，我不知道您做了这么多年。

吴：做得不好（笑）。

刘：您谦虚了！吴教授很有想法，您所论述的关于中西哲学比较的深层次的理解和架构，我很受启发，真的很值得我们学习。

吴：谢谢，谢谢。

刘：中西比较不是拿几个概念出来作简单比较。

吴：对对。

刘：那是思想的碰撞。

吴：对对对。

刘：嗯，我们就是思想的碰撞。

吴：谢谢刘老师（鼓掌）。

《比较哲学与比较文化论丛》
征稿启事

由湖北省人文社科重点研究基地"比较哲学与文化战略研究中心"和武汉大学哲学学院主办、中国社会科学出版社出版发行的学术丛刊《比较哲学与比较文化论丛》,以倡导和推动比较哲学与比较文化研究、促进中西文化对话与融通为宗旨,至今已出版 10 辑。为加快这一事业的发展,现竭诚向各界征稿。欢迎各位道友惠赐大作。

从第 8 辑起,本论丛将特设"学术新人"栏目,欢迎广大博士研究生踊跃投稿。

来稿选题以比较哲学与比较文化研究为主,参考栏目如下:

1. 中外比较哲学与比较文化历史回顾与总结;

2. 比较哲学与比较文化研究方法论;

3. 中外哲学和文化中的重要概念、命题、理论、思潮或事件的比较研究;

4. 借鉴西方理论与方法,对中国传统思想展开新的阐释;

5. 中外哲学史上哲学家的比较思想与学术成就研究;

6. 比较哲学与比较文化研究动态研究;

7. 其他与比较相关的研究。

来稿请附 300 字以内的内容提要、关键词及作者简介与通信地址,邮箱与手机号或 QQ 号；采用页下注；以 Word 文档提交至 hbphhs@126.com。来稿一经采用，将支付薄酬。

湖北省人文社科重点研究基地"比较哲学与文化战略研究中心"

武汉大学哲学学院

《比较哲学与比较文化论丛》编委会

2017 年 10 月 30 日